Research Highlights in Technology and Teacher Education 2012

Senior Book Editors

Cleborne D. Maddux
The University of Nevada, Reno

David Gibson
simSchool

Book Editors

Matthew J. Koehler

John Lee

Ron McBride

Punya Mishra

Paul Resta

Raymond Rose

David Slykhuis

Jeremy Wendt

Society for Information Technology and Teacher Education
site.aace.org

Research Highlights in Technology and Teacher Education 2012

Preface 5

Forward 11

Peer Review Panel 13

Articles

TPACK: TECHNOLOGICAL, PEDAGOGICAL, CONTENT KNOWLEDGE

Testing an Instrument Using Structured Interviews to Assess Experienced Teachers' TPACK
  Judi Harris, Neal Grandgenett, and Mark Hofer (USA) 15

Using TPACK for Analysing Teachers' Task Design: Understanding Change in a 1:1-Laptop Setting
  Martin Tallvid, Johan Lundin and Berner Lindström (Sweden) 23

TPACK Research with Inservice Teachers: Where's the TCK?
  Mark Hofer and Judi Harris (USA) 31

SIMULATIONS IN TEACHER EDUCATION

Teacher Education with simSchool
  David Gibson (USA) 37

Simulating Students with Learning Disabilities in Virtual Classrooms: A Validation Study
  Sita Periathiruvadi, Tandra Tyler-Wood, Gerald Knezek, and Rhonda Christensen (USA) 45

Situated Online: Theoretical Underpinnings of Field Experiences in Virtual School Settings
  Leanna Archambault and Kathryn Kennedy (USA) 53

STEM TEACHING AND LEARNING

New Technology Tools for Science Teachers to Consider: A Case Study of an Online Biology Lab
  Gregory MacKinnon, Eric Alcorn, and Trevor Avery (USA) 61

The Virtual Boat: Design Team Issues in the Development of a Virtual Simulations for High School Science
  Teresa Franklin, Sertac Ozercan, Chang Liu, and Nathan Andre (USA) 69

Effective Use of Online Quizzes in Science Courses
  William Stowe and Lin Lin (USA) 77

Using Technology in Training Elementary Mathematics Teachers, The Development of TPACK Knowledge
  Beth Bos and Kathryn S. Lee (USA) 83

WEB 2.0 AND SOCIAL NETWORKING

Developing Pre-Service Teachers´ Competencies in Using Technologies in the Classroom: An Example From Portugal
  Clara Pereira Coutinho (Portugal) 91

Using Online Learning Networks to Promote Self-Regulated Learning in Primary Teacher Education
Emmy Vrieling, Theo Bastiaens and Sjef Stijnen (Netherlands) 101

Preservice Teachers' Personality, Motives, Motivation, and Attitudes Associated with the Use of Social Network Services: Facebook Case
Oğuzhan Atabek (Turkey) 109

INFORMAL LEARNING

InteractiveSchoolWall: A Digital Enriched Learning Environment for Systemic-Constructive Informal Learning Processes
Thomas Winkler, Martina Ide, and Michael Herczeg (Germany) 117

Parents' Influence on Adolescent Children' Media-multitasking Attitudes and Behaviors
Lin Lin, Kim Nimon, and David Bonner (USA) 127

IMPACT STUDIES

Examining the Impact of the Professional Development Model for International Educators on Greek Teachers
Debra R Sprague, Anastasia Kitsantas, Beverly Shaklee, and Maria Katradis (USA and Greece) 133

Interactive white boards: Is it worth it? Use in Four Western PA K-12 Schools
Yehuda Peled, Mandy Medvin and Linda Domanski (Israel and USA) 141

Issues in the Transformation of Teaching with Technology
Shelley Goldman and Robert Lucas (USA) 149

A Study of the Effectiveness of Technology Integration Training on Student Achievement
Scott Elliot and Cathy Mikulas (USA) 157

ONLINE AND BLENDED LEARNING

Cognitive Presence Characteristics of Online and Face-to-face Discussions in a Blended Course
Petrea Redmond (Australia) 167

Generalized Checklist Significance in Improving Timeliness in Asynchronous Distance Education
Terence Cavanaugh, Marcia Lamkin, and Haihong Hu (USA) 175

Learning Motivation and Student Academic Dishonesty – A Comparison Between Face-To-Face And Online Courses
Yehuda Peled, Casimir Barczyk, Yovav Eshet, and Keren Grinautski (Israel) 181

Teacher Credibility: How Presentation Modalities Affect Teacher Education Students' Perceived Credibility of Information
Jenna L. Sexton and Cleborne D. Maddux (USA) 189

Research Highlights in Technology and Teacher Education 2012
(ISBN # 1-880094-96-7) is published by the Society for Information Tecnology & Teacher Education (SITE),
an international, educational, nonprofit organization.
Published by: SITE, PO Box 1545, Chesapeake, VA 23327-1545, USA
757-366-5606; Fax: 703-997-8760; E-mail: info@aace.org
© Copyright 2012 by Site
site.aace.org
Available at http://www.aace.org/bookshelf.htm

PREFACE

The seven themes of research highlighted this year are a mixture of rising ideas; some that are beginning to organize the professional discussions of the society and others that are long-standing themes of teacher education in the information age.

Beginning in 2006 with the publication of "Technological Pedagogical Content Knowledge: A New Framework for Teacher Knowledge" by Mishra and Koehler, a body of research has begun to grow leading to the book's first section.

TPACK

Judi Harris, Neal Grandgenett, and Mark Hofer developed, tested, and released a reliable and valid instrument in 2012 that can be used to assess the quality of inexperienced teachers' TPACK by examining their detailed written lesson plans. In the first chapter "Testing an Instrument Using Structured Interviews to Assess Experienced Teachers' TPACK" that instrument was validated for use in the context of experienced teachers' planning. Interrater reliability was computed on scores of spoken responses to semi-structured interview questions, using both Intraclass Correlation (.870) and a score agreement (93.6%) procedure. Internal consistency (using Cronbach's Alpha) was .895. Test-retest reliability (score agreement) was 100%. Taken together, these results demonstrate that the rubric is robust when used to analyze experienced teachers' descriptions of lessons or projects offered in response to the interview questions, which are provided for interested readers.

In "Using TPACK for Analysing Teachers' Task Design: Understanding Change in a 1:1-Laptop Setting" three researchers from Sweden, Martin Tallvid, Johan Lundin and Berner Lindström, use the TPACK-framework as a lens for understanding not only how information technologies play an additional part in the design of tasks, but also for analyzing how teachers address the integration of pedagogy and content in the use of technology. The chapter provides guidelines for task design in a 1:1 setting, usable for both pre- and in-service teacher education.

Mark Hofer and Judi Harris return in chapter three "TPACK Research with Inservice Teachers: Where's the TCK?" to discuss the patterns of research in studies that have begun to distinguish teacher knowledge in TPACK's subdomains, including technological pedagogical knowledge (TPK) and technological content knowledge (TCK). In reviewing this literature, they report that teachers' TPK is documented considerably more often than their TCK. The chapter reviews the studies that together illustrate this trend, offering potential explanations and suggestions for further investigation.

Simulations in Teacher Education

In the 2012 Horizon Report for Higher Education, one of the trends predicted to emerge within the next two to three years is games and simulations, a topic that the society has been following for several years. Three chapters illustrate some of the best recent work going on in the society.

In "Teacher Education with simSchool" David Gibson discusses how some of the systemic challenges of teacher education in the U.S can be addressed through simulation-based teacher education. The chapter outlines a rationale for the new approach based in self-direction and personal validation in a complex but repeatable practice environment, supported by emergent interdisciplinary knowledge stemming from the unique affordances of digital media assessment and social media. The online simulation simSchool is used as an example model that embodies the new paradigm.

It is often difficult to provide experience for pre-service teachers to work with students with learning disabilities. Can a simulation accurately depict a classroom experience that a future teacher might encounter in today's inclusion classroom? In chapter five, "Simulating Students with Learning Disabilities in Virtual Classrooms: A Validation Study," Sita Periathiruvadi, Tandra Tyler-Wood, Gerald Knezek, and Rhonda Christensen of the University of North Texas explored the validity of using a simulation as a tool to train future teachers to work with a student with a learning disability in an inclusion classroom. An actual student with a learning disability was observed in an inclusion classroom. Using those observations, a simulated version of the student was built into the simSchool program. Comparison of various attributes including behavior and personality revealed important findings concerning the ability of the simulation to accurately depict students with learning disabilities.

Providing a theoretical lens for research on virtual school settings in teacher education, Leanna Archambault and Kathryn Kennedy describe the historical, practical, and theoretical underpinnings behind an essential component of teacher preparation, the field experience. Their chapter, "Situated Online: Theoretical Underpinnings of Field Experiences in Virtual School Settings" explores the theory of situated cognition as it applies to online teaching and learning and discusses the basis for the development of field experiences in K-12 virtual schools. Various online models are described, as well as implications for teacher education programs.

STEM Teaching and Learning

The theme of integrating technology in order to improve teaching and learning in science, technology, engineering and mathematics subjects has been a long-term interest at SITE. Several special interest groups in the disciplines are active leaders of the society, and other researchers, such as those with an interest in games and simulations or other innovative learning technologies often apply their findings to STEM teaching and learning. Four chapters address STEM issues in this year's book.

In chapter seven, "New Technology Tools for Science Teachers to Consider: A Case Study of an Online Biology Lab" Gregory MacKinnon, Eric Alcorn, and Trevor Avery offer a case study of an online biology lab that highlights three technologies to supplement or replace traditional approaches. Using a mixed-methods, action research approach with about 200 students, the relative impact of virtual reality models, animations and simulations was sampled. Surveys, interviews and focus groups established that while face-to-face laboratories were preferred by students, most felt it was acceptable that 30% of their labs be online, and of those, virtual reality models were the least favored when compared to animations and simulations. In addition, it was found that at the 95% confidence level, there was no significant difference in the laboratory scores between students who did online versions of the labs and those that face-to-face versions of the same laboratories. This is a promising finding in that a problem of limited space can be solved through technology without compromising student learning.

Games and simulations intersect with STEM again in chapter eight, "The Virtual Boat: Design Team Issues in the Development of a Virtual Simulations for High School Science" by Teresa Franklin, Sertac Ozercan, Chang Liu, and Nathan Andre. The Virtual Boat is part of a National Science Foundation GK-12 grant called the Boat of Knowledge in the Science Classroom. The challenges of *design* and *team* are discussed to provide insights into game design and the teamwork often required for the building of a 3-D virtual environment for learning.

William Stowe and Lin Lin, authors of chapter nine, "Effective Use of Online Quizzes in Science Courses" investigated ways to effectively incorporate online quizzes in college biology courses. A total of 151 college students participated in this experimental study, taking online quizzes, lecture exams, and surveys. The study indicates that a 30-minute delay between online quiz attempts effectively creates a study time for the student to read the feedback, locate the material related to the missed questions, and reread that material before attempting the quiz again.

The STEM issue of mathematics intersects with TPACK issues in chapter ten by Beth Bos and Kathryn S. Lee, "Using Technology in Training Elementary Mathematics Teachers, The Development of TPACK Knowledge." Their study examined the effects of a problem-based Elementary Mathematics Specialist Program on mathematical, technological, and pedagogical knowledge. A questionnaire was used with a matched pair t-test for pre- and post-test data and revealed statistically significant gains with good effect sizes. The data shows that growth in TPACK knowledge flourished in this content-based program.

Web 2.0 and Social Networking

Clara Pereira Coutinho of Portugal writes about 32 preservice teachers in chapter eleven "Developing Pre-Service Teachers´ Competencies in Using Technologies in the Classroom: An Example From Portugal." For data collection, several sources of evidence were used: an electronic questionnaire, an individual written reflection on the learning experience and direct observation. The chapter describes the program, reflects on the results and discusses guidelines for future research.

Chapter twelve, "Using Online Learning Networks to Promote Self-Regulated Learning in Primary Teacher Education" presents seven design principles for teacher education, and shows the results of implementing these principles in informal learning contexts. Based on positive results of their implementation process, Emmy Vrieling, Theo Bastiaens and Sjef Stijnen of the Netherlands describe emerging trends for self-regulated learning networks to enhance further use in pre-service teacher learning programs.

Social network services simulate and may even emulate existing social networks on an abstract level and reflect them in the electronic world, says Oğuzhan Atabek of Turkey, author of "Preservice Teachers' Personality, Motives, Motivation, and Attitudes Associated with the Use of Facebook." This chapter reports the findings from the quantitative part of an ongoing research study on Turkish preservice teachers. To investigate the factors that influence their Facebook use, 641 preservice students of the Middle East Technical University in Turkey were surveyed. Four regression analyses were used to describe the results of the collected data.

Informal Learning

"InteractiveSchoolWall: A Digital Enriched Learning Environment for Systemic-Constructive Informal Learning Processes" by Thomas Winkler, Martina Ide, and Michael Herczeg of Germany is one of two chapters focusing on informal learning. The interactive wall is a hypermedia presentation and interaction platform, publicly accessible in the lobby of a secondary school in northern Germany that extends learning spaces in a new way. The technical construction of the wall follows the logic of a novel digital network environment framework that allows the use of personalized and semantic enriched multimedia objects as a specific multimedia-learning environment. Teachers' reactions are included in a discussion of the reflective handling of complex knowledge, with the potential to impact and enhance teaching models in teacher education and in-service teacher education programs. What new perspectives may emerge for management, organization, and school development processes?

Another study of technology in informal learning is presented in chapter fifteen "Parents' Influence on Adolescent Children' Media-multitasking Attitudes and Behaviors" by Lin Lin, Kim Nimon, and David Bonner. Their study of 104 mothers' influence on their paired adolescent children's media multitasking attitudes and behaviors utilized three surveys including the Media Multitasking Self Efficacy, Media Multitasking Attitude, and Media Multitasking Index in addition to demographics. Results showed that the adolescents had more favorable attitudes and active behaviors towards media multitasking than their mothers. Girls had more favorable attitudes and active behaviors than boys, and the boys had slightly better self-efficacy towards media multitasking. Results from the study offer implications for parenting, teaching and learning.

Impact Studies

Four studies are grouped together as impact studies, although several of the chapters just introduced could have as easily been included in this group.

An international study by Debra R Sprague, Anastasia Kitsantas, Beverly Shaklee, and Maria Katradis entitled "Examining the Impact of the Professional Development Model for International Educators on Greek Teachers" is offered first. This chapter examines the long-term effects of the Professional Development Model for International Educators.

The model encompasses an academic program, field experiences in diverse secondary schools, cultural exchanges and trips to provide the international educators with a vast array of tools, technologies, and perspectives for introducing and sustaining innovative educational practices upon their return to their home country. Nineteen Greek educators participated in the eight-week project in which they were engaged in innovative teaching practices such as integrating technology, which led them to higher levels of self-efficacy and pedagogical knowledge.

Chapter seventeen, "Interactive white boards: Is it worth it? Use in Four Western PA K-12 Schools" reports on work by an international team of researchers. Yehuda Peled of Israel, with Mandy Medvin and Linda Domanski of the United States examine teacher attitudes and fears about implementing interactive whiteboards in classrooms to enhance student engagement and achievement. Nearly 78 percent of all teachers surveyed reported using the whiteboard either "Often" or "All the time" and 75 percent of them reported using it for two or more years, factors that were strongly related to levels of training and support the teachers believed they received, teachers' sense of self-efficacy and the perceived value of the technology as a useful tool, and teachers' perceptions about the positive effect that integrating whiteboards had on student achievement.

Teacher perceptions and attitudes is also the subject of the chapter by Shelley Goldman and Robert Lucas. They write in "Issues in the Transformation of Teaching with Technology" about a semi-structured protocol used to interview 25 teachers from 11 states and four international sites. Using open coding and a constant comparative method, the teachers' most significant issues, accomplishments, and thoughts were identified. Almost every teacher felt pressured to cover standards and prepare students for tests, and they saw those demands as a higher priority than engaging in 21st century teaching and learning. They used a variety of technologies but generally had not transformed their teaching with them. The teachers expressed a hope for teacher education and professional development that would point them to the future with technology and new kinds of learning.

Does online technology integration training for teachers impact student achievement? Do students in classes whose teachers use online technology integration training achieve greater increases in Reading and Mathematics skills than a comparable group of students in classes whose teachers do not use online technology integration training? Scott Elliot and Cathy Mikulas, report in "Improving Student Learning Through Teacher Technology Training: A Study of the Effectiveness of Technology Integration Training on Student Achievement" that students in classes whose teachers used technology integration training show greater learning gains in reading and mathematics than students in classes whose teachers did not use the online technology integration training.

Online and Blended Learning

The last cluster of chapters we've categorized as studies of online and blended learning. Petrea Redmond of Australia leads the section with a focus on "Cognitive Presence Characteristics of Online and Face-to-face Discussions in a Blended Course." The chapter describes the cognitive presence that pre-service teachers demonstrated during online and face-to-face discussions in a blended Early Childhood Leadership course. Using cognitive presence indicators from the Community of Inquiry Framework, her study found that cognitive presence was more frequent at the exploration level in both face-to-face discussions and online posts. The study also found that having a third party analyze the online and face-to-face elements of the course and report the results back to the instructor provided a powerful tool for instructor reflection and catalyst for change in pedagogical practice.

In the chapter "Generalized Checklist Significance in Improving Timeliness in Asynchronous Distance Education," Terence Cavanaugh, Marcia Lamkin, and Haihong Hu address the problem of novice online learners in distance learning courses submitting work late and missing elements of various assignments. Their generalized assessments checklist was designed using the READ-DO checklist design standards and distributed to students by email on a weekly basis. The checklist was found to be statistically significant as a strategy in improving submission times for asynchronous distance learning students.

Researchers from Israel authored chapter twenty-two, "Learning Motivation and Student Academic Dishonesty – A Comparison Between Face-To-Face And Online Courses." Yehuda Peled, Casimir Barczyk, Yovav Eshet, and Keren

Grinautski explore student academic dishonesty in the context of traditional and distance-learning courses in higher education. Data from 1,376 Students enrolled in colleges or universities in the U.S. and Israel were surveyed to assess their motivational orientation and their willingness to commit various acts of academic misconduct. Findings indicate that students' propensity to engage in academic dishonesty is explained by an extrinsic motivational orientation, participation in face-to-face type courses, and their age. Students were inclined to commit acts of dishonesty if they were (1) extrinsically, rather than intrinsically motivated to learn; (2) engaged in traditional face-to-face, rather than online courses; and (3) younger in age, rather than older. In addition, students in face-to-face courses had a statistically significantly higher propensity to engage in academic dishonesty than their counterparts in distance learning courses – a finding similar in both the U.S. and Israel.

In this year's final chapter, "Teacher Credibility: How Presentation Modalities affect Teacher Education Students' Perceived Credibility of Information," Jenna L. Sexton and Cleborne D. Maddux, of the University of Nevada, Reno examine whether or not, all else being equal, the modality of information delivery has an impact on its perceived credibility among teacher education students of two age groups: (>25 and <25). A piece of fabricated information was formatted, with the exact same content and from the same source, into three modalities; (a) face-to-face lecture (b) print via paper, and (c) print via World Wide Web. The formatted information was delivered separately to three randomly assigned groups of undergraduate and graduate teacher education students. After the information was delivered the students completed a self-report survey instrument that recorded their perceptions of the credibility of the formatted information. No significance was found between the mean differences in the credibility scores of participants in the two age groups. However, significant main effects for modality were found. The credibility scores were significantly higher for the print via paper modality than both the face-to-face lecture and the print via World Wide Web modalities.

We trust that you'll find many gems in this year's collection! We'd like to thank the many reviewers and the authoring teams for their willingness to work together to create another outstanding collection of research highlights.

The Editors
Cleborne D. Maddux
David C. Gibson

EdITLib
EDUCATION & INFORMATION TECHNOLOGY DIGITAL LIBRARY

- Journal Articles
- Conference Papers
- Special Topic Books
- Conference Invited Speaker Talks
- Videos
- Conference Presentation Slides

EdITLib is your source for 15+ years (with your subscription) of peer-reviewed, published articles (20,000+) and papers on the latest research, developments, and applications related to all aspects of Educational Technology and E-Learning.

Ten (10) Academic Journals including:

- *Journal of Educational Multimedia and Hypermedia*
- *International Journal on E-Learning*
  (Corporate, Government, Healthcare, & Higher Education)
- *Journal of Computers in Mathematics and Science Teaching*
- *Journal of Interactive Learning Research*
- *Journal of Technology and Teacher Education*
- *AACE Journal*
  (electronic)
- *Contemporary Issues in Technology & Teacher Education*
  (electronic)

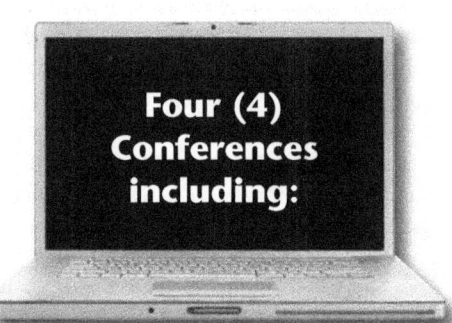

Four (4) Conferences including:

- **ED-MEDIA** – World Conference on Educational Multimedia, Hypermedia & Telecommunications
- **E-Learn** – World Conference on E-Learning in Corporate, Healthcare, Government, and Higher Education
- **SITE** – Society for Information Technology and Teacher Education International Conference

Adding soon!
- **Global Learn Asia Pacific** – Global Conference on Learning and Technology
- **Global TIME** – Global Conference on Technology, Innovation, Media & Education

Individual subscriptions $19/month

Does Your Library Subscribe?

Free access to abstracts so you can try the Digital Library at no cost!
- Conduct research • Keep current on the latest research and publications in your field
- Access and fully search publications • Create and store personal collections of articles by topic
- Receive table of contents alerts prior to journal publication
- Share article abstracts and search results with colleagues via email and include your comments
- Export citations to BibTex, EndNote, and RefWorks

www.EdITLib.org

Association for the Advancement of Computing in Education

Email: info@aace.org • Phone: 757-366-5606 • Fax: 703-997-8760

FOREWARD

In its fourth year of publication, the Research Highlights in Technology and Teacher Education journal of the Society for Information Technology (SITE) has become one of the "most viewed" journals in the extensive holdings in the AACE digital library (EdITLib). Based on the international scholarship represented at SITE's annual conference, Research Highlights serves as a critical journal that highlights key trends in practice and research in the area of learning technologies. At the March 2012 conference, held in Austin, Texas about 1300 scholars from 54 countries shared their expertise with colleagues from across the world. Research Highlights represents the best of that work.

Research Highlights was developed and launched under the leadership of former SITE presidents Gerald Knezek and Ian Gibson, AACE CEO Gary Marks and senior editor Cleb Maddux. Under Dr. Maddux's stewardship, the quality of the journal improves with each year's publication.

Each year, SITE designates leaders from its membership to serve as co-editors for the Research Highlights. This year, Cleb Maddux and David Gibson served as Senior Editors and were assisted by editors Drs. Matthew Koehler, John Lee, Ron McBride, Punya Mishra, Paul Resta, Raymond Rose, David Slykhuis, Jeremy Wendt and other SITE leaders, in producing the 2012 Research Highlights in Technology and Teacher Education. To be considered for publication in Research Highlights, a submission first has to be accepted as a "full paper" at the annual SITE conference. Subsequently, those full papers undergo additional rigorous review and editing—no papers are published simply on the basis of their "full paper" status alone. Authors are always required to do additional edits and revisions to meet the high standards of Dr. Maddux and his team. This year, a total of 75 submissions, from the 841 accepted as conference "full papers" were considered. Of those, only 23 were selected for publication in the 2012 Research Highlights in Technology and Teacher Education.

In the end, a successful journal succeeds only based on the quality and rigor of the work submitted for publication. SITE's Research Highlights is fortunate to have an outstanding cohort of international researchers and practitioners who have chosen to share their innovative work in this volume. I trust you will be as impressed as I am by the array of research and quality of scholarship represented here.

Reflecting an outstanding conference, SITE is honored to publish the 2012 Research Highlights in Technology and Teacher Education.

Regards,

Michael Searson, Ph.D.
President, Society for Information Technology & Teacher Education (SITE)

SITE BOOK REVIEWERS 2012

Peter Albion, University of Southern Queensland, Australia
Marsha Alibrandi, Fairfield University, United States
Cindy Anderson, Roosevelt University, United States
Leanna Archambault, Arizona State University, United States
Young Baek, Boise State University, United States
Savilla Banister, Bowling Green State University, United States
Michael Barbour, University of Georgia, United States
Sally Beisser, Drake University, United States
Beth Bos, Texas State University, United States
Bonnie Bracey-Sutton, The Power of US Foundation, United States
Vicki Brown, Florida Atlantic University, United States
Glen Bull, University of Virginia, United States
Livia D'Andrea, University of Nevada-Reno, United States
Niki Davis, University of Canterbury, New Zealand
Lisa Dawley, Boise State University, United States
Aaron Doering, University of Minnesota, United States
Vanessa Earp, Kent University, United States
Candace Figg, Brock University, United States
Teresa Franklin, Ohio University, United States
Adam Friedman, Wake Forest University, United States
Penny Garcia, University of Wisconsin-Oshkosh, United States
Robert Jason Hancock, Southeastern Louisiana University, United States
Mark Hofer, College of William and Mary, United States
Natalie Johnson, Arkansas State University, United States
Kioh Kim, University of Louisiana-Monroe, United States
Lesia Lennex, Morehead State University, United States
Lin Lin, University of North Texas, United States, United States
Carolyn Lowe, Northern Michigan University, United States
Ron McBride, Northwestern State University of Louisiana, United States
Karen McFerrin, Northwestern State University of Louisiana, United States
Sara McNeil, University of Houston, United States, United States
Chrystalla Mouza, University of Delaware, United States, United States
Priscilla Norton, George Mason University, United States
Marilyn Ochoa, University of Florida, United States
Tim Pelton, University of Victoria, Canada
David Pugalee, University of North Carolina at Charlotte, United States
Mark Rodriguez, Sacramento State, United States
Dina Rosen, Kean University, United States
Merryellen Schulz, College of Saint Mary, United States
Melanie Shoffner, Purdue University, United States
Scott Slough, Texas A&M University, United States
Debra Sprague, George Mason University, United States
James Telese, University of Texas-Brownsville, United States
Tandra Tyler-Wood, University of North Texas, United States
Hans van Bergen, Hogeschool Utrecht, Netherlands
Lawrence Walker, University of Canterbury, United States
Scott Waring, University of Central Florida, United States
Roberta Weber, Florida Atlantic University, United States
Jana Willis, University of Houston-Clear Lake, United States
Thomas Winkler, Institute for Multimedia and Interactive Systems, Germany
Harrison Yang, State University of New York-Oswego, United States
Melda Yildiz, Kean University, United States
Carl Young, North Carolina State University, United States

SOCIETY FOR INFORMATION TECHNOLOGY & TEACHER EDUCATION

MEMBERSHIP INFORMATION

Advancing Instructional Technology in Teacher Education

http://site.aace.org/

Mission: The Society for Information Technology and Teacher Education is an international association of individual teacher educators, and affiliated organizations of teacher educators in all disciplines, who are interested in the creation and dissemination of knowledge about the use of information technology in teacher education and faculty/staff development.

The Society seeks to promote research, scholarship, collaboration, exchange, and support among its membership, and to actively foster the development of new national organizations where a need emerges. SITE is the only organization that has as its sole focus the integration of instructional technologies into teacher education programs.

SITE promotes the development and dissemination of theoretical knowledge, conceptual research, and professional practice knowledge through the SITE conference, books, collaborative projects with other organizations, and the *Journal of Technology and Teacher Education*.

Join SITE Today!

You are invited to join SITE and receive the following benefits of professional membership. And, as a member of SITE, you automatically become of member of the Association for the Advancement of Computing in Education (AACE).

Benefits of SITE membership:

- Subscription to the *Journal of Technology and Teacher Education*
- Subscription to the AACE member periodical [electronic]
- Early announcements on Calls for Papers and CITE electronic journal issues
- SITE Conference registration discounts
- Discounts on all other AACE journals and conference proceedings
- Opportunities to work and collaborate with members on activities in areas of common interest and concern

Professional Membership: $115 (US); $130 (non-US)
Student Membership: $35 (US); $50 (non-US)

To join SITE, see **http://site.aace.org/membership/**

Join Us at Next Year's SITE Conference
http://site.aace.org/conf/

International Headquarters: SITE
PO Box 1545, Chesapeake, VA 23327-1545 USA
Tel: 757-366-5606 • Fax: 703-997-8760 • E-mail: info@aace.org

Testing an Instrument Using Structured Interviews to Assess Experienced Teachers' TPACK

Judi Harris
School of Education
College of William & Mary
Williamsburg, Virginia USA
judi.harris@wm.edu

Neal Grandgenett
Department of Teacher Education
University of Nebraska at Omaha
Omaha, Nebraska USA
ngrandgenett@mail.unomaha.edu

Mark Hofer
School of Education
College of William & Mary
Williamsburg, Virginia USA
mark.hofer@wm.edu

Abstract: In 2010, the authors developed, tested, and released a reliable and valid instrument that can be used to assess the quality of inexperienced teachers' TPACK by examining their detailed written lesson plans. In the current study, the same instrument was tested to see if it could be used to assess the TPACK evident in experienced teachers' planning in the form of spoken responses to semi-structured interview questions. Inter-rater reliability was computed using both Intraclass Correlation (.870) and a score agreement (93.6%) procedure. Internal consistency (using Cronbach's Alpha) was .895. Test-retest reliability (score agreement) was 100%. Taken together, these results demonstrate that the rubric is robust when used to analyze experienced teachers' descriptions of lessons or projects offered in response to the interview questions that appear in the Appendix.

Assessing TPACK

During the past three years, scholarship that addresses the complex, situated, and interdependent nature of teachers' technology integration knowledge—known as "technological pedagogical content knowledge," or TPACK (Mishra & Koehler, 2006; Koehler & Mishra, 2008)—has focused increasingly upon how this knowledge can be assessed. In 2009, only five reliable and valid TPACK assessment instruments or frameworks had been published: two self-report surveys (Archambault & Crippen, 2009; Schmidt, Baran, Thompson, Koehler, Shin & Mishra, 2009), a discourse analysis framework (Koehler, Mishra & Yahya, 2007), and two triangulated performance assessments (Angeli & Valanides, 2009; Groth, Spickler, Bergner & Bardzell, 2009). By early 2012, at least eight more validated self-report survey instruments had appeared (Burgoyne, Graham, & Sudweeks, 2010; Chuang & Ho, 2011; Figg & Jaipal, 2011; Landry, 2010; Lee & Tsai, 2010; Lux, 2010; Sahin, 2011; Yurdakul, et al., 2012), along with two validated rubrics (Harris, Grandgenett & Hofer, 2010; Hofer, Grandgenett, Harris & Swan, 2011) and multiple types of TPACK-based content analyses (e.g., Graham, Borup & Smith, 2012; Hechter & Phyfe 2010; Koh & Divaharan, 2011) and verbal analyses (e.g., Mouza, 2011; Mouza & Wong, 2009) that demonstrated at least adequate levels of inter-rater reliability. Given the complexities of the TPACK construct (Cox & Graham, 2009), and the resulting challenges in its reliable and valid detection and description (cf. Koehler, Shin & Mishra, 2012), scholarship that develops and tests methods for TPACK assessment will probably continue for some time.

Our work in this area has focused upon developing and testing what Koehler et al. (2012, p. 17) term "performance assessments." These assessments "evaluate participants' TPACK by directly examining their performance on given tasks that are designed to represent complex, authentic, real-life tasks" (p. 22). Since no TPACK-based performance assessment for preservice teachers had been developed and published by mid-2009, we created and tested a rubric that can be used to assess the TPACK evident in teachers' written lesson plans (Harris, Grandgenett & Hofer, 2010). Five TPACK experts confirmed the instrument's construct and face validities prior to reliability testing. The instrument's interrater reliability was examined using both Intraclass Correlation (.857) and a percent score agreement procedure (84.1%). Internal consistency (using Cronbach's Alpha) was .911. Test-retest reliability (percent score agreement) was 87.0%.

Given the importance of assessing both planned and enacted instruction, we then developed and tested another TPACK-based rubric that can be used to assess observed evidence of TPACK during classroom instruction (Hofer, Grandgenett, Harris & Swan, 2011). Seven TPACK experts confirmed this observation instrument's construct and face validities. Its interrater reliability coefficient was computed using the same methods applied to the lesson plan rubric, with both Intraclass Correlation (.802) and percent score agreement (90.8%) procedures. Internal consistency (Cronbach's Alpha) for the observation rubric was .914. Test-retest reliability (score agreement) was 93.9%.

Experienced vs. Inexperienced Teachers' Planning

Our TPACK-based observation instrument (Hofer, et al., 2011) was tested using unedited classroom videos of equal numbers of both experienced and inexperienced teachers teaching. Considering this, and given the reliability and validity results summarized above, the observation rubric is sufficiently robust to be used to observe either preservice or inservice teachers. Our previous instrument (Harris, et al., 2010), however, was tested only with inexperienced teachers' lesson plans. Therefore, it was demonstrated to be a reliable and valid tool to use to assess only preservice teachers' written instructional plans. In the current study, we sought a similarly succinct, yet robust measure of experienced teachers' instructional planning with reference to the quality of their technology integration knowledge, or TPACK.

Studies of experienced teachers' lesson planning show it to be quite different from that of inexperienced teachers (Leinhardt, 1993). Inservice teachers' written plans rarely encompass everything that the teacher expects to happen during the planned instructional time, and they are not often written in a linear sequence from learning goals to learning activities to assessments (Clark & Peterson, 1986). They tend to focus upon guiding students' thinking moreso than inexperienced teachers' plans do, anticipating difficulties that students might have with the content to be taught. Experienced teachers also tend to be able to think simultaneously about their own actions, while also attending to and predicting their students' probable misconceptions and actions. Novice teachers generally do not plan or teach "in stereo" in this way, as inservice teachers do, and their actions during teaching don't always address the learning goals of the lesson completely (Leinhardt, 1993). Many experienced teachers can address the content of a lesson while meeting planned instructional objectives, connecting the content taught to larger issues, and anticipating students' probable confusions and difficulties. Inexperienced teachers tend to have much more limited knowledge of the nature of student learning, and experience difficulty in finding ways other than those that reflect their own thinking patterns to explain concepts to their students (Livingston & Borko, 1990).

Inservice teachers' written lesson plans tend to comprise brief notes only (Leinhardt, 1993), though their authors are able to explain at length the content foci, assessment strategies, targeted student thinking, alternative explanations, and "Plan B" learning activities that those limited written notes represent. Given the brevity and idiosyncrasy of experienced teachers' written planning documents, we realized that we could not assess their lesson plans in the same way that we assessed inexperienced teachers' planning artifacts. Instead, we devised a 20" – 30" semi-structured lesson interview protocol (see Appendix) that we used with volunteer inservice teachers to record essential information about their technology integrated lesson plans. These audiorecordings then became the data to which our "scorers" listened. For each interview, the scorers completed a copy of the Technology Integration Assessment Rubric (see Appendix), using it to assess the quality of the interviewed teachers' TPACK. In this way, we tested the existing rubric for reliability and validity when it was used to assess the quality of TPACK represented in experienced teachers' interactive descriptions of particular technology-infused lessons or projects.

Instrument Testing Procedures

Twelve experienced technology-using teachers (described in Table 1 below) and district-based teacher educators in two different geographic regions of the United States tested the reliability of the lesson plan instrument when it was used to individually assess 12 inservice teachers' audiorecorded interviews about self-selected, technology-infused lessons that they planned and taught. These two groups of scorers met at two different universities during either July or August of 2011 for approximately 3 hours to learn to use the rubric with two sample lesson plan interviews, then applied it within the following two weeks to evaluate of each of the audiorecorded 12 lesson interviews. The planning interviews addressed varying content areas and grade levels.

After the scorers used the existing rubric to individually assess each of the audiorecorded lesson interviews, they answered seven free-response questions that requested feedback about using the rubric with this type of data. We also asked each scorer to re-score three assigned lesson interviews one month after scoring them for the first time, and used these data to calculate the test-retest reliability of the instrument.

Scorer	Years Taught	Content Specialty	Grade Levels Taught	Years Teaching w/ Digital Techs.	Ed Tech PD Hours: Prev. 5 Years	Ed Tech Expertise Self-Assess.
A	20	Social Studies	9-12	20	220	Advanced
B	11	Elementary gifted learners	3, 5, 6, 8	5	65	Advanced
C	12	Elementary; Science	3-6	12	70	Advanced
D	39	Math	K-12	19	300	Intermediate
E	5	Physics	9-12	5	35	Intermediate
F	11	Technology Integration	K-8	6	150	Advanced
I	4	Elementary, Reading	2	4	100	Intermediate
J	14	Special Education	5-12	9	200	Advanced
K	12	English	10-12	11	300	Advanced
L	11	Math, Technology Integration	K-12	11	520	Advanced
M	30	Gifted Ed., Technology Integration	K-12 & college	25	120	Advanced
N	9	Math, Gifted Ed.	K-1, 7-8	7	90	Advanced

Table 1: Study participants working at pseudononymous Midwestern and Southeastern (shaded) Universities.

Validity Analysis

The construct and face validities of the instrument were examined when the instrument was first tested with preservice teachers' lesson plans (Harris, Grandgenett & Hofer, 2010). We used two strategies that are recommended for rubric validation (cf. Arter & McTighe, 2001; Moskal & Leydens, 2000). Construct validity reflects how well an instrument measures a particular construct of interest, which in this study was TPACK, as it is represented in educational lesson plans. As explained above, construct validity was examined in this study using expert reviews. Face validity, or whether an instrument appears to informed observers to measure what it is designed to measure, was examined using the experienced teachers' (scorers') responses to the seven-item survey, also described above.

Construct validity was a particularly important aspect of this rubric for us to test, since it was developed with TPACK as a central and unifying construct. The six experts consulted when the rubric was first developed and tested had strong qualifications for this review process, which included extensive experience with the TPACK framework as both researchers and teacher educators. In addition, two of the reviewers authored chapters in the *Handbook of Technological Pedagogical Content Knowledge (TPCK) for Educators* (AACTE, 2008), and one had recently released a TPACK-based preservice textbook. The researchers were asked to gauge how well TPK, TCK and TPACK were represented in the rubric, how well technology integration knowledge might be ascertained overall when using the rubric to evaluate a lesson/project plan, and what changes might be made to the rubric to help it to better reflect evidence of TPACK in teachers' planning documents. The rubric's construct validity was supported strongly by comments from five of the six expert reviewers. The sixth expert did not agree that the quality of technology integration (and therefore teachers' TPACK) could be ascertained overall for any instructional plan. Instead, this reviewer suggested creating specific questions to be answered about the appropriateness of technology use in different aspects of an instructional plan, such as the communication of content, the instruction itself, and the assessment.

The rubric's face validity was determined by analyzing the scorers' feedback on both the process of using the rubric and its perceived utility. All of the scorers' written comments during each of the two rubric tests (in 2009 and 2011) supported its ability to help teacher educators to assess the quality of TPACK-based technology integration inferred from lesson plans/interviews. Some also offered suggestions for minor changes to the wording in some of the rubric's cells, several of which were used to create the version of the rubric that appears in the Appendix.

Reliability Analysis

The reliability analyses for the rubric when it was used to assess audio interviews were conducted in July and August of 2011 with 12 teachers participating: six at Southeastern University and six at Midwestern University. The same rubric was used at each of the two locations. Scorers at both locations were chosen purposively, based upon their experience in integrating use of digital technologies into their teaching and their diverse professional backgrounds in both content areas and grade levels. Using the data generated, reliability across both locations was calculated using four different strategies: 1) interrater reliability, computed using the Intraclass Correlation Coefficient (ICC), 2) interrater reliability, computed using a second percent score agreement procedure, 3) internal consistency within the rubric, computed using Cronbach's Alpha, and 4) test-retest reliability as represented by the percent agreement between scorings of the same videos examined one month apart by the same teachers. The reliability procedures used for this study were similar to those used to validate the rubric for written lesson plan review (Harris, Grandgenett & Hofer 2010) and, in an expanded form, for the review of video observations of classes,(Hofer, Grandgenett, Harris & Swan, 2011). The statistical procedures were selected in consultation with three expert statisticians specializing in psychometrics.

Similar to our previous studies, the statistical procedures for the review of the rubric's reliability for audio interviews were selected based on each procedure's particular advantages for examining rubric reliability (or for that of similar scoring instruments). For example, the Intraclass Correlation Coefficient flexibly examines relationships among members of a class (Field, 2005; Griffin & Gonzalez, 1995; McGraw & Wong, 1996) and is becoming comparatively well known in instrument validation studies. It is now a scale analysis option in *SPSS* software. In this particular study, the educators scoring the audio interviews were essentially designated as a class, with rubric scores considered to be random effects, and the educators themselves representing fixed effects for the ICC calculations. Percent agreement was used to further document the extent of interrater reliability, systematically pairing scores from two different judges at a time on each video, then computing the mean percent of agreement across all judges. Adjacent scoring was used to represent this scorer agreement, and was defined as two scores with no more than one rubric category of difference. In this way, rubric scores of 3 and 4 would be considered to be in agreement, while scores of 2 and 4 would be identified as out of agreement. Percent of agreement has long been used for criterion-referenced scoring (Gronlund, 1985; Litwin, 2002); it was a useful way to further check the interrater reliability of the rubric in this study.

The rubric's internal consistency in assessing the TPACK evident in audio interviews was again examined using the well-established and commonly used Cronbach's Alpha procedure (Allen & Yen, 2002; Cronbach, Gleser, Nanda, & Rajaratnam, 1972). In this procedure, the rubric scoring data set was transposed within the SPSS data file to permit an examination of the consistency of participants' scores between each of the four rows of the rubric.

To analyze the rubric's test-retest reliability, a percent of adjacent agreement strategy was used again. The educators' scores for three of the audio files were compared to their scores for the same three audio files scored one month earlier. Each individual row's score, as well as the rubric's total scores, were compared, and an average percent agreement score was computed. The three audio interviews selected for a second scoring process were identified as a possible "check set" of audio files that the researchers expected to be scored as representing high, medium, and low levels of demonstrated TPACK. The three recordings also represented a range of content that included elementary science, high school mathematics, and middle school foreign language.

Finally, to provide some context on the scorers' own perceptions of expertise to do such scorings adequately, the scorers assessed their expertise levels at both the time of the initial scoring and when rescoring interviews to determine if their self-perceptions of technology expertise had changed from one scoring to the next. The scorers' self-assessments confirmed their perceptions of adequate expertise. The 12 scorers all ranked themselves similarly from the first scoring to the second, with 9 scorers ranking themselves as "advanced" on the first scoring, and three ranking themselves as "intermediate." At the time of the rescoring one month later, one of the scorers increased their ranking from intermediate to "expert," while all others scorers retained their original self-perceived levels of expertise within the intermediate and advanced categories.

Reliability Results

To complete the Intraclass Correlation reliability calculation, the scores for each row of the rubric were recorded individually, with a total score for all four rows computed by adding the scores for each of the individual rows. Using the ICC procedure incorporated into SPSS software, the resulting statistics for the 12 scorers were: Row 1 = .651, Row 2 = .814, Row 3 = .681, Row 4 = .853, and Total Rubric = .818. This was a comparatively strong finding for ICC, which is a statistical procedure that can produce rather conservative results for reliability computations. However, upon further examination of the correlations among individual scorers, it was noted that one scorer was negatively correlated with all other scorers on all row scores, as well in the total scores. When that single scorer was removed, the ICC coefficients increased significantly, with Row 1 = .750, Row 2 = .850, Row 3 = .771, Row 4 = .886, and Total Rubric = .870. Upon reflection on the background this single scorer, it was determined that he was relatively unique among the set of judges in his perspective (with lower scores for many of the planning interviews), and had just assumed a full-time administrative post in his local school district. Thus, his "unique administrative perspective" on the audio lessons was different enough to warrant the removal of his scores from the data set.

The percent of agreement among the 12 scorers was also computed. This statistic is known to be less sensitive to the "direction" of how judges' scores align. Instead, it considers exclusively how "close" judges' scores are to each other. The percent agreement for the rubric scoring procedure across all scorers was computed to be 91.7%, further supporting the reliability of the rubric as first calculated using ICC statistics. When the negatively correlated scorer mentioned previously was removed, than the percent of adjacent agreement between scorers increased slightly to 93.6.

The computed internal consistency of the rubric was also quite promising, calculated as .895 (Cronbach's Alpha) for the rubric as tested across the 12 scorers. The rescoring of the three check set videos, which also used a percent agreement calculation, further supported the rubric's reliability. The percent agreement between the two separate scorings of the check set videos one month apart attained 100% adjacent agreement, showing strong consistency in the separate scorings of the check set videos for all scorers.

Conclusion

Given the results of reliability testing with 12 scorers using ICC calculations, percent agreement computations, and the Cronbach's Alpha measure, we conclude that this instrument has comparatively strong reliability for examining audio interviews describing lessons and projects in which educational technologies are incorporated, and we feel confident in recommending it for further use. The rubric's reliability calculations, along with its validity evaluations, suggest that we can now offer it to other researchers and educators to assess the TPACK evident in structured interviews done with experienced teachers. It has been released under a Creative Commons License, and is available on the Learning Activity Types Web site (http://activitytypes.wm.edu/).

We are pleased to place the interview prompts used with this instrument into the public domain, also via a Creative Commons (attribution, noncommercial, no derivatives) license, and encourage consideration of their use for both research and professional development. Given the increasing variety of tested TPACK-based instruments currently available, it is now possible to more accurately and comprehensively assess teachers' TPACK in authentic ways. We hope that the work described in this chapter will support that ongoing effort within future well-triangulated studies of teachers' TPACK.

References

Abbitt, J. (2011). Measuring technological pedagogical content knowledge in preservice teacher education: A review of current methods and instruments. *Journal of Research on Technology in Education, 43*(4), 281–300.

Allen, M. J. & Yen, W. M. (2002). *Introduction to measurement theory*. Long Grove, IL: Waveland Press.

American Association of Colleges of Teacher Education (Eds.).(2008). *The handbook of technological pedagogical content knowledge for educators*. New York: Routledge.

Angeli, C., & Valanides, N. (2009). Epistemological and methodological issues for the conceptualization, development, and assessment of ICT–TPCK: Advances in technological pedagogical content knowledge (TPCK). *Computers and Education, 52*(1), 154-168.

Archambault, L., & Crippen, K. (2009). Examining TPACK among K-12 online distance educators in the United States. *Contemporary Issues in Technology and Teacher Education, 9*(1). Retrieved from http://www.citejournal.org/vol9/iss1/general/article2.cfm

Arter, J., & McTighe, J. (2001). *Scoring rubrics in the classroom*. Thousand Oaks: Corwin Press, Inc.

Britten, J.S., & Cassady, J.C. (2005). The Technology Integration Assessment Instrument: Understanding planned use of technology by classroom teachers. *Computers in the Schools, 22*(3), 49-61.

Burgoyne, N., Graham, C.R. & Sudweeks, R. (2010). The validation of an instrument measuring TPACK. In D. Gibson & B. Dodge (Eds.), *Proceedings of Society for Information Technology & Teacher Education international conference 2010* (pp. 3787-3794). Chesapeake, VA: AACE. Retrieved from http://www.editlib.org/p/33971

Chuang, H-H, & Ho, C-J. (2011). An investigation of early childhood teachers' technological pedagogical content knowledge (TPACK) in Taiwan. *Journal of Kirsehir Education Faculty, 12*(2), 99-117. Retrieved from http://www.doaj.org/doaj?func=abstract&id=782294&recNo=6&toc=1&uiLanguage=en

Clark, C., & Peterson, P. (1986). Teachers' thought processes. In M. C. Wittrock (Ed.), *Handbook of research on teaching* (3rd ed., pp. 255-296). New York: Macmillan.

Cronbach, L. J., Gleser, G. C., Nanda, H., & Rajaratnam, N. (1972). *The dependability of behavioral measurements: Theory of generalizability of scores and profiles*. New York: Wiley.

Field, A.P. (2005). Intraclass correlation. In Everitt, B.S. & Howell, D.C. (Eds.). *Encyclopedia of statistics in the behavioral sciences* (pp. 1296-1305). Chichester, England: Wiley.

Figg, C. & Jaipal, K. (2011). Developing a survey from a taxonomy of characteristics for TK, TCK, and TPK to assess teacher candidates' knowledge of teaching with technology. In M. Koehler & P. Mishra (Eds.), *Proceedings of Society for Information Technology & Teacher Education international conference 2011* (pp. 4330-4339). Chesapeake, VA: AACE. Retrieved from http://www.editlib.org/p/37012

Graham, C. R., Borup, J., & Smith, N. B. (2012). Using TPACK as a framework to understand teacher candidates' technology integration decisions. *Journal of Computer Assisted Learning*. doi: 10.1111/j.1365-2729.2011.00472.x

Griffin, D., & Gonzalez, R. (1995). Correlational analysis of dyad-level data in the exchangeable case. *Psychological Bulletin, 118,* 430-439.

Gronlund, N.E. (1985). *Measurement and evaluation in teaching* (5th ed.), New York: McMillian.

Groth, R., Spickler, D., Bergner, J., & Bardzell, M. (2009). A qualitative approach to assessing technological pedagogical content knowledge. *Contemporary Issues in Technology and Teacher Education, 9*(4). Retrieved December 5, 2009, from http://www.citejournal.org/vol9/iss4/mathematics/article1.cfm

Hammond, T. C., Alexander, R. C., & Bodzin, A. M. (2012). Assessment in authentic environments: Designing instruments and reporting results from classroom-based TPACK research. In R. N. Ronau, C. R. Rakes, & M. L. Niess (Eds.), *Educational technology, teacher knowledge, and classroom impact: A research handbook on frameworks and approaches* (pp. 32-57). Hershey, PA: IGI Global. doi: 10.4018/978-1-60960-750-0.ch003

Harris, J., Grandgenett, N., & Hofer, M. (2010). Testing a TPACK-based technology integration assessment rubric. In C. D. Maddux (Ed.), *Research highlights in technology and teacher education 2010* (pp. 323-331). Chesapeake, VA: Society for Information Technology & Teacher Education (SITE).

Hechter, R. & Phyfe, L. (2010). Using online videos in the science methods classroom as context for developing preservice teachers' awareness of the TPACK components. In D. Gibson & B. Dodge (Eds.), *Proceedings of the Society for Information Technology & Teacher Education international conference 2010* (pp. 3841-3848). Chesapeake, VA: AACE.

Hofer, M., Grandgenett, N., Harris, J., & Swan, K. (2011). Testing a TPACK-based technology integration observation instrument. In C. D. Maddux (Ed.), *Research highlights in technology and teacher education 2011* (pp. 39-46). Chesapeake, VA: Society for Information Technology & Teacher Education (SITE).

Koehler, M.J., & Mishra, P. (2008). Introducing TPACK. In AACTE Committee on Innovation & Technology (Eds.). *Handbook of technological pedagogical content knowledge for educators* (pp. 3-29). New York, NY: Routledge.

Koehler, M.J., & Mishra, P. (2005). Teachers learning technology by design. *Journal of Computing in Teacher Education, 21*(3), 94-102.

Koehler, M.J., Mishra, P., & Yahya, K. (2007). Tracing the development of teacher knowledge in a design seminar: Integrating content, pedagogy, & technology. *Computers & Education, 49*(3), 740-762.

Koehler, M. J., Shin, T. S., & Mishra, P. (2012). How do we measure TPACK? Let me count the ways. In R. N. Ronau, C. R. Rakes, & M. L. Niess (Eds.), *Educational technology, teacher knowledge, and classroom impact: A research handbook on frameworks and approaches* (pp. 16-31). Hershey, PA: IGI Global. doi: 10.4018/978-1-60960-750-0.ch002

Koh, J. H. L., & Divaharan, S. (2011). Developing pre-service teachers' technology integration expertise through the TPACK-Developing Instructional Model. *Journal of Educational Computing Research, 44*(1), 35-58. doi: 10.2190/EC.44.1.c

Landry, G. A. (2010). *Creating and validating an instrument to measure middle school mathematics teachers' technological pedagogical content knowledge (TPACK)* (Doctoral dissertation, University of Tennessee - Knoxville). Retrieved from http://trace.tennessee.edu/utk_graddiss/720

Lee, M. H. & Tsai, C. C. (2010). Exploring teachers' perceived self-efficacy and technological pedagogical content knowledge with respect to educational use of the World Wide Web. *Instructional Science, 38*(1), 1-21.

Leinhardt, G. (1993). On teaching. In R. Glaser (Ed.), *Advances in instructional psychology* (Vol. 4, pp. 1-54). Hillsdale, NJ: Lawrence Erlbaum Associates.

Litwin, M.S. (2002). How to assess and interpret survey psychometrics. *The Survey Kit Series* (Vol. 8). Thousand Oaks, CA: Sage Publications.

Livingston, C., & Borko, H. (1990). High school mathematics review lessons: Expert-novice distinctions. *Journal for Research in Mathematics Education, 21*(5), 372-387.

Lux, N. J. (2010). *Assessing technological pedagogical content knowledge* (Doctoral dissertation). **Retrieved from ProQuest Dissertation and Theses.** (AAT 3430401)

McGraw, K.O., & Wong, S.P. (1996). Forming inferences about some intraclass correlation coefficients, *Psychological Methods, 1*(1), 30-46.

Mishra, P., & Koehler, M. J. (2006). Technological pedagogical content knowledge: A new framework for teacher knowledge. *Teachers College Record. 108*(6), 1017-1054.

Moskal, B. M., & Leydens, J. A. (2000). Scoring rubric development: Validity and reliability. *Practical Assessment, Research & Evaluation, 7,* 71-81.

Mouza, C. (2011). Promoting urban teachers' understanding of technology, content, and pedagogy in the context of case development. *Journal of Research on Technology in Education, 44*(1), 1–29.

Mouza, C. & Wong, W. (2009). *Studying classroom practice: Case development for professional learning in technology integration.* Journal of Technology and Teacher Education, 17(2), 175-202.

Sahin, I. (2011). Development of survey of Technological Pedagogical and Content Knowledge (TPACK). *Turkish Online Journal of Educational Technology, 10*(1), 97-105.

Schmidt, D., Baran, E., Thompson, A., Koehler, M.J., Shin, T, & Mishra, P. (2009, April). *Technological pedagogical content knowledge (TPACK): The development and validation of an assessment instrument for preservice teachers.* Paper presented at the 2009 Annual Meeting of the American Educational Research Association, San Diego, CA. Retrieved from http://mkoehler.educ.msu.edu/unprotected_readings/TPACK_Survey/Schmidt_et_al_Survey_v1.pdf

Yurdakul, I. K., Odabasi, H. F., Kilicer, K., Coklar, A. N., Birinci, G., & Kurt, A. A. (2012). The development, validity and reliability of TPACK-deep: A technological pedagogical content knowledge scale. *Computers & Education 58*(3), 964–977. doi: 10.1016/j.compedu.2011.10.012

Appendix: Interview Protocol and Assessment Rubric

Interview Protocol

LESSON DESCRIPTION:
Describe the content and/or process topic(s) for the lesson.
Describe the student learning goals/objectives addressed in the lesson. (These will not necessarily be state or national standards. Participants should describe these in their own words.)
Describe your students (e.g. grade level, and specific learning needs/preferences).
Walk me through the lesson/project as it unfolded in the classroom.
What educational technologies (digital and non-digital) did you use and how did you and/or your students use them?
Describe any contextual information (e.g. access to a computer lab, materials and resources available; particular departmental/school-wide initiatives) that influenced the design or implementation of the lesson/project.

TPACK-SPECIFIC QUESTIONS:
How and why do the particular technologies used in this lesson/project "fit" the content/process goals?
How and why do the particular technologies used in this lesson/project "fit" the instructional strategies you used?
How and why do the learning goals, instructional strategies, and technologies used all fit together in this lesson/project?

Assessment Rubric

Criteria	4	3	2	1
Curriculum Goals & Technologies (Curriculum-based technology use)	Technologies selected for use in the instructional plan are <u>strongly aligned</u> with one or more curriculum goals.	Technologies selected for use in the instructional plan are <u>aligned</u> with one or more curriculum goals.	Technologies selected for use in the instructional plan are <u>partially aligned</u> with one or more curriculum goals.	Technologies selected for use in the instructional plan are <u>not aligned</u> with any curriculum goals.
Instructional Strategies & Technologies (Using technology in teaching/learning)	Technology use <u>optimally supports</u> instructional strategies.	Technology use <u>supports</u> instructional strategies.	Technology use <u>minimally supports</u> instructional strategies.	Technology use <u>does not support</u> instructional strategies.
Technology Selection(s) (Compatibility with curriculum goals & instructional strategies)	Technology selection(s) are <u>exemplary</u>, given curriculum goal(s) and instructional strategies.	Technology selection(s) are <u>appropriate, but not exemplary</u>, given curriculum goal(s) and instructional strategies.	Technology selection(s) are <u>marginally appropriate</u>, given curriculum goal(s) and instructional strategies.	Technology selection(s) are <u>inappropriate</u>, given curriculum goal(s) and instructional strategies.
"Fit" (Content, pedagogy and technology together)	Content, instructional strategies and technology <u>fit together strongly</u> within the instructional plan.	Content, instructional strategies and technology <u>fit together</u> within the instructional plan.	Content, instructional strategies and technology <u>fit together somewhat</u> within the instructional plan.	Content, instructional strategies and technology <u>do not fit together</u> within the instructional plan.

Using TPACK for Analysing Teachers' Task Design: Understanding Change in a 1:1-Laptop Setting

Martin Tallvid
Johan Lundin
Berner Lindström
University of Gothenburg
Sweden
martin.tallvid@educ.goteborg.se

Abstract: This paper investigates teachers' task design in a 1:1-setting. The analysis draws on a longitudinal study in two secondary schools in Sweden. The TPACK-framework is used as a lens for understanding not only how information technologies play an additional part in the design of tasks, but also for analysing how teachers address the integration of pedagogy and content in the use of technology. The teacher's and the students' continuous access to laptops enabled an arena for collective knowledge building. The results show how the original task was expanded in unanticipated ways. The paper also provides guidelines for task design in a 1:1 setting, usable for both pre- and in-service teacher education.

Introduction

Substantial efforts have been made during the past decades to push ICT into educational settings. The reasons given for designing, or employing new technologies are mainly to enhance and support students' learning. Large-scale projects have been initiated in the US, as well as huge investments in, for example, the UK, Singapore and Germany, in developing and implementing educational technology infrastructures (Selwyn, 2000). Even though some studies point to enhanced learning possibilities with ICT (Bebell & Kay, 2010; Penuel, 2006), and a general drive to include ICT in education, schools seem to struggle with implementing technology in everyday practices of teachers and students (Cuban, 2001; Dynarski et al., 2007; O'Shea & Koschmann, 1997; Zhao & Frank, 2003).

Since the beginning of the 21-century there seem to be a gradual change in schools towards including mobile technologies, such as laptops. For example, a number of reports show a significantly increased interest in laptop use in education (Balanskat, Blamire, & Kefala, 2006; Fried, 2008; Lowther, Ross, & Morrison, 2003; Warschauer, 2006). This can have several explanations, but the reduced costs, the higher performance, battery capacity as well as the reduced size and weight made this development possible. It would be rather naïve to not also consider the growing interest from computer manufacturers in the emergent market for computers in schools. E.g. Apple and Microsoft have made substantial investments aimed at education and have departments whose main task is increasing the use of computer-based education.[1] Both have also been driving forces behind the first large-scale investments in laptops in classrooms (Rockman, 1998; Silvernail & Lane, 2004). Classrooms where students use laptops are today increasingly common in schools all over the western world (Valiente, 2010).

One trend is to provide students with a laptop each, to use as a daily tool in all their educational activities, so called 1:1-projects. The number of 1:1-projects are growing rapidly in Sweden as well. In 2011 more than 180 municipalities (out of 290) have on-going 1:1-projects in one, several or all schools and the number of 1:1-schools is growing[2]. This change puts many teachers in new and challenging positions. One main challenge is to design meaningful and educationally relevant activities for learners with laptops. In this paper we focus on how teachers engage in task design and perform educational activities, and how this performance can be related to their knowledge in pedagogy, technology and

[1] http://www.apple.com/education/ ; http://www.microsoft.com/education/teachers/default.aspx

[2] http://www2.diu.se/framlar/

the subject content. When designing a task the teacher has a specific content to be learned in mind, they have to use their understanding of student learning in the design, and construct a task framed by the technical resources at hand. Subsequently, the students' involvement in the tasks provides feedback on the design. Previous research on mobile technologies in classrooms, tends to be design oriented, experimental or short-term evaluations (Underwood, 2004). With a few exceptions (Bate, 2010; Orlando, 2009) there is a lack of longitudinal studies focusing on how teachers redesign their tasks in relation to the technical development. This paper aims to address this gap and provide results from a four-year study, where all students and teachers in two secondary schools were equipped with a personal laptop.

We used the TPACK framework (Mishra & Koehler, (2006), to analyse teachers' task design in a 1:1-setting. The introduction of new technologies into educational settings has an impact on not only the pedagogical approaches a teacher can use, but also the content presentation. This is often neglected when investigating ICT and education. The TPACK framework stresses the importance of formulating teacher competence as an integration of pedagogical, content and technical knowledge. In our analysis we investigate how these three (pedagogical, content and technical knowledge) are integrated in teachers' task design. Based on this we will provide tentative guidelines for teachers' designing educational tasks for 1:1 classroom settings.

The remainder of the paper is organised as follows: first we present the TPACK framework and discuss it as a tool for analysing task design. After this we describe the set-up of the study. This is followed by a description of a task design for the 1:1 classroom, drawing on one particularly illustrative instance from the collected data. Finally we provide a conclusions and a discussion, including guidelines for task design in a 1:1 setting.

The TPACK framework

What constitutes applicable teacher competence and training is under debate (Afshari, 2009; Fullan, 2006; Giavrimis, Giossi, & Papastamatis, 2011). The demands change as the organisation of schools change, but also as our understanding of learning, different subject contents and as the technical possibilities change. Shulman (1986, 1987) formulated a framework suggesting that successful teachers integrate content knowledge with pedagogical knowledge in their teaching.

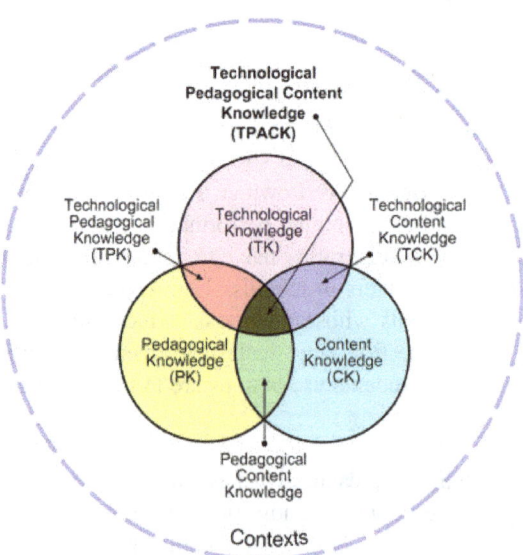

Figure 1: TPACK (Mishra & Koehler, 2006)

The TPACK model is a development of Shulman's model describing the relation between pedagogy and subject content, i.e. "pedagogical-content knowledge" (Shulman, 1986). Knowledge of how to use technology is added in the

TPACK-framework, arguing that all three are crucial in teaching, but also emphasizing the importance of taking advantage of expanding technical recourses available (Mishra & Koehler, 2006). Technological knowledge relates to technology and its use in education. Mishra and Koehler (2006) argue that useful technological knowledge is constantly changing due to rapid technological development, and regard the development technological knowledge an "open-ended interaction with technology" (Mishra, Koehler, & Kereluik, 2009, p. 115). Cox and Graham (2009) argue that the meaning of "technologies" in the TPACK framework is not fully defined, and propose a definition rather focus "emerging technologies" (ibid p. 63). TPACK is presented as the integration that expands the three components (Koehler & Mishra, 2008). This means that TPACK is developed and performed in interaction with these three; the teachers need to be able to simultaneously integrate their knowledge of pedagogy, content and technology into their daily teaching. What this interaction is, and how it emerges in teaching practice is less well defined. It is possible to regard TPACK as a "way to explain the complexity of teaching integration as a unique type of teacher knowledge" (Polly & Brantley-Dias, 2009), i.e. a way to express and think of a specific teachers´ knowledge, which gives a holistic perspective on technology integration into education.

Method

The data used in this paper is part of a larger study carried out from 2007 to 2011 in two Swedish secondary schools (14-16 year old students). Data in the larger study were produced using surveys, interviews and classroom observations. Three web surveys (2007, 2008, 2010) were followed up by both group interviews (2007) and individual interviews (2009, 2010) with students, teachers, headmasters and parents. Twenty-five classroom observations were conducted. The classes were observed during lessons and during breaks, and in some cases also videotaped. Detailed results from the study are described in three reports (Hallerström & Tallvid, 2008; Tallvid, 2010; Tallvid & Hallerström, 2009). This provides data on how the students performed the tasks and how the teacher instructed the students during their work. In some cases teachers described the task design in advance, and in some cases we asked about specific observations in the interviews. Data were presented in group analysis sessions, looking for observable and distinguishable integration of TPACK in task design, and tasks being implemented classrooms. The analysis presented in this paper is based on the total body of data from the interviews and the observations, supplemented with video. However, in the presentation below, we use one narrative to convey these main findings.

Understanding task design through TPACK

When designing a task teachers usually first consider the content and then what method to use (Harris & Hofer, 2011; John, 2006). In this section we will, for illustrative purposes, use the design and execution of one specific task. The findings draw on observations from several different subjects. This narrative concerns math, i.e. drawing in scale. We will deconstruct the task using the TPACK framework.

Designing the task "Build your dream house"

The learning objective for this task is to understand scale drawing, through moving between virtual representations and actual physical spaces. The Swedish curriculum states that students should manage to make drawings in scale for two and three dimensional objects (Skolverket, 2010). The math teacher is an experienced teacher and he stated that he have had problems with presenting scale drawing to the students as comprehensible as desired. The traditional way is to use the textbook in mathematics where the students are supposed to make changes in previously prepared drawings, either making them bigger or smaller. But now, when all students had personal laptops, the teacher wanted to try a new way of presenting learning scales.

The teacher designed a task that included making a vision of your personal "dream house". The dream house was to be sketched using 3D-software and then built in cardboard in scale of 1:10. The teacher described that he, after only a couple of minutes searching on the internet, found a free 3D-software that would make it possible to make complete drawings of a house . With this 3D-software it would be achievable to first create a house plan on the laptop and then student would build a cardboard model of the "dream house". The teacher considered letting the students work in pairs or in groups, but finally decided to let the students work alone using their laptops. This decision was based on his experience from teaching scale drawing where he realized that "some of the students didn't really grasp the solutions". He had tried to explain the correlation between e.g. a house and a floor plan in different ways, but he had been forced to realize that many students still have had problems understanding this relation. He identified the particularly challenging aspects of the tasks and he tried to find ways to present the task in a motivating way. When the teacher prepared this segment of the curriculum he used the Internet to find inspiration and new ideas. Before 1:1, he usually used the Teachers' Guide, supplementing the math-book. Now he had heard from colleagues that there was free software that could be used for drawing a floor plan in a scale. This explorative way of engaging in the design process demands an understanding of what content that needs to be learned. He then moved on to formulating a setup of the activity, which is closely interlinked with available technical resources. In this work he needed technical, pedagogical and content knowledge, but also an understanding of how these related to each other in the specific design.

With the new situation at hand (one laptop per student) teachers can be certain that all students have the same technical resources and therefore the inclusion of the laptops is always a feasible option. The teachers' planning now, compared with before the 1:1-project, is different for a number of reasons. Since they can be sure of that all students have his or her personal laptop they do not have to consider whether they all have access to a computer. The interviews with teachers confirmed that it was possible to realize many of the tasks before the 1:1-project, but then they had to book a computer hall in advance. And even if they did, they couldn't be certain that all computers were fully functioning and therefore they often refrained from tasks that demanded computer access. But as they now knew that all students had ubiquitous access to online laptops, and the fact that the students could retain their material on their own laptops, it facilitated and promoted the development of tasks like this. This is a shift in driving force behind a change worth to mention. Before 1:1 teachers designed the task first and then added the technology to make it more motivating. But since they now knew that all students had a laptop the technology became an influential driving force integrated in task design.

Implementation of "designing your dream house"

The observations are made in an 8th grade class in a 1-1 school. The class has 24 students; 14 boys and 10 girls. The observation was carried out during two 60 minutes-lessons in mathematics. The classroom is equipped with ordinary school desks put up in rows and at front a teacher's desk and a white board. The excerpt below is from the classroom observation notes. (translation from Swedish):

> "Arrival at 8.35 am. Lesson starts at 8.40. The teacher gives instructions for today's task: "Continue to work on your dream houses". The students are supposed to continue from where they finished their work the previous lesson. The students work calmly and quietly. They take out their personal laptops and put them on their desks. All the students seem to be familiar with the task and they begin to work immediately. They express that they like the task "because it's different from just using the book" (girl 8th grade). The classroom is spacious – the students have their own desks with their own building material, with cardboard, scissors and glue. Everyone is focused on the task, I see no browsing the web or chatting. They have made drawings of their dream home in 3D - software on the laptops. They look at the drawing on the laptop screen and build a copy of their dream home in cardboard. They constantly return to the laptop drawing to check if the measuring is correct."

Figure 2 & 3: 8th grade student building cardboard model using 3D-plan on laptop.
(Excerpts from video recorded during classroom observation.)

The students worked individually on their personal dream house, but there was also a lot of cooperation going on, e.g. students giving each other hints on usable webpages. The aim with the task was to understand scale drawing, but the task developed to something else as well, without the teacher's involvement. The students started to equip their homes with luxurious Jacuzzis and expensive television sets with surround sound systems. The teacher accepted the development with the remark that they had to make an appropriate budget and keep track of their total expenditures. The students also elaborated the task by finding examples of wallpaper on the web that could be printed out and used in their cardboard models, and they found out that they could use the furniture retailers' webpages to find nice photos of pieces of furniture. This resulted in, that in addition to making a model in a scale, the students were obliged to calculate how many square meters of wallpaper they would need and how much this would cost. They were also forced to find out the estimated cost for the desired furniture and multimedia equipment.

The teacher had previously used the task of building a dream home, but not in a 1:1 classroom. But even though he had tried earlier to illustrate the correlation between the physical world and representations in a drawing he described the difference when he knew that every student had their own laptop.

> " ... for those students who have difficulties in understanding this part the personal laptop makes it easier to try it over and over again. After a couple of attempts they "see the light" and understand how to solve the problem". (male mathematics teacher)

This shows that teachers' TPACK is not the only decisive factor in the realisation of task design. While observing the realisation of the task in the classroom we saw the need for competent execution of the task among the students. They need to learn new content to complete the task, but also mastering task design, as well as the tools included. There is also a collective expansion of competence as the task unfolds in the students' elaboration and development of the task and the trial- and error use of the software. The teacher was not an expert on using either the software or the Internet, but he was technically competent enough to encourage the student in trying to explore the possibilities. This resulted in unanticipated use of the tools and led to an extension and development of the task. The use of the laptops also challenged the idea of what really were the content and the learning object of the task. The original aim was negotiated and the students' willingness to elaborate the task was accepted by the teacher.

The different demands of the technical knowledge in this narrative are several and they together have an impact on the teacher's strategies for designing the task. Initially he must know that it is possible to find tools that can be applied in line with the expected outcome of the task and he needs to know how to find and download the software. Secondly he needs the skills to articulate a task where the software meets the pedagogical demands and thereby supports student learning. Thirdly he must be aware of the eventuality that the students will within minutes of working on the laptop be on the borderline of off-task activities, and have strategies for dealing with this.

Discussion and conclusions

In this paper we set out to investigate the use of the TPACK framework as an analytical lens for investigating teachers task design, as well as provide some guidelines for teachers design of educational tasks for a 1:1 classroom setting.

When planning lessons there are methods and strategies that are predictable and possible to train during both pre- and in-service teacher education. The 1:1 environment affords many different outcomes that are impossible to predict. This study shows that teachers must be prepared for the unforeseen and have different strategies to handle new situations in the classroom.

When analysing results from the implementation phase of the designed task it is possible to distinguish two different patterns in the outcomes. The teacher's expected outcome from the design was that students should work with sketching in 3D and then build a model in cardboard of their drawing in scale 1:10. The students fulfilled this aim, but there was also a not negligible unexpected outcome from the design. The students engaged not only in learning scales, but also in developing the task, making the different outcomes impossible to anticipate. The teacher's and the students' continuous access to the laptops made it possible to elaborate and search on the Internet for resources. Even though students were mainly using one application the laptop functioned as an open-ended tool where new web-resources and applications can be involved as they are needed and discovered. This arena for collective knowledge building gave both the teacher and the students' new insights. Having knowledge of the integration of content, pedagogy and technology makes it possible for the teacher to anticipate and handle the unexpected outcomes in a 1:1 environment. In line with what is argued by Mifsud and Mörch (2010) we see how activities not defined by the teacher from the beginning, proved to be a valuable development of the task.

The different parts of the task design	Suggested by teacher	Suggested by students
Predefined curriculum-based content	Using the 3D program to design the house, building a house in cardboard	Furnishing the house, making calculations of the size of furniture
Spin-off content - off task	Making the house aesthetically pleasing (choosing wallpaper, calculations of wall paper-size)	Making the house functionally pleasing (choosing media equipment, calculations of costs)

Table 1: Different parts of the task design

It proves complex to define what can be understood as part of the task. In this sense the setup proposes that we understand the task design as an on going, collective activity. The teachers' design suggested pure sketching and building of a house, but as the students elaborated the task they introduced off-task (however curriculum-based) activities, such as measuring wallpaper and doing estimates of the prices for media equipment. The most common way to handle these unavoidable unexpected outcomes among less TPACK-confident teachers in a 1:1- environment is to confine or forbid off-task activities. Apparently students with laptops also occasionally engage in other activities such as using Facebook or gaming. In this paper we do not explore how to understand and deal with unwanted activities, merely unexpected.

From this analysis it is possible to formulate the following guidelines for task design in a 1:1 environment:

Firstly: teachers must continuously expand their competence in anticipating different scenarios. This closely connects with their TPACK, and with experience and training teachers develops competence and methods in task design, allowing for an increased possibility for anticipating the possible outcomes. The one thing he or she can be sure of is that in the 1:1 setup allows for many unexpected outcomes, which are more diverse and create a larger spectrum of new situations to deal with.

Secondly: since teachers can be sure that the unexpected always occurs, it is wise to have different strategies for addressing changes in task design. Because it is impossible to predict what is going to happen in an educational situation, and particularly in a 1:1 environment, this is one of the most important aspects relating to TPACK. As we see in the example above, unintended activities are sometimes supportive and connect to the learning goals. Such unexpected development is one of the possible advantages with a 1:1 environment since it often gives an opportunity to take benefit of the students' curiosity and willingness to learn. However, a teacher must constantly evaluate the re-design of the task.

Thirdly: The 1:1 classroom can be regarded as a joint arena for learning, where teachers and student have an interchange of information. The most TPACK-confident teacher has no problem with being unable to answer all kinds of questions or not being the laptop-specialist in the class. The guideline is to be aware of this and to be mentally prepared for not being in total control of the development of the task. Some of the teachers in the interviews compared it with being confident enough to dare to make a parachute jump.

"It's scary in the beginning, but after a while it is wonderful and you will be rewarded". (excerpt from interview with female language teacher)

As Mishra and Kohler (2006) state, it is impossible for teachers to be constantly updated on the latest technological development. As the mobile technology always is evolving and changing it designates that, in settings where all teachers and all students are provided with a personal laptop, tasks need to be reformulated and constantly developed. The main concern for the teacher is to be aware of, and have an open mind to the persistently changing map of technology in education.

Fourthly: Understanding task design as an on-going process involving the students it is even more important that the students understand what content is in focus in the particular activity, i.e. what particular content is to be learned. If this is not transparent to the students, they will not be able to have this as a resource when re-designing and suggesting alternative takes on the task at hand, allowing for more spin-off activities not related to the content.

Concluding remarks

The interviews with the teachers made it explicit that the teachers need further in-service training to be able to develop their TPACK. Every situation in the classroom is unique and to solve the problems the teachers have to navigate between the three fundamentals of teaching with technology. To merely regard pedagogy, content and technology as separate components is a "real disservice to good teaching"(AACTE, 2008). In the analysis of the construction and the execution of the tasks we have used the TPACK framework as a tool for understanding the relation between the pedagogical, content and technological knowledge, that are suggested to be crucial to provide an educationally effective use of the emerging educational technologies. The framework was useful for understanding not only how technology plays an additional part in the design of tasks, but also how teachers address the integration of pedagogy and content in the use of technology. In some cases the integration is done without reflection of the role that technology might play, such as when writing on the laptop rather than by hand (or typewriter). In these cases teachers rarely feel a need to innovate or transform tasks to fit. In other cases they find possibilities for transforming previous tasks in the integration. By using the TPACK framework as a lens, the observations, interviews and the results from the surveys altogether paint the picture of teachers reformulating the tasks due to the unlimited access to technical devices. The TPACK framework pointed out relevant foci when analysing task design in a 1:1 classroom.

References

AACTE (Ed.). (2008). The handbook of technological pedagogical content knowledge (TPCK) for educators. New York: Taylor & Francis Group for the American Association of Colleges for Teacher Education.
Afshari, M. (2009). Factors affecting teachers' use of information and communication technology. International Journal of Instruction, 2(1), 77-104.
Balanskat, A., Blamire, R., & Kefala, S. (2006). The ICT impact report: A review of studies of ICT impact on schools in Europe. European Schoolnet. http://ec.europa.eu/education/pdf/doc254_en.pdf.
Bate, F. (2010). A longitudinal study of beginning teachers' pedagogical identity and their use of ICT. Murdoch University, Perth.
Bebell, D., & Kay, R. (2010). One to one computing: A summary of the quantitative results from the Berkshire wireless learning initiative. Journal of Technology, Learning and Assesment, 9(2).
Cox, S., & Graham, C. R. (2009). Using an elaborated model of the TPACK framework to analyze and depict teacher knowledge. TechTrends, 53(5), 6 -67.
Cuban, L. (2001). Oversold and underused: Computers in the classroom. Cambridge, MA: Harvard University Press.
Dynarski, M., Agodini, R., Heaviside, S., Novak, T., Care, N., Campuzano, L. (2007). Effectiveness of reading and mathematics software products: Findings from the first student cohort . Report to Congress. Washington DC: US Department of Education.
Fried, C. B. (2008). In-class laptop use and its effect on student learning. Computers and Education, 50(3), 9.
Fullan, M. (2006). The future of educational change: System thinkers in action. Journal of Educational Change(7), 113 - 122.
Giavrimis, P., Giossi, S., & Papastamatis, A. (2011). Teachers' attitudes towards training in ICT: A critical approach. Quality Assurance in Education, 19(3), 283-296.
Hallerström, H., & Tallvid, M. (2008). En egen dator som redskap för lärande. Research Report in Sociology of Law. Lund: Sociology of Law.

Harris, J., & Hofer, M. (2011). Technological pedagogical content knowledge (TPACK) in action: A descriptive study of secondary teachers' curriculum-based, technology-related instructional planning. Journal of Research on Technology in Education, 43(3), 211-229.

John, P., D. (2006). Lesson planning and the student teacher: Re thinking the dominant model. Journal of Curriculum Studies, 38(4), 483-498.

Koehler, M., J., & Mishra, P. (Eds.). (2008). Introducing TPCK. AACTE Committee on Innovation and Technology (Ed.), The handbook of technological pedagogical content knowledge (TPCK) for educators (pp. 3-29). New York: Routledge.

Lowther, L., Deborah, Ross, S., M., & Morrison, G., M. (2003). When each one has one: The influences on teaching strategies and student achievement of using laptops in the classroom. Educational Technology Research and Development, 51(3), 23-44.

Mishra, P., & Koehler, M., J. (2006). Technological pedagogical content knowledge: A framework for teacher knowledge. Teachers Collage Record, 108(6), 1017 - 1054.

Mishra, P., Koehler, M., J., & Kereluik, K. (2009). The song remains the same: Looking back to the future of educational technology. TechTrends 53(5), 48-54.

O'Shea, T., & Koschmann, T. (1997). The children's machine: Rethinking school in the age of the computer. Journal of the Learning Sciences 6(4), 401-415.

Orlando, J. (2009). Understanding changes in teachers' practices. A longitudinal perspective. Technology, Pedagogy and Education, 18(1), 33-44.

Penuel, W. (2006). Implementation and effects of one-to-one computing initiatives: A research synthesis. Journal of Research on Technology in Education, 38(3), 20.

Polly, D., & Brantley-Dias, L. (2009). TPACK: Where do we go now? TechTrends, 53(5), 46-47.

Rockman. (1998). Anytime, anywhere learning with laptops: Results from a Microsoft/Toshiba pilot program. THE Journal, 25(8).

Selwyn, N. (2000). Researching computers and education: Glimpses of the wider picture. Computers & Education(34), 93-101.

Shulman, L. (1986). Those who understand: Knowledge growth in teaching. Educational Researcher, 15(2), 4-14.

Silvernail, D. L., & Lane, M. L. (2004). The impact of Maine's one-to-one laptop program on middle school teachers and students. Portland, MA: Maine Education Policy Research Institute, University of Southern Maine Office.

Skolverket. (2010). Kursplan för grundskolan. Retreived from http://www.skolverket.se/forskola_och_skola/Grundskoleutbildning/2.3072/kursplaner/grundskolan/matematik

Tallvid, M. (2010). En-till-en Falkenbergs väg till framtiden? Falkenberg: Falkenbergs Kommun.

Tallvid, M., & Hallerström, H. (2009). En egen dator i skolarbetet:Redskap för lärande? Falkenberg.

Underwood, J. (2004). Research into information and communication technologies: Where now? Technology, Pedagogy and Education, 13(2), 135-143.

Valiente, O. (2010). 1-1 in education: Current practice, international comparative research evidence and policy implications, OECD education working papers (Vol. 44), OECD Publishing.

Warschauer, M. (2006). Laptops and literacy: Learning in the wireless classroom. New York: Teachers College Press.

Zhao, Y., & Frank, K. (2003). Factors affecting technology uses in schools: An ecological perspective. American Educational Research Journal, 40(4), 807-840.

TPACK Research with Inservice Teachers: Where's the TCK?

Mark Hofer
School of Education
College of William & Mary
Williamsburg, Virginia USA
mark.hofer@wm.edu

Judi Harris
School of Education
College of William & Mary
Williamsburg, Virginia USA
judi.harris@wm.edu

Abstract: Researchers are increasingly exploring the development and expression of experienced teachers' technological pedagogical content knowledge (TPACK). While the majority of extant studies focus on evidence and growth of TPACK holistically, some have begun to distinguish teacher knowledge in TPACK's subdomains, including technological pedagogical knowledge (TPK) and technological content knowledge (TCK). In reviewing this literature, one pattern has become apparent: teachers' TPK is documented considerably more often than their TCK across studies that have disaggregated results according to these subdomains. This paper reviews the studies that together illustrate this trend, offering potential explanations and suggestions for further investigation.

Since the appearance of the technological pedagogical content knowledge (TPACK) framework (Mishra & Koehler, 2006), more than 500 TPACK-based studies of teachers' technology integration knowledge have been presented and published. The majority of these studies have focused upon development of preservice teachers' TPACK. Increasingly, however, researchers have begun to explore how this knowledge develops with inservice teachers. Given experienced teachers' greater familiarity with teaching and curriculum, the nature and acquisition of their technological pedagogical (TPK), technological content (TCK) and technological pedagogical content (TPACK) knowledge are distinct from that of their more novice colleagues in many ways.

Although many studies do not seek to distinguish among teachers' knowledge in TPACK's subdomains—technological (TK), pedagogical (PK), content (CK), pedagogical content (PCK), technological pedagogical (TPK), and technological content knowledge (TCK) —TPACK scholarship within the past two years has begun to examine these related, but arguably distinct, aspects more closely. Some of this work has debated the external consistency of many of the subdomain constructs (e.g., Archambault & Barnett, 2010; Lux, 2010); more has suggested alternate ways to conceptualize and represent TPACK (e.g., Angeli & Valanides, 2009; Cox & Graham, 2009; Niess, 2011; Robertson, 2008). Even as this refinement of the construct continues, one pattern has already become apparent: teachers' TPK is documented considerably more often than their TCK across studies that have disaggregated results according to TPACK's subdomains.

Why might this be so? What does this pattern of results suggest for future TPACK research? To address these questions, we will first review the studies that together illustrate this trend.

Studies of Experienced Teachers' TPK & TCK

Of the twelve studies located in late 2011 that explored experienced teachers' TPACK, nine focused on teachers' knowledge during or after engaging in professional development experiences. Only one examined teachers' learning during university coursework related to TPACK. In a study of five classroom teachers enrolled in a graduate course on cognition and technology, Mouza & Wong (2009) explored writing action research-like technology integration cases as a means to build participants' TPACK. Following an analysis of the cases the teachers wrote, their course-related online discussions, and interviews conducted with each individually, the researchers concluded that though all participants developed their TPACK, the greatest change manifested within the teachers' PK. Specifically, development of the teachers' TPK was more prevalent than growth in their TCK.

The majority of the studies of experienced teachers that distinguished between TPK and TCK focused upon content-specific professional development efforts taught outside of university coursework. In science education, for example, Graham, Cox, & Velasquez (2009) reported on a pre/post study of fifteen elementary through high school classroom teachers during a university-based professional development experience focused upon content, inquiry-oriented pedagogy, and educational technologies. Participants completed a 31-item TPACK confidence questionnaire that focused on TK, TPK, TCK, and TPACK. The participants reported significant increases in all four areas. Of the four domains measured, however, TCK had the lowest mean.

In a study of ten mathematics teachers participating in a four-week summer professional learning experience designed to help them to develop their TPACK through the use of spreadsheets, Niess, Lee, Sadri, & Suharwoto (2006) analyzed pre/post questionnaire responses, course assignments, journal entries, observation notes, and peer teaching feedback. The authors reported that participants noted TPK development primarily. In only one case did a participant reference using TCK-related knowledge that resulted from participation in the professional development experience. In a similar study of two elementary mathematics teachers' learning from a 30-hour summer professional development experience, Polly (2011a) drew upon interviews and classroom observations to gauge the growth of teachers' TPACK. He reported that both teachers were confident in their CK, PCK and TPK, but they reported needing additional TCK and TPACK development.

In social studies education, Harris & Hofer (2011) explored the TPACK growth of seven classroom teachers during a university-based curriculum development project. Through an analysis of pre/post interviews, unit plans, and written reflections, the authors noted that participants' knowledge development focused primarily on TPK-related concerns, with comparatively little emphasis on TCK, despite the reported primacy of curriculum content during the teachers' instructional planning. Swan & Hofer (2011) arrived at similar conclusions in their study of eight secondary economics teachers following a summer professional development experience in which participants explored ways to integrate podcasting into their teaching. After analyzing project plans, structured reflections, interviews and classroom observation notes, the authors reported that participating teachers demonstrated strong TPK in planning and implementation, but only limited TCK. Even after direct prompting, only one of the participants was able to offer a TCK-based rationale for their instructional design.

Two studies examined a mentoring model for TPACK development. Shafer (2008) reported on a year-long, one-on-one apprenticeship experience with a math teacher that focused on integrating use of *Geometer's Sketchpad* in her classroom. Through an analysis of field notes, classroom observations, and an exit interview, Shafer reported almost exclusively on the teacher's growth in TPK, despite the mathematics content focus of the work. In another study of an individual mathematics teacher's efforts to integrate use of a content-specific digital tool—the TI Nspire graphing calculator—into classroom instruction, Özgün-Koca, Meagher, & Edwards (2011) analyzed the teacher's reflective journals, classroom observation notes, and instructional materials, finding much more evidence of TPK than TCK development. They note the teacher's "TCK did not come into play that much during this specific experience, and this domain [did] not … develop to a great extent" (p. 222).

Another two studies explored teachers' existing practices regarding technology integration knowledge, rather than differences that emerge following professional development or coursework. Richardson (2009) designed her dissertation study to determine how teachers draw upon their TPACK in planning and implementing technology-enhanced classroom lessons. In her interpretivist study of twelve fifth, sixth, and seventh grade teachers, she determined that each domain of TPACK was evident in their practice. Through an analysis of interviews, observations, and planning documents, Richardson concluded that despite the evidence of each TPACK subdomain in the participating teachers' thinking, TPK took precedence, while TCK was "the weakest area of knowledge reported" (p. 133). Also seeking to understand veteran teachers' knowledge for technology integration, Hervey (2011) designed a two-phase dissertation study in which 81 secondary teachers first self-assessed their TPACK using Schmidt, Baran, Thompson, Mishra, Koehler & Shin's (2009) self-report survey. From these respondents, Hervey identified six teachers, two of whom reported particularly strong TCK, TPK and TPACK, respectively. She then developed case studies for each of the six teachers, using videotapes of classroom instruction, stimulated recall activities, semi-structured interviews, and observational field notes. Though the six participants reported drawing upon all three domains of knowledge in their instructional planning and implementation, analysis of their survey responses indicated slightly lower levels of self-reported TCK when compared with TPK and TPACK.

Only two of the twelve studies located that examined experienced teachers' TPACK via the construct's subdomains reported results *other than* the predominance of TPK over TCK. Polly (2011b) provided fifth and sixth-grade teachers with thirty hours of instruction to assist them in developing technology-rich instructional materials to support higher-order thinking tasks for students. Following limited classroom implementation of the materials, he interviewed the fourteen teachers, coding their comments according to the subdomains of TPACK represented in each. Interestingly, TCK-coded responses were the third most frequent (16.34%), following only TK (26.12%) and CK (17.65%). By comparison, TPK codes represented only 5.23% of responses. Somewhat similar results were obtained with teachers of even younger children. Chuang and Ho (2011) adapted the Schmidt et al. (2009) survey by translating it into Chinese and adding items to address early childhood teaching. After conducting a pilot test of the revised instrument to ensure validity and reliability, 335 early childhood teachers in Taiwan completed the survey. The researchers found that teachers' self-reported TK and TCK (but not TPK) correlated with the amount of time they reported using digital tools in their teaching. Specifically, those participants who reported teaching with technologies for at least 20 hours per week had significantly higher self-reported TK and TCK than those who used technologies instructionally for fewer than 5 hours per week. However, time spent using technology in the classroom was *not* correlated with higher levels of self-reported TPACK.

These twelve studies demonstrate that participating teachers drew upon multiple subdomains of TPACK knowledge as they thought about, planned for, and implemented technologically integrated teaching. Most of the studies also found that teachers were able to build their TPACK in documentable ways. Yet with only two exceptions, it appears that teachers' TPK was more fully developed and/or more frequently displayed than their TCK. It is unclear why this is so. In the following section, we offer both suggestions for why demonstrated and self-reported TCK may lag behind TPK, and tentative recommendations for future TPACK research efforts that we hope will explore these particular aspects of teachers' technology integration knowledge.

Discussion

As we began our literature search, we noted that the majority of studies of experienced teachers' TPACK do not discuss the expression or development of TPK or TCK separately. In most studies, researchers focus their analysis and discussion around the integrated knowledge represented by the TPACK construct. This may be due, in part, to the challenges involved in teasing out particular domains of applied knowledge that are interdependent (Mishra & Koehler, 2006) within a larger and more complex framework. Some researchers even go so far as to suggest that some or all of TPACK's postulated subdomains of knowledge may not exist in practice. Archambault & Barnett (2010), for example, were able to identify only TK in their study of almost 600 K-12 online teachers. Lux (2010) was not able to identify TCK in the data generated to test his TPACK survey. Robertson (2008) used a theoretical argument to determine that TCK does not exist in the pragmatic application of teachers' technology integration knowledge, saying

> ...the astute will notice that this modified model purports there is no such thing as an educationally-important "TC:" one cannot have meaningful expressions of technological content in education without first having a specific set of students, goals, and environment in mind (pedagogy). (p. 2219)

In those studies that do attempt to isolate and describe knowledge in each of TPACK's subdomains, however, TPK is considerably more evident than TCK in explorations of experienced teachers' technology integration knowledge. Assuming that these results are accurate, why might this be so? At least five possible explanations can be suggested.

1. Practicing teachers may focus more of their attention upon pedagogy than content, therefore being more aware of technological pedagogical (TPK) than technological content knowledge (TCK). This may be particularly true as they participate in technology-focused professional development efforts. In the Swan and Hofer (2011) study, for example, the technology choice (podcasts) was pre-determined. It fell to the teachers then to find ways to integrate this technology in their instructional practice. This may explain the focus on TPK-related thinking displayed by the teachers. This same emphasis on TPK was also reflected in the other studies conducted in the context of educational technology professional development experiences.

   Experienced teachers may unknowingly include their technological content knowledge within their content/curriculum knowledge, since, as Deng (2007) and others have indicated, school curricula are not comprised primarily of disciplinary (or "content") knowledge. Instead, school curricula are situated, applied constructions existing almost exclusively within school environments. Teachers may, for example, accept the use of the primary source documents available digitally online in secondary-level history classes as a part of the curriculum for which they are responsible. Indeed, multiple curricula are beginning to be written to specify use of particular technological tools (e.g., MSDE, 2006).Recent analyses of Shulman's PCK construct (e.g., Henze, van Driel, & Verloop, 2008; Park & Oliver, 2007) have similarly suggested that teachers' knowledge of students is encompassed within their PK and PCK. In this conceptualization, knowledge of educational uses for technologies is also incorporated within PCK.

2. Similarly, inservice teachers' technological content knowledge (TCK) may be a subdomain of their pedagogical content knowledge (PCK), given the curriculum-specific nature of tools such as graphing calculators, scientific probeware, and historical primary source documents. In this sense, the tools and resources become curricular materials similar to textbooks, data sets, collections of documents, and other "thinking tools."

3. Professional development in technology integration is still largely technocentric (Harris, Mishra & Koehler, 2009) and focused upon use of general-purpose technologies, rather than content-specific implementations. Given this emphasis and its 30 year history, teachers may be focusing more upon "how to teach with the tools" rather than "what to teach with which tools" out of habit.

4. Many of the teachers who participated in these studies may either not have access to a sufficient variety of tools from which to choose for use in their teaching, or may be unaware of many of the content-specific ways in which general productivity tools can be used instructionally. Either or both of these reasons could cause less identifiable TCK to be used in a teacher's instructional plan.

Suggestions for Future Research

While some suggest that attempting to tease out TPK and TCK in research about teachers' practice is difficult, if not impossible, we argue that findings from those studies that do focus on these subdomains can be helpful in both understanding teachers' technology integration practices and in identifying opportunities for targeted professional development experiences.

However, different researchers have defined TCK differently, and this presents a considerable challenge. For example, in their seminal article on TPACK, Mishra & Koehler (2006) define TCK as, "…knowledge about the manner in which technology and content are reciprocally related. Teachers need to know not just the subject matter they teach but also the manner in which the subject matter can be changed by the application of technology" (p. 1028). In contrast, Polly (2011a) defines TCK as "knowledge about how technology aligns to various [curriculum] concepts" (p. 40). In their study of TPACK development in science, Graham, Cox, & Velasquez (2009) suggested that "TCK in science represents knowledge of the technologies and representations that are relevant to functioning within a scientific domain" (p. 74). These different conceptualizations of TCK, and the ten more identified by Cox (2008), undoubtedly lead to inconsistencies in research findings. It is possible that with a more concrete and applied definition of TCK, future studies may be better able to identify, describe, and measure how teachers think about technologies vis-à-vis curriculum content.

It is also possible that some of the current approaches to measuring and interpreting teachers' technology integration knowledge that were used in the studies included in this review are simply not sensitive enough to identify specific instances of teachers' thinking related to TPK and TCK with sufficient reliability. As the TPACK research community continues to develop more content-specific ways to assess and understand TPACK, it may be possible to more closely examine and identify with better reliability and validity the subdomains of knowledge included within the TPACK framework. Using more precise instruments, more focused interview prompts, more accurate stimulated recall techniques, and more effective data analysis methods, researchers may be better able to understand both the composition and the complexities of teachers' applied TPACK.

References

Angeli, C., & Valanides, N. (2009). Epistemological and methodological issues for the conceptualization, development, and assessment of ICT-TPCK: Advances in technological pedagogical content knowledge (TPCK). *Computers & Education, 52*(1), 154-168.

Archambault, L. M., & Barnett, J. H. (2010). Revisiting technological pedagogical content knowledge: Exploring the TPACK framework. *Computers & Education, 55*(4), 1656-1662.

Chuang, H.-H., & Ho, C.-J. (2011). An investigation of early childhood teachers' technological pedagogical content knowledge (TPACK) in Taiwan. *Journal of Kirsehir Education Faculty, 12*(2), 99-117. Retrieved from http://www.doaj.org/doaj?func=abstract&id=782294&recNo=6&toc=1&uiLanguage=en

Cox, S. (2008). *A conceptual analysis of technological pedagogical content knowledge* (Doctoral dissertation). Retrieved from ProQuest Dissertations and Theses database. (UMI No. 3318618)

Cox, S., & Graham, C. R. (2009). Diagramming TPACK in practice: Using an elaborated model of the TPACK framework to analyze and depict teacher knowledge. *TechTrends: Linking Research & Practice to Improve Learning, 53*(5), 60-69.

Deng, Z. (2007). Transforming the subject matter: Examining the intellectual roots of pedagogical content knowledge. *Curriculum Inquiry, 37*(3), 279-295.

Graham, C., Cox, S., & Velasquez, A. (2009). Teaching and measuring TPACK development in two preservice teacher preparation programs. In I. Gibson, R. Weber, K. McFerrin, R. Carlsen, & D. A. Willis (Eds.), *Proceedings of Society for Information Technology Teacher Education international conference 2009* (pp. 4081-4086). Chesapeake, VA: AACE. Retrieved from http://www.editlib.org/p/31297

Harris, J. B., & Hofer, M. (2011). Technological pedagogical content knowledge (TPACK) in action: A descriptive study of secondary teachers' curriculum-based, technology-related instructional planning. *Journal of Research on Technology in Education, 43*(3), 211-229.

Harris, J., Mishra, P., & Koehler, M. J. (2009). Teachers' technological pedagogical content knowledge and learning activity types: Curriculum-based technology integration reframed. *Journal of Research on Technology in Education, 41*(4), 393-416.

Henze, I., van Driel, J. H., & Verloop, N. (2008). Development of experienced science teachers' pedagogical content knowledge of models of the solar system and the universe. *International Journal of Science Education, 30*(10), 1321-1342.

Hervey, L. G. (2011). *Between the notion and the act: Veteran teachers' TPACK and practice in 1:1 settings* (Doctoral dissertation). Retrieved from ProQuest Dissertations and Theses database. (UMI No. 3463705)

Lux, N. J. (2010). *Assessing technological pedagogical content knowledge* (Doctoral dissertation). Retrieved from ProQuest Dissertations and Theses database. (UMI No. 763640461)

Maryland State Department of Education (MSDE). (2006). *State curriculum: Social studies*. Retrieved from http://mdk12.org/instruction/curriculum/social_studies/vsc_toolkit.html

Mishra, P., & Koehler, M. J. (2006). Technological pedagogical content knowledge: A framework for teacher knowledge. *Teachers College Record, 108*(6), 1017-1054.

Mouza, C., & Wong, W. (2009). Studying classroom practice: Case development for professional learning in technology integration. *Journal of Technology & Teacher Education, 17*(2), 175-201.

Niess, M. L. (2011). Investigating TPACK: Knowledge growth in teaching with technology. *Journal of Educational Computing Research, 44*(3), 299-317.

Niess, M. L., Lee, K., Sadri, P., & Suharwoto, G. (2006, April). *Guiding inservice mathematics teachers in developing TPCK*. Paper presented at the American Education Research Association Annual (AERA) Conference, San Francisco, CA.

Özgün-Koca, S. A., Meagher, M., & Edwards, M. T. (2011). A teacher's journey with a new generation handheld: Decisions, struggles, and accomplishments. *School Science and Mathematics, 111*(5), 209-224.

Park, S., & Oliver, J. S. (2007). Revisiting the conceptualisation of pedagogical content knowledge (PCK): PCK as a conceptual tool to understand teachers as professionals. *Research in Science Education, 38*(3), 261-284.

Polly, D. (2011a). Examining teachers' enactment of technological pedagogical and content knowledge (TPACK) in their mathematics teaching after technology integration professional development. *Journal of Computers in Mathematics and Science Teaching, 30*(1), 37-59. Retrieved from http://www.editlib.org/f/34610

Polly, D. (2011b). Teachers' learning while constructing technology-based instructional resources. *British Journal of Educational Technology, 42*(6), 950-961.

Richardson, K. W. (2009). *Looking at/looking through: Teachers planning for curriculum-based learning with technology* (Doctoral dissertation). Retrieved from ProQuest Dissertations and Theses database. (UMI No. 3371354)

Robertson, T. (2008). When outcomes attack: Technology introduction decisions focusing on results instead of uses through the TPACK educator knowledge model. In K. McFerrin, R. Weber, R. Carlsen, & D.A. Willis (Eds.), *Proceedings of Society for Information Technology & Teacher Education International Conference 2008* (pp. 2217 - 2222). Chesapeake, VA: AACE. Retrieved from http://www.editlib.org/p/27537

Schmidt, D. A., Baran, E., Thompson, A. D., Mishra, P., Koehler, M. J., & Shin, T. S. (2009). Technological pedagogical content knowledge (TPACK): The development and validation of an assessment instrument for preservice teachers. *Journal of Research on Technology in Education, 42*(2), 123-149.

Shafer, K. G. (2008). Learning to teach with technology through an apprenticeship model. *Contemporary Issues in Technology and Teacher Education, 8*(1), 27-44. Retrieved from http://www.editlib.org/d/26135/article_26135.pdf

Swan, K., & Hofer, M. (2011). In search of technological pedagogical content knowledge: Teachers' initial forays into podcasting in economics. *Journal of Research on Technology in Education, 44*(1), 75-98.

Teacher Education with simSchool

David Gibson
Curveshift
Stowe, Vermont
david.gibson@curveshift.com

Abstract: This chapter discusses how some of the systemic challenges of teacher education in the U.S can be addressed through simulation-based teacher education. The chapter outlines a rationale for the new approach based in self-direction and personal validation in a complex but repeatable practice environment, supported by emergent interdisciplinary knowledge concerning the unique affordances of digital media assessment and social media. The online simulation simSchool is used as an example model that embodies the new paradigm.

Introduction

The plan of the chapter is to briefly outline some of the key problems with teacher education in the U.S. Then the narrative presents the characteristics of a new model of self-directed teacher education supported in a game-like simulation context. The plan is to demonstrate that such a context has unique affordances compared with the alternatives, which entails describing how such an environment teaches as well as how it offers evidence for assessing whether someone has learned how to teach. The chapter is supported by an example – simSchool - a flight simulator for teachers.

Some problems with teacher education

About half of all new teachers quit by the end of their third year. The National Commission on Teaching and America's Future estimates that the national cost of public school teacher turnover could be over $7.3 billion a year. In addition to the nation losing billions of dollars, the constant churn of teachers drains resources, diminishes teaching quality, and undermines our ability to close global and even local student achievement gaps (Carroll, 2007). In 2004 most U.S. teachers were 52 years old and the average age was 43, but by 2008 most teachers were 28 years old (Carroll & Foster, 2010). This dramatic change in the demographics of teaching in the U.S. implies two things: 1) there is a need to prepare, mentor and support a much larger percentage of the teaching workforce for a longer period of time than at any other time in history and longer than formal education has traditionally been prepared to address, and 2) the current teaching workforce has grown up in an environment where technology, including access to the Internet and digital games, has been ubiquitous, informal and embedded in their lives (Beck & Wade, 2004). These implications point to the need for a scalable, informal online support environment that is available at all times to augment human performance in education. How are current formal and informal teacher education systems set up to accept, respond to and deliver this capability? To examine the situation, we'll briefly review gaps in formal program quality and policies.

Quality of programs and experiences (and thus the teachers produced) varies widely. Formal teacher preparation programs have come under attack for many years and are seen as unprotected by the higher education establishment because, according to some analysts, they are "basement" offerings that were fit historically for lower status women, and are seen as cash cows at most institutions (Maher, 2002). Data collected by the U.S. Department of Education Title 2 process (Higher Education Opportunity Act, 2008) suggests that in spite of the self-reported high pass rates, the actual quality and effectiveness of programs for ensuring the quality of teaching to meet existing needs varies widely putting students at risk in various ways depending on where they live. Until fundamental changes in the status of teaching take hold, with changes in incentives, career opportunities, school resource availability in low-income locations, and the cessation of waiver-based policies, the wide variance in teacher quality is likely to continue in the U.S. Dramatic shifts are needed in the policies that shape how educators are identified, recruited into the profession, made ready to teach, and supported in the field of service.

Policies and practices in the U.S. compare poorly with other countries, as do our student results. The U.S. lags behind other countries in student results, teacher support, and technology vision for education. Poor student results are well-known; news and national reports since the early 1980's have lamented the situation, warned and chided policymakers, and painted a picture of dire circumstances (Broad, 2005; COSEPUP, 2006; NCEE, 1983; TIMSS, 2003). International comparisons of teacher support are just as dire; in some other countries teachers enter teaching being paid as much as beginning doctors, that are supported by mentor teachers and have fifteen or more hours a week to work and learn together (Strauss, 2011). A global comparison of technology leadership fares no better; South Korea for example announced in early July 2011 that it plans to spend over $2 billion developing digital textbooks, replacing paper in all of its schools by 2015 (Honig, 2011). These examples highlight the gaps, lack of vision and the impact of both the de-professionalized status of teaching in America and the lack of investment and focus on the role of advanced technologies such as games and simulations in informal and formal education, including teacher education, which is out of step with the strategies pursued by the world's educational leaders, a point made clear in 2011 at the first International Summit on Teaching (Stewart, 2011). These gaps suggest some policy areas in need of attention.

One area concerns how and where student teachers practice what they have learned. Teacher educators have trouble finding enough appropriate placements with mentor teachers who can provide effective critical feedback about a student teacher's instructional skills and effectiveness (Grossman, 2010). In our work with teacher education programs in nearly 100 institutions that are using simSchool, we've learned that in certain parts of the country, student teachers do not have field placements within driving distance of their college that provide experiences with diversity of race, socioeconomic differences, and special education conditions. In addition, student teachers cannot "experiment" with students during these field experiences; mentor teachers sometimes only allow a small amount of control, or small amounts of time, for the student teacher to be in total control (Gibson & Kruse, 2011). Many student teachers thus only get a handful of hours in highly constrained conditions, which may be contributing to the high rate of turnover and low productivity of teacher preparation programs (Carroll, 2007).

Another policy area concerns the relationship of self-direction to motivation and engagement in learning, which is absent in typical professional development systems and mirrored in many K-12 systems. This is in spite of the fact that the literature on self-directed professional development has noted the value and necessity of choice for building personal relevance and effectiveness (Mezirow, 1997; NSDC, 2001). In order to develop the habits of self-direction and to carry those habits forward from professional development into K-12 settings, student teachers need experiences with setting professional development goals and self-monitoring progress toward those goals, as well as in developing modules and lesson plans that utilize similar approaches with their own future students (Zimmerman, 2000). The culture of games and simulations has a natural fit with this sort of empowered decision-making (Prensky, 2001) and thus has great potential to help. The next section discusses the characteristics of a changed viewpoint consistent with the need for new methods of teacher education that are innovatively online, scalable, personalized, data-rich, well-suited to the gamer teacher generation, and adaptable for many different levels of expertise that are acquired over a lifetime of learning to teach.

Formalizing informal online experiences and the future of learning

How the U.S. national technology plan of 2010 connects teaching, learning and assessment. The vision of teaching in the U.S. national technology plan (USDOE, 2010) connects the elements of teaching and learning in three ways; (1) teams rather than solo teachers guide learners, (2) data on student performance and analysis tools are always available, and (3) there are online resources always at hand to help act on insights. Learning is "powered by technology" to be engaging, relevant and empowering. Finally, assessment is viewed as diagnostic and designed for multi-stakeholder collaboration for continuous improvement.

This vision of teaching, learning and assessment is congruent with a shift to informal education and a simulation-based vision of teacher education. A key example of the shift can be found in simulation based learning, where the technology of a computational model and the web-based freedoms of informal education can be combined with the needs of formal education. The premise of teacher education with simSchool is that a flight simulator for teachers can provide a new way of learning how to teach. The next section describes what sets simulation-based learning apart, how a simulation works, and in particular how simSchool works and what evidence exists for it as a model of teaching and learning.

Can someone learn to teach by practicing with a classroom simulation?

A simulation of a classroom with enough complexity to educate teachers stretches the imagination, so it is important to begin with an illustration of some of the affordances and limitations of all simulation models. Imagine that an elementary teacher is teaching a lesson in earth science. As a constructivist and inquiry-oriented teacher, she gives the students a bare lamp bulb on a stand as a light source, a basketball and a softball, and challenges the students to turn down the lights and experiment with these objects until they find a way to show the phases of the moon. After several minutes of playing with these objects, the students discover several facts about the sun-earth-moon system in spite of the fact that the light source is too small to represent the true size of the sun and the room is too small to represent the distances involved among the three bodies. Even though the relative positions, sizes and shapes of the balls are not an accurate representation of the earth or moon, the students discover important truths about some of the dynamics, geomechanics and perspectives from the earth that lead to the observable phases of the moon.

This vignette illustrates that the affordances and limitations of a model such as *simSchool* offer benefits for learning. One benefit is *shearing away details in a simplification of a real system*. Models allow us to hold, in our hands and minds, some aspects of a system that cannot otherwise be experienced. Connected to and entailed by the characteristic of simplification is *increased safety* (e.g. a pilot in training can crash a virtual plane and a beginning teacher can crash a student or a class), *decreased costs* (e.g. virtual materials are more easily built and shared), and *enhanced focus on the relationships* among the simplified features (e.g. making a theory operational and amenable to manipulation). Simulations also provide *multiple chances to practice*, including making attempts with higher risks and causing spectacular failures, and to learn, retry and master new skills more rapidly and with less effort than through experiences that are not mediated by computers (Holland, 1995; Wolfram, 2002). This is part of the reason that simulations are used in aviation, medicine and the military with increasing frequency and effectiveness (Prensky, 2001). In teacher preparation, simulations that provide targeted feedback can develop teachers' understanding and practice and may be as effective as field experience (Christensen, Knezek, Tyler-Wood, & Gibson, 2011).

Limitations of models include the fact that *they are not full substitutes for real experience*, and as simplifications, there is *a danger that something vital may have been left out*. However, the progress of science attests to the fact that despite these limitations, models are vital parts of the advancement of knowledge. Happily, recent policy recommendations for teacher professional development now mention simulations among the promising new tools (Carroll, 2000, 2009; Dede, 2009; Grossman, 2010). This recognition leads to an important principle in the underlying theory of learning in simSchool; practice in a variety of settings builds expertise – and virtual settings may be as good as real ones in certain circumstances, due to the characteristics and benefits of models.

How a simulation of a classroom can entail enough realism to be a worthwhile learning environment for teachers. What teachers do in the classroom matters a great deal and is part of a causal network that brings about student learning as evidenced in their skill- and knowledge-based performances (Darling-Hammond, 1997; Darling-Hammond & Youngs, 2002; Rice, 2003). Teacher decisions can be thought of as independent variables in an ongoing experiment in their own classrooms that builds expertise over time (G. Girod, Girod, & Denton, 2006; M. Girod & Girod, 2006). A simulated classroom like simSchool provides cycles of experimentation and practice with few of the dangers associated with mistakes made on real students in real classrooms.

The "classroom experiment" metaphor is represented with four kinds of variables in *simSchool*: Observable, Hidden, Independent and Dependent variables (Figure 1).

a) The observable variables are what the teacher can see, which includes a typical student record passed down from teacher to teacher and kept on file in the school data system (e.g. grades, comments, psychological profile), behaviors in class including students' talking and body positions. In the simulator, unlike in real classrooms, the teacher can also see dynamic trailing indicator clusters that show the immediate result of the interaction of a current task or a teacher's talking behavior on the student's learning, happiness and self-efficacy/sense of power.

b) The hidden variables include detailed factor-level views of the individual variables of the student profile that are changing every instant in response to tasks and teacher talk. These variables, are also hidden in real classrooms, but are revealed in *simSchool* during the after-action reflection to help analyze why the student learned and behaved in a particular way.

c) The independent variables are the teacher's selection and timing of tasks and decisions about whether to talk and how to say things. This is the area where a teacher's knowledge and practice repertoire make a difference in student learning.

d) The dependent variables are the trailing indicators, which are revealed at the end of a session to allow a detailed reflection and analysis of the moment-by-moment interactions and effects caused by the teacher's decisions.

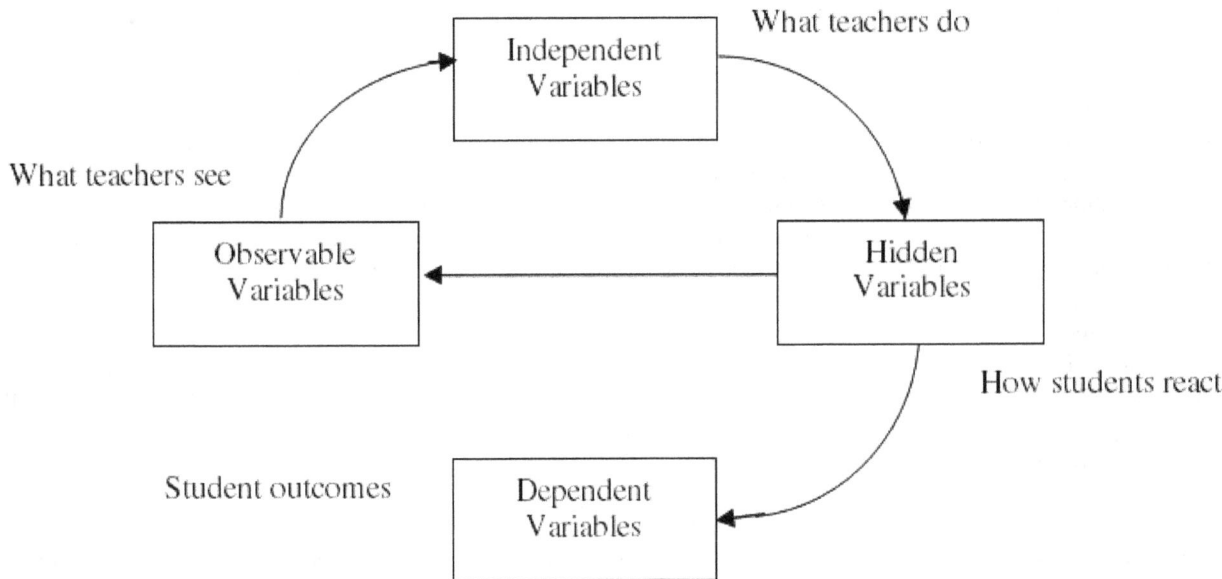

Figure 1. An experimental framework for developing teaching expertise

How simSchool works and what research has shown are its main effects. People who practice with a simulator develop *heuristic knowledge* of the underlying theories because the immersive multimedia experience taps into physical, emotional as well as cognitive pathways, heightening the sense of importance of the experience (Dede, Gibson, & Damon, 2007; Gee, 2004; Shaffer, 2007; Squire, 2006). Heuristic knowledge is readily accessible and probabilistic in nature; it develops from experience and while not guaranteeing a result, does make a desired result more likely. A heuristic approach to solving a problem is one that is followed when there are too many choices to exhaustively search for the best solution; examples include educated guesses, rules of thumb, and intuitive judgments.

Independent research teams have found initial evidence indicating the development of heuristic knowledge of teaching. In one study for example, preservice teachers could not articulate what they had learned, but outscored non-players on teaching skills that had been developed through exposure to simSchool (Christensen, Knezek, Tyler-Wood, & Gibson, 2011).

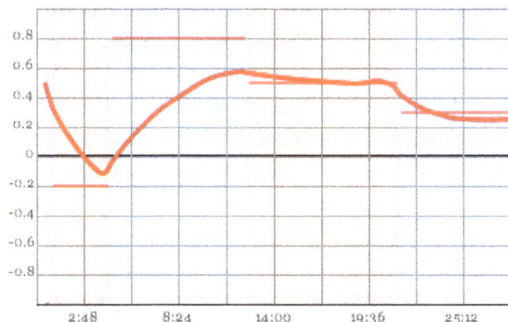

Figure 2. Task expectations

The example of academic output from a simulation in Figure 2 represents about four minutes of real time and simulates about 26 minutes of class time. It provides a way to discuss the learning opportunity for developing habits of teaching. The lighter constant lines during task time represent each tasks' academic expectation level. When a task is given with a certain academic requirement, the simulated learner responds by attempting to perform to the task's requirements. Tasks with low expectations elicit low performance and tasks above the students' current performance level require time to struggle with the task in order to make gains.

What are the possible heuristic lessons from a preservice student's choice of tasks? A task's academic impact might be rationalized by the user in terms of the difficulty of the task, or the timing of introducing this task, or the lack of effective preparatory tasks or talking, all of these are possibilities for interpretation in part or in some combination, since they are all equally true. The point being made here is that teaching is complex, layered and multicausal and that actual user performance and detailed documentation in a simulation provides a window into these subtleties.

While there are no easy completely "right" answers, there are hosts of partially right ones, and this facet of simulation is evidence for the development of heuristic knowledge. What has to be learned, instead of verbalized pat answers, is a set of estimations, educated guesses, and rules of thumb for similar situations. A user can actually re-run this simulation many times to try out alternatives and build up a history of interaction-based knowledge. Does talking sooner help more? Would a different task better set up the student for success? Of the available tasks, which one would be the best "first" task? Of the available ways to talk to the student, which ones have the best effect during this particular task? There are sets of answers to these questions that are clearly better than other answers, and since the sets overlap in complex ways, the knowledge that builds up as one develops them is heuristic.

Knowing what students know

Assessing teaching with simSchool is shaped by three approaches to digital media assessment: evidence-centered design, portfolios, and complex systems modeling. First, the Evidence-Centered Design (ECD) framework (Almond, Steinberg, & Mislevy, 2002; Mislevy, Steinberg, & Almond, 1999, 2003) stems from a program of research and application development first carried out at Educational Testing Service. ECD is a principled framework for designing, producing, and delivering educational assessments. Special attention is given to assessments that incorporate interactive and adaptive features such as those found in digital media learning applications. The design process includes domain analysis and modeling, two stages that are engaged to meet the product requirements of a specific assessment (e.g. an assessment of problem-solving skill in chemistry), which are then made operational in a three-part structure: a student model, task model and evidence model. The objects and specifications in that structure provide a blueprint for 1. Creating tasks and the computational models used to infer from performance of the tasks, 2. Implementing the assessment (operating it and collecting data from it) and 3. Analyzing data and reporting results.

Second, Gibson (2004) proposed a three-dimensional model of the decision-making space that includes "Audiences," "Reflective Purposes" and "Artifacts" - areas that intersect to form key questions in the creation of an assessment.

The three-dimensional model follows closely the Activity Theory of Leontev (1896 – 1934), which depicts all purposeful human activity as interactions among subjects (audiences), artifacts (tools), and objects (purposes). The model provides a source for principled inquiry into the nature of the interaction of an assessment's creators and users, the artifacts that stand as evidence of what people know and can do, and the inferences one might make about learners. The answers to the key questions in the model also contain a number of irresolvable dilemmas that designers need to live with and maximize or minimize, as their needs demand. The intersection of *audience* (self, trusted others, the public) with *purposes* (mirror, map, sonnet) and *artifacts* (configuration complexity, intentional content, affordances and constraints of the media) suggests a multidimensional analysis space for considering design and implementation issues (Gibson, 2004, 2006). More research is needed that applies this framework to digital media assessment planning processes and specific embedded implementations. Negotiating among the questions inherent in the three-part structure, an assessment designer or design team must settle on sets of decisions that change for different audiences, purposes and artifact types. These negotiated configurations form an institutional design fingerprint that shapes the assessments in the system. The challenge of multi-dimensional assessments extends to teachers designing assessments for their own classrooms, and to professors designing courses about assessment in teacher preparation programs.

Third and finally, since the problem of assessing performances in digital media learning environments involves several types of knowledge and action, often dynamically integrated to accomplish a nontrivial task, it is a complex matter. Complexity science offers new tools of theory and analysis for digital media assessments, as it encompasses several interdisciplinary theoretical frameworks in the search for patterns and causes in adaptive, changeable systems (Bar-Yam, 1997; Bechtel, 1993; Holland, 1995). Some of complexity science's analysis frameworks are coalescing around network theory, which has been found useful in a wide variety of fields from biology, e.g. (Kauffman, 2000) space and physical sciences, e.g. (Prigogine, 1980), to social and economic sciences, e.g. (Beinhocker, 2006), to neurosciences, e.g. (Sporns, 2011). Complexity and network approaches have also been noted for their potential in evaluation and educational assessment (Dexter, 2003; Gibson, 2003; Patton, 2011). The new methods include network analysis, artificial neural nets, Bayesian nets, coherence nets, ontologies and semantic nets, data mining techniques and methods, and knowledge engineering (Gibson & Jakl, in preparation). In simSchool, for example, the crowd-sourced performance of various groups is data mined to form network images of the knowledge-in-action or performance representation of the groups. These can then be compared with an individual performance to make adaptations in the digital experience as well as make inferences about what the user knows and can do.

Summary

When using a simulation platform such as simSchool to prepare teachers, the conceptions of teaching and learning, the organization of knowledge, assessment practices and results, and the engagement communities of practice stand in dramatic contrast with traditional course-based online learning experiences. The new paradigm focuses on the development of heuristic knowledge through direct experience, guided by self-direction and personal validation in a complex but repeatable environment. New methods of automated data gathering and analysis help address some of the important unmet challenges of teacher education by supporting emergent interdisciplinary knowledge and leveraging the unique affordances of digital and social media.

References

Almond, R., Steinberg, L., & Mislevy, R. (2002). Enhancing the design and delivery of assessment systems: A four process architecture. *The Journal of Technology, Learning, and Assessment*, 1(5).
Bar-Yam, Y. (1997). *Dynamics of complex systems*. Reading, MA: Addison-Wesley.
Bechtel, W. (1993). *Discovering complexity: decomposition and localization as strategies in scientific research*. Princeton, NJ: Princeton University Press.
Beck, J., & Wade, M. (2004). *Got game: How the gamer generation is reshaping business forever*. Boston, MA: Harvard Business School Press.
Beinhocker, E. (2006). *The origin of wealth: Evolution, complexity and the radical remaking of economics*. Boston, MA: Harvard Business School Press.
Broad, W. (2005, Oct 13). Top advisory panel warns of an erosion of the U.S. competitive edge in science. *New York Times*.

Carroll, T. (2000). If we didn't have the schools we have today, would we create the schools we have today? Keynote address presented at *Society for Information Technology and Teacher Education 2000 International Conference*, San Diego.

Carroll, T. (2007). *The high cost of teacher turnover*. National Commission on Teaching and America's Future.

Carroll, T. (2009). Transforming schools into 21st century learning environments. *eSchool News*.

Carroll, T., & Foster, E. (2010). *Who will teach? Experience matters*. Washington, DC: National Commission on Teaching and America's Future.

Christensen, R., Knezek, G., Tyler-Wood, T., & Gibson, D. (2011). SimSchool: An online dynamic simulator for enhancing teacher preparation. *International Journal of Learning Technology*.

COSEPUP. (2006). *Rising above the gathering storm: Energizing and employing America for a brighter economic future*. The National Academy of Sciences, The National Academy of Engineering, The Institute of Medicine.

Darling-Hammond, L. (1997). Quality teaching: The critical key to learning. *Principal*, 77, 5-6.

Strauss, V. (2011) Darling-Hammond: U.S. vs highest-achieving nations in education. *Washington Post,* March 22, 2011.

Darling-Hammond, L., & Youngs, P. (2002). Defining "Highly Qualified Teachers": What Does "Scientifically-Based Research" Actually Tell Us? *Educational Researcher*, 31(9), 13-25.

Dede, C. (2009). Address to the ITEST Summit 2009. Unpublished Lecture - slide show. *National Science Foundation*.

Dede, C., Gibson, D., & Damon, T. (2007). Learning games and simulations (video podcast), 2007 *National Educational Computing Conference* (Vol. 2009). Atlanta, GA.: International Society for Technology in Education.

Dexter, S. (2003). The Promise of Network-based Assessment for Supporting the Development of Teachers' Technology Integration and Implementation Skills. Paper presented at the *Society for Information Technology and Teacher Education 2003 International Conference,* New Orleans.

Garoian, C. (1999). *Performing pedagogy: Toward an art of politics*. Albany, NY: SUNY Press.

Gee, J. (2004). *What Video Games Have to Teach Us About Learning and Literacy*. New York: Palgrave Macmillan.

Gibson, D. (2003). Network-based assessment in education. Contemporary Issues in Technology and Teacher Education, 3(3).

Gibson, D. (2004). E-Portfolio Decisions and Dilemmas. Paper presented at the *Society for Information Technology in Teacher Education 2004 International Conference*, Atlanta, GA.

Gibson, D. (2006). Elements of Network-Based Assessment. In D. Jonson & K. Knogrith (Eds.), *Teaching Teachers to Use Technology* (pp. 131-150). New York: Haworth Press.

Gibson, D., & Jakl, P. (in preparation). Measuring teaching skills with a simulation: simSchool with Leverage. *Journal of Educational Data Mining*.

Gibson, D., & Kruse, S. (2011). Personal Communications with LEVEL 3 Partnership Colleges. *simSchool Modules EDUCAUSE Project*. Stowe, VT.

Girod, G., Girod, M., & Denton, J. (2006). Lessons learned modeling "connecting teaching and learning". In D. Gibson, C. Aldrich & M. Prensky (Eds.), *Games and simulations in online learning: Research & development frameworks*. Hershey, PA: Idea Group.

Girod, M., & Girod, J. (2006). Simulation and the need for quality practice in teacher preparation. Paper presented at the *American Association of Colleges for Teacher Education*. from http://www.allacademic.com/meta/p36279_index.html

Grossman, P. (2010). *Learning to practice: The design of clinical experience in teacher preparation*. Washington DC: Partnership for Teacher Quality (AACTE and NEA).

Higher Education Opportunity Act, H.R. 4137 1125 (2008).

Holland, J. (1995). *Hidden order: How adaptation builds complexity*. Cambridge, MA: Perseus Books.

Honig, Z. (2011). South Korea plans to convert all textbooks to digital, swap backpacks for tablets by 2015 [Electronic Version]. *Engadget*, from http://www.engadget.com/2011/07/03/south-korea-plans-to-convert-all-textbooks-to-digital-swap-back/

Kauffman, S. (2000). *Investigations*. New York: Oxford University Press.

Knezek, G., & Christensen, C. (2009). Preservice educator learning in a simulated teaching environment. In C. Maddux (Ed.), *Research Highlights in Technology and Teacher Education* (Vol. 1, pp. 161-170).

Maher, F. (2002). The attack on teacher education and teachers. *Radical Teacher*, 64(5), 5-8.

Mezirow, J. (1997). Transformative Learning: Theory to Practice. *New Directions for Adult and Continuing Education, 1997*(74), 5-12.

Mislevy, R., Steinberg, L., & Almond, R. (1999). *Evidence-Centered Assessment Design*. Educational Testing Service.

Mislevy, R., Steinberg, L., & Almond, R. (2003). On the structure of educational assessments. *Measurement: Interdisciplinary Research and Perspectives*, 1, 3-67.

NCEE. (1983). *A nation at risk*. Washington, DC: National Commission on Excellence in Education.

NSDC. (2001). *National standards for online learning*. National Staff Development Council.

Patton, M. (2011). *Developmental evaluation: Applying complexity concepts to enhance innovation and use*. New York, NY: The Guilford Press.

Prensky, M. (2001). *Digital game-based learning*. New York: McGraw-Hill.

Prigogine, I. (1980). *From being to becoming: time and complexity in the physical sciences*. San Francisco: W.H. Freeman.

Rice, J. (2003). *Teacher quality: Understanding the effectiveness of teacher attributes*. Washington, DC: Economic Policy Institute.

Shaffer, D. (2007). Epistemic games [Electronic Version]. *Innovate*, 1, from http://innovateonline.info/pdf/vol1_issue6/Epistemic_Games.pdf

Sporns, O. (2011). *Networks of the brain*. Cambridge:MA: MIT Press.

Squire, K. (2006). From content to context: Videogames as designed experience. *Educational Researcher*, 35(8), 19-29.

Stewart, V. (2011). *Improving teacher quality around the world: The international summit on the teaching profession*. New York, NY: Asia Society and U.S. Department of Education.

TIMSS. (2003). *International report on achievement in the mathematics cognitive domains*. June 29, 2006, from http://timss.bc.edu/timss2003i/mcgdm.html

USDOE. (2010). *Learning powered by technology: Transforming American education*. Washington, DC: U.S. Department of Education

Wolfram, S. (2002). *A new kind of science*. Champaign, IL: Wolfram Media.

Zimmerman, B. (2000). Attaining self-regulation: A social-cognitive perspective. In M. Boekaerts, P. Pintrich, & M. Zeichner (Eds.), *Handbook of self-regulation* (pp. 13-39). Orlando, FL: Academic Press.

Simulating Students with Learning Disabilities in Virtual Classrooms: A Validation Study

Sita Periathiruvadi
sitaperi@gmail.com

Tandra Tyler-Wood
Tandra.wood@unt.edu

Gerald Knezek
gknezek@gmail.com

Rhonda Christensen
University of North Texas, USA
rhonda.christensen@gmail.com

Abstract: This study explores the validity of using a simulation as a tool to train future teachers to work with a student with a learning disability in an inclusion classroom. Often, it is difficult to provide experience for pre-service teachers to work with students with learning disabilities. This study seeks to determine if a simulation can accurately depict a classroom experience that a future teacher might encounter in today's inclusion classroom. Specifically, the purpose is to validate the use of simSchool, a web-based classroom simulation program for training pre-service and in-service teachers to teach students with special needs. An actual student with a learning disability was observed in an inclusion classroom. Using those observations, a simulated version of the student was built into the simSchool program. Comparison of various attributes including behavior and personality revealed important findings concerning the ability of the simulation to accurately depict students with learning disabilities.

In light of the dramatic shortage of teachers trained to work with students with special needs, and our need to prepare teachers across a wide range of competencies, there is an urgent need to find new ways in which we can help teachers develop the broad range of skills and knowledge necessary to teach children with special needs (COPSSE, 2006). A three-year project supported at a large southwestern university by the National Science Foundation-Research in Disabilities Education award (NSF-RDE), has demonstrated success in using a classroom simulation called simSchool to assist in preparation of pre-service teachers for inclusion classrooms (McPherson, Tyler-Wood, McEnturff, & Peak, 2011). The current study aims to validate the use of simSchool for training teachers by examining how well the simulation can depict real students with disabilities.

Theoretical Framework

The simulation implements mathematically modeled representations of how people learn and what teachers do when teaching. The actions of the classroom teacher are likened to a causal network that results in student learning (Rice, 2003). It is important to consider the affordances and limitations of any simulation model (Gibson, 2008; Gibson, 2009). Although over-simplification is an inherent limitation of modeling a real classroom environment, factors such as a safe environment for practicing teaching, and obtaining targeted feedback about teaching outweighs the limitations. A diagrammatic representation (Fig. 1) shows how teacher-related and student-related variables interact in a classroom. What teachers see in the classroom such as a student's academic performance or student comments are observed variables in the classroom. The independent variables are how teachers select and assign tasks in the classroom. The student-related variables include both hidden (how students react to the teacher comments and tasks assigned) and dependent variables (student outcomes as a result of teacher actions and teaching).

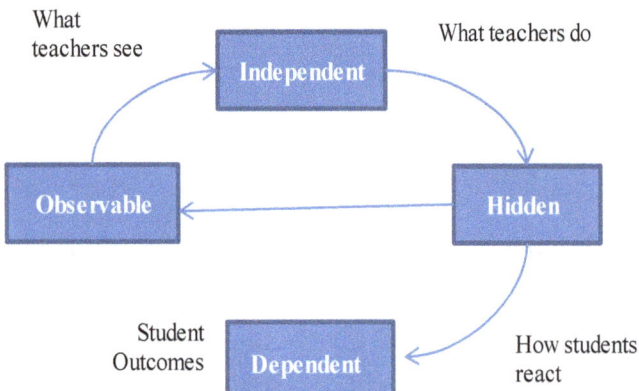

Figure 1. Interaction between Teacher-related and Student-related Variables (Gibson, 2009).

Review of Literature

Effective teacher induction programs help teachers succeed and increase their intentions to remain in special education (COPSSE, 2006). In addition, professional development in teaching students with special needs was associated to a moderate extent with being well prepared in pedagogy and well prepared in classroom management (Boe, Cook, & Sunderland, 2008). It is important to explore methods that provide teachers with an opportunity to receive training in working with special populations while enrolled in teacher training programs and during the first critical years of teaching.

Students with Learning Disabilities

Although learning disabilities are the most frequent category of disability found in an inclusion classroom (Turnbull, Turnbull & WehMeyer, 2009), this disability is often difficult for individuals entering the educational profession to understand. For the most part, students with learning disabilities physically resemble other students in the inclusion classroom. The cognitive abilities of students with learning disabilities are usually in the average range. It is difficult for many beginning teachers to understand the issues with limits in academic achievement, which students with learning disabilities display.

A learning disability is a disorder that affects how individuals absorb, express or retain information. A learning disability manifests as a deficit in one or more of the following areas: oral expression, auditory processing, written expression, reading decoding, reading comprehension, or math calculations (Turnbull et al., 2009). Students with learning disabilities may experience difficulty with sustained attention, time management, social interactions and executive functions. These characteristics are not readily observable in most learning environments (Taylor, Smiley, & Richards, 2008). A plethora of best practices have been developed (Fuchs & Deshler, 2007). Without a thorough understanding of such practices, implementing required federal mandates such as the documentation of response to intervention (RTI) may well be beyond the capabilities of teachers during the induction years (Oliver & Reschly, 2007). Experience in a simulated classroom might provide more rapid and concentrated training with best practices for beginning teachers.

Simulations in Teacher Education

With the increase in online teacher education programs and the enormous potential of online environments, it is important to explore innovative practices in teacher education. Incorporating technology into teacher education programs can range from using a tool (computer activities or online course portal), a medium (video conferencing and online discussion forums for collaboration), or using environments such as simulations and multi-user virtual environments. The current generation of digital games has seen a shift towards simulations requiring the player to solve real world problems. Simulation games can be more effective than traditional instruction methods because the games simultaneously engage players' affective and cognitive processes (Sitzmann, 2011).

The definitions of simulations and online virtual worlds have largely been overlapping. Kapp (2007) noted the main difference between simulation and other online worlds was based on the type of interaction – in simulations one player interacts with the program behind the simulation while in online worlds the players interact with other players simultaneously in the virtual environment or with pre-programmed agents. Empirical studies have evaluated the use of simulations in teacher preparation (Girod & Girod, 2008; McPherson et al., 2011). Teacher candidates who worked with a web-based classroom simulation, *Cook School District*, reported more gain in understanding individual student needs, and were better able to align the instruction not just to state standards but to other factors such as student's learning and assessment (Girod & Girod, 2008). Another classroom simulation, simSchool, the focus of the current study (www.simSchool.org), allows teachers to create a student avatar, assign tasks and then reflect on why the lesson was or was not successful in meeting the needs of the learner (Gibson, Christensen, Tyler-Wood & Knezek, 2011).

Methods

Case study methodology was chosen for the current study as an in-depth and intricate investigation of the simulation of students with disabilities was required (Tellis, 1997). The subject in this study was Ana, a third grader who participated in a summer science program organized in a large southwestern university. Ana's academic performance was rated as average by her classroom teacher. She was described as a sympathetic and warm person who loved to work with her peers. Ana was usually very relaxed and her class work was well organized most of the time. However, Ana preferred to have a pre-planned routine and was not curious about new ideas. The following research questions were asked to compare the real and simulated student:
   1. How do the personality attributes of the simulated student compare with those of the real student with a learning disability?
   2. How does the simulation depict the off-task behavior of the real student?
   3. Can the simulation capture student-initiated interactions with the teacher as observed in a real inclusion classroom?

To compare the real student data with the virtual data, an observation of the real student was performed in an inclusion classroom in a summer science program for one week. Once the data collection on the real student was completed, the sim-version of the student was built into the simulation and the simulation output was compared with the data collected on the real student. The output of the simSchool program is a graph which provides immediate feedback on the personality and academic attributes of the simulated student. The off-task behavior and student - teacher interaction were observed in the simulation using the same rating system which was used to make classroom observations.

A simple way to describe the working of the simulation is to consider two entities: the student and the task (the lesson). How well the teacher (player of the game) matches and adapts the task and interacts with the student avatar determines the simulated student's outcomes and subsequent rating of the teacher's instructional performance. Therefore, data collection from the classroom should provide data for
- creating the student in the simulation,
- creating the task in the simulation,
- real classroom observations of the real student, and
- virtual classroom observations of the student avatar.

First, the student's attributes were entered in the "create a student" function in the simulation. Ratings for the student were obtained from the student's teacher-of-record from the previous academic year. Three pieces of information constituted the student's attributes which include: personality attributes, physical attributes and academic performance information. Using the *Ten Item Personality Instrument* [TIPI] (Gosling, Rentfrow & Swann, 2003) (described in the Instruments section), the teacher rated the personality attributes of the student. The TIPI instrument has 10 items which group into five factors of personality (described in the Instruments section) (Gibson, 2009). The reason the data obtained from the TIPI was used was to make sure that some arbitrary information was not entered for each of the five personality factors.

Using the instrument allowed a reliable and valid measure of the student's personality. The physical attributes were rated on a scale of -1 to +1 (low to high) for three variables: visual, kinesthetic and auditory characteristics of the student. The third piece of information was the academic performance on a scale from -1 to +1 (low to high). These three pieces of information enabled researchers to create the student in simSchool.

Second, to create the lesson task in the simulation, information was needed about the title of the task, task difficulty, personality expectations of the task, and the physical attributes needed to complete the task. This information was rated by the classroom-teacher of the summer program. For the nature of the task, the teacher chose from 4 options ranging from recall, skill, strategic thinking and extended thinking. For the personality expectations of the task, the TIPI instrument was used to rate the lesson task. The physical attributes were rated on a scale of -1 to +1 (low to high) to for three variables: visual, kinesthetic and auditory characteristics needed for completion of the task by the student. The tasks and their description are shown below (Tab. 1).

Task Type	Skill	Skill	Recall	Skill	Strategic
Task Name	Property of Water	Bottom of the Pond	Build a Watershed	Catching Fish	Stream Race
Task Description	Students learn properties of water such as surface tension and cohesion	Students collect materials to fill bottom of the pond	Students build their own watershed	Students caught fish for their watershed	Boys and girls competed to block water stream using materials near the pond.
Activity Type	Lecture	Group	Individual	Individual	Group

Table 1. Lesson Tasks in the Summer Program

Third, the research team of four members observed the student during different lesson tasks and rated the personality attributes, academic performance at each instance, and on-task behavior of the student using an interval-recording method. Care was taken to make sure that the researchers' presence did not intrude or negatively impact the student's behavior. For instance, the research team wore the same summer-program T-shirts as the student assistants, and they were present from the beginning of the summer program.

Finally, once the real student observations were completed, the research team then created the student avatar and the lesson tasks in the simulation. Prior to teaching a lesson, the student's behavior, personality attributes, interactions with the teacher were recorded internally by the simulation. These data were analyzed by the research team once the simulation run was completed. Each of the lesson-tasks was run for 2 minutes in the simulation equating to 12 minutes in real classroom time. The data for the virtual personality attributes were obtained from numerous recorded data points that the simSchool engine collects for the duration of the simulation run. The four data points in equal intervals were selected for plotting the graph. The on-task behavior was observed by the research team and recorded using interval-recording for every 10 seconds. For the student-initiated interactions, every time the student asked a question or said something in the simulation, it was noted along with the actual comment made by the student. The data collected in steps (c) and (d) were plotted in graphs to compare the trends of the real student and his/her avatar in personality, on-task behavior and student-initiated interactions.

Instruments

Three instruments (Tab. 2) were used for data collection. Three attribute groups were measured for both the real and virtual student. They were personality, off-task behavior, and student-initiated interaction with the teacher. To measure the student's personality characteristics, we used the Ten-Item-Personality Instrument [TIPI] (Gosling, et al., 2003). The simulation employs the *Five Factor* model of personality, which represents personality in abstract level using five factors: openness, conscientiousness, extraversion, agreeableness, and neuroticism (OCEAN). The personality attributes were measured at three separate instances as mentioned in the methods section. One measure was for a student's general personality ratings by his/her classroom teacher, one for each of the lesson tasks to determine what the task expectations were, and for the observation of the real student's personality change over the duration of the lesson. The TIPI instrument was selected because it was shorter and met the project needs to make quick and accurate observations. This instrument includes 10 items which group in to the five OCEAN factors of personality. An abstract personality factor, extraversion was measured using two facets representing opposite poles of the factor such as being enthusiastic and being quiet. The content validity of the instrument was verified and approved by a project evaluation team. To ensure the observations were reliable, two researchers rated the student's personality attributes. The percent agreement between the two raters was 96%. The observations with mis-matched readings were not included in the final data for analysis.

Construct	Instrument
Personality attributes	Ten-Item-Personality Instrument [TIPI] (Gosling, Rentfrow, & Swann, 2003).
Off-Task Behavior	Interval recording of the operationally defined behavior
Student-initiated interaction w/ the teacher	Event Recording and classification of behavior using Bloom's Taxonomy.

Table 2. Instruments for Measuring Student Attributes

To record the off-task behavior, two members of the research team observed the student for the lesson task duration (10-15 minutes depending on the lesson) using an interval recording procedure. Interval recording is used for data collection when the behavior cannot be observed continuously for the given duration or when the behavior does not have a clear start/end. The observation duration was divided into intervals each lasting 30 seconds and the presence or absence of the behavior was recorded using a partial interval recording method. The researchers operationally defined the off-task behavior as: student not listening to the teacher, not working on the given assignment or talking to peers when not allowed. The research team was seated at a distance from the students, and if they could not distinguish student interaction with peers as essential or irrelevant, the benefit of doubt was given to the student and it was not marked as an off-task behavior. This was specifically considered in lesson tasks where outdoor activities were involved. Inter-rater reliability (kappa= 0.715) and percent agreement = 97% was found to be in the substantial agreement range (0.6 to 0.8) (Vierra & Garrett, 2005). The research team considered if the mismatch was an error in understanding and if not resolvable, the observations were removed from the data.

To record the student-initiated interaction, every time the student raised a question or initiated a conversation with the teacher, the interaction was categorized into one of the six Bloom's categories of cognitive thinking (Bloom, Mesia, & Krathwohl, 1964). Bloom's taxonomy classified cognitive skill levels into six categories ranging from the ability to just simply recall the tasks to being able to evaluate the value of information. The six categories include *Knowledge, Comprehension, Application, Analysis, Synthesis and Evaluation* (Clark, 2010). The research team observers were provided with verbs corresponding to each of the cognitive domains (Horner et al, 2005) and rated the student comment accordingly. For instance, if the student comment reflected just their recalling or describing, it was rated as knowledge. If the student could identify an example or use what they had learned in their activities, it was recorded as application. The inter-rater reliability was found to be (kappa= 0.745; percent agreement = 98.3%) and is considered as substantial agreement between the raters (Vierra & Garrett, 2005).

Findings

Comparison of OCEAN Attributes

A graphical representation (Fig. 2) of the findings on personality comparison between the real and simulated student are described below.

Expected scores on the extroversion scale for all three observed tasks were in the positive range. In the simulation, the student's extroversion scores tended to move towards the scores predicted by the simulator. However, in the real classroom, the extroversion scores for Ana showed a decrease on observations one, three, and four when the student was on her own silently performing the given task with not much interaction with her peers and teachers.

The data on the agreeableness variable reflected mixed findings: for tasks 1 and 3, the real student showed higher agreeableness while her virtual counterpart's agreeableness more closely matched the agreeableness factor of the task. However, for task 2, the simulated student's agreeableness almost matched that of the real student. Further investigation is required to understand why the simulation reacts differently for tasks with similar difficulty levels.

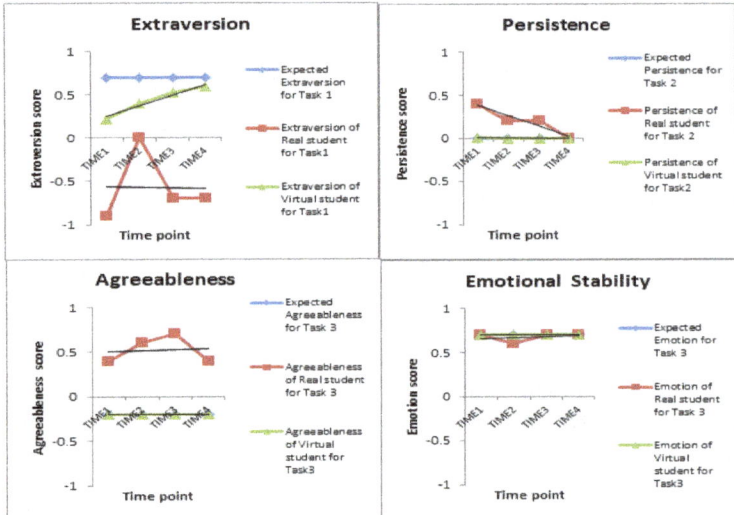

Figure 2. Comparison of Personality Attributes.

The findings on the intellectual open-ness to learning attribute showed that the real student with learning disabilities showed a decrease in score for task 2 and 3 while the virtual student showed an increasing score. In both the real and virtual cases, the expected scores on the intellect variable associated with the task were higher when compared to the scores exhibited by the student. Again, the simulated students' intellect observations tended to approach the expected intellect for the given task.

The virtual student's score on the persistence (conscientiousness) variable matched that of the task expectation for all three tasks. Whereas, the real student showed a persistence score higher than what was predicted by the simulator. The scores for the persistence variable for the real student indicated that for tasks 1 and 2 (skill/concept level tasks), the persistence variable decreased and for task 3 (recall task), the score increased.

The simulation could successfully capture the emotional stability (neuroticism) attribute for the student for tasks 2 and 3 (activity type tasks) as both the real and virtual student's emotional trend and scores were similar. For Task 1 (lecture mode task), the real student measured a higher emotional state than that predicted by the simulator, while the virtual student's emotion matched the simulator's prediction.

Off-task Behavior

Ana's real and virtual off-task behavior were compared for three tasks. During the first task, the students watched their teacher's model and built their own water sheds. For the second task, students were asked to catch fish in a stream of water, and for the third task students divided into two groups and participated in a stream race. The off-task behavior (Fig. 3) for the individual activities was similar. However, for the group activity, the simulation showed that Ana was off-task for most of the time in contrast to what was observed in the real classroom. In fact, Ana was part of the winning team and made significant contribution to her team's success. Overall, the group activity was more difficult than the other two tasks as it required strategic thinking while the other two tasks merely required the students to learn/exhibit a concept or skill.

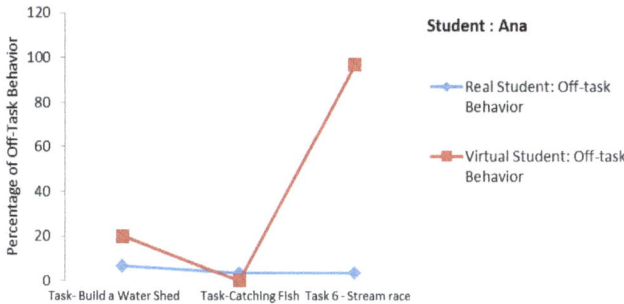

Figure 3. Comparison of Off-Task Behavior

Student Initiated Classroom Interactions

In the real classroom, the researcher noted that student initiated discussions were an integral part of the classroom experience. However, in the simulation, the student-initiated comments were limited to conversational comments such as "What are we doing here?" It should be noted that the simulation does a good job of capturing student behaviors and the comments made by the students in the simulation convey their state of happiness and learning of the given task.

Discussion

This validation study is a preliminary attempt to understand how real students can be depicted accurately in the simulation. The findings indicate that in the simulation, the personality attributes of the virtual student have a tendency to reach or overlap with the expected personality attributes of the task. Although, the current validation study could not reveal conclusive findings on the depiction accuracy, it has revealed several considerations for future studies. For instance, is this tendency of virtual student towards the task expectation only observed for students with learning disabilities? How does the simulation behave for a student without a disability? What impact does the nature and difficulty level of a task have on the personality trends? For the off-task behavior comparison, the simulation did not take into account the interactions and experiences of a student in a group activity. Future modifications to the simulator might need to consider group interactions. Care should be taken before generalizing the findings of this study as only a single case was explored. In addition, the case study, Anna will not represent all students with learning disabilities. Another limitation in this study is that the lesson tasks were considered as a single unit although each task could be divided into sub-tasks for more accurate comparison. It should also be noted that this study was conducted on the initial version of simSchool. Future studies can replicate these analyses in the newer version of simSchool with modules.

With the advancement in gaming technology, there is a great potential for innovative computer simulations to provide teachers a more realistic and enriching experience before stepping into the real classroom. However, there is a need for systematic and conceptual frameworks to guide the use of simulations (Girod & Girod, 2008). The research on simulated classrooms is important for two main reasons. Most novice teachers do not have the opportunity to work with a variety of students during their student teaching (Tyler-Wood & Periathiruvadi, 2010) and so a virtual practicum can provide pre-service teachers with important learning experiences. Second, new teachers can use a simulated, inclusive classroom as a safe practice ground, instantly receiving feedback on how their teaching matches their students' learning. Teacher educators should provide teacher candidates with extension opportunities to coordinate and collaborate with peers to reinforce what they learn after playing the simulation. As Girod and Girod (2008) suggested simulations should not only focus on helping teacher candidates making intellectual solutions but also emotional aspects of the problem observed in real classrooms. More research on using simulations and multi-user virtual environments will help to enhance the online teacher education experiences.

References

Boe, E. E., Cook, L. H., & Sunderland, R. J. (2008). *Teacher turnover: Examining exit attrition, teaching area transfer, and school migration. Exceptional Children, 75*, 7-31.

Bloom, B., Mesia, B., & Krathwohl, D. (1964). *Taxonomy of educational objectives*. New York, NY: David McKay.

Clark, D. (2010). Bloom's taxonomy of learning domains. Retrieved June 13, 2011 from http://www.nwlink.com/~donclark/hrd/bloom.html

Center on Personnel Studies in Special Education [COPSSE] (2006). Special education teacher attrition: What we know, what we can do? Retrieved from http://copsse.education.ufl.edu/copsse/

Fuchs, D., & Deshler, D. D. (2007). What we need to know about responsiveness to intervention (and shouldn't be afraid to ask). *Learning Disabilities Research & Practice, 22*, 129–136.

Gibson, D. (2008). Modeling classroom cognition and teaching behaviors with COVE. In D. Gibson & Y. Baek (Eds.), Digital simulations for improving education. Hershey, PA: IGI Global.

Gibson, D. (2009). Designing a computational model of learning. In R. Ferdig (Ed.), Handbook of research on effective electronic gaming in education (Vol. 2, pp. 671-701). Hershey, PA: Information Science Reference.

Gibson, D., Christensen, R., Tyler-Wood, T. & Knezek, G. (2011). SimSchool: Enhancing Teacher Preparation through Simulated Classrooms. *Society for Information Technology & Teacher Education International Conference*, 2011, Association for the Advancement of Computing in Education, Chesapeake, VA, 1504-1510.

Girod, M., & Girod, G. R. (2008). Simulation and the need for practice in teacher preparation. *Education, 16*, 307-337.

Gosling, S. D., Rentfrow, P. J., & Swann, W. B., Jr. (2003). A very brief measure of the big five personality domains. *Journal of Research in Personality, 37*, 504-528.

Kapp, K. (2007). *Gadgets, games, and gizmos for learning: Tools and techniques for transferring know-how from boomers to gamers.* New York, NY: Pfeiffer.

Knezek, G., Christensen, R., & Tyler-Wood, T.L. (2008). Assessing Learning In a Simulated Teaching Environment, *Hawaii Educational Research Association, 2008*.

McPherson, R., Tyler-Wood, T., McEnturff, A. & Peak, P. (2011). Using a computerized classroom simulation to prepare pre-service teachers. *Journal of Technology and Teacher Education, 19*(1), 93-110. Chesapeake, VA:AACE. Retrieved from http://www.editlib.org/p/31438.

Oliver, R. M., & Reschly, D. J. (2007). Effective classroom management: Teacher preparation and professional development. Retrieved June 30, 2008, from http://www.tqsource.org/topics/effectiveClassroomManagement.pdf

Rice, J. (2003). *Teacher quality: Understanding the effectiveness of teacher attributes*. Washington, DC: Economic Policy Institute.

Sitzmann, T. (2011). A meta-analytic examination of the instructional effectiveness of computer-based simulation games. *Personnel Psychology, 64*, 489-528. doi:10.1111/j.1744-6570.2011.01190.x

Tyler-Wood, T. & Periathiruvadi, S. (2010). Virtual Practicum in E-Learning for Teacher Preparation. *World Conference on E-Learning in Corporate, Government, Healthcare, and Higher Education, 2010*, Association for the Advancement of Computing in Education, Chesapeake, VA, 2249-2253.

Taylor, R., Smiley, L., & Richards, S. (2008). Exceptional Students: Preparing Teachers for the 21st Century, McGraw-Hill Co., NY, NY.

Tellis. W. (1997). Application of a case study methodology. *The Qualitative Report, 3*(3). Retrieved from http://www.nova.edu/ssss/QR/QR3-3/tellis2.html

Turnbull, A. P., Turnbull, H. R., & WehMeyer, M.L, D. (2009). *Exceptional lives: Special education in today's schools*. Upper Saddle River, NJ: Merrill.

Vierra, J., & Garrett, J.M. Understanding interobserver agreement: The kappa statistic. *Family Medicine, 37*, 360-363.

Situated Online:
Theoretical Underpinnings of Field Experiences in Virtual School Settings

Leanna Archambault
Arizona State University
USA
leanna.archambault@asu.edu

Kathryn Kennedy
Georgia Southern University
USA
kmkennedy@georgiasouthern.edu

Abstract: This paper describes the historical, practical, and theoretical underpinnings behind an essential component of teacher preparation, the field experience. It explores the theory of situated cognition as it applies to online teaching and learning which advances the notion that learning requires a contextualized, authentic setting with the participant engaged in direct interaction and reflection (Brown, Collins & Duguid, 1989). Discussed is the basis for the development of field experiences in K-12 virtual schools. Various models that have emerged to address the need for teacher preparation within K-12 online settings are described, and implications for teacher education programs are also addressed.

Introduction

As K-12 online education continues to expand, it is necessary to examine the various policies, standards, and theoretical underpinnings that are influencing the field as a whole. A growing number of states have added specific educational policy governing virtual schooling. For example. several states have added high school graduation requirements for students to complete an online learning experience as part of their coursework. These states include Michigan (2006), Alabama (2008), New Mexico (2009), Indiana (2011), and Idaho (Bonner, 2011). In addition to requirement statutes, Florida has one of the most progressive stances on virtual schooling, mandating that all school districts offer some form of online learning, whether it be internally created or offered through an external organization such as Florida Virtual (Florida Senate, 2011). In addition, the Idaho State Board of Education adopted online teacher standards in 2010 and has recently passed a state-level teaching endorsement, becoming the second state after Georgia to do so. Connecticut (2010) now allows teachers to be certified in any state, a significant development since it supports licensing reciprocity, potentially allowing teachers licensed and living outside of one state to teach students in another.

With these national, state, and district-level developments concerning virtual schooling, the field continues to gain acceptance while expanding and transforming today's educational landscape. Because of this expansion, including increases in blended learning and homegrown school-district-level online learning programs (Watson, Murin, Vashaw, Gemin, & Rapp, 2011), a growing number of qualified educators will be required to meet the demands. Consequently, it is important that teachers be prepared in their teacher education programs to serve an increasing number of online students. To accomplish this goal, teacher education programs will need to consider creating relevant course work and practica to prepare teachers entering blended, hybrid, and fully online classrooms. The purpose of this paper is to describe the historical, practical, and theoretical underpinnings behind an essential component of teacher preparation, the field experience.

History of Field Experience

The process of preparing teachers has taken varying routes throughout the history of teacher education. As early as the 19th century, theorists and practitioners explored preparatory practices (Beijaard, Verloop, & Vermunt, 2000; Borrowman, 1956; Walkington, 2005). The overarching name for these preparatory practices is practica. (Cattley, 2007). Under the umbrella term of practica are a plethora of models. These include observational learning (Koran, Snow, & McDonald, 1971), internships (Gardner & Henry, 1968), microteaching (Allen & Eve, 1968), field experiences (Zeichner, 1984), self-evaluations (Beijaard et al., 2000), reflection (Hatton & Smith, 1995), immersion (Wiggins, Follo, & Eberly, 2007), and mentoring (Ballantyne & Hansford, 1995).

These experiences are the heart and soul of teacher education programs, allowing pre-service teachers first-hand guided work in the classroom before they venture out to assume their roles as full-fledged education professionals (Aiken & Day, 1999; Buck, Morsink, Griffin, Hines, & Lenk, 1992; Harlin, 1999; Joyce, Yarger, Howey, Harbeck, & Kluwin, 1977; Wiggins & Follo, 1999). Practica were so vital that as of the 1970s, the U.S. state departments of education established them as required parts of the teacher certification process (Moore, 1979). According to the 2002 NCATE standards, pre-service teachers taking part in practica are required to have dispositions that acknowledge, understand, and uphold social justice, responsibility, academic honesty, professionalism, fairness, equality, caring, and empathy (NCATE, 2002). In addition to these dispositions, preservice teachers must possess skills in classroom management, motivational techniques, reflective teaching, and differentiation.

While teacher education programs typically require preservice teachers to do their practica in traditional, face-to-face, brick-and-mortar classrooms, a handful of programs have started offering field experiences in virtual schools and other K-12 online learning environments. Several skills taught in these settings include managing online classrooms, interacting with students and encouraging interaction between students, motivating students in the online classroom, translating teaching from face-to-face to online format, navigating the course management system, learning to build relationships with students, discovering the various models of K-12 online learning programs, creating online content, and differentiating lessons and providing one-on-one assistance to students (iNACOL, 2008).

Standards for Field Experience

The National Council for Accreditation of Teacher Education (NCATE, 2007) and the Teacher Education Accreditation Council (TEAC, 2010) standardize the preparation of teachers for classrooms and have been doing so for 57 and 14 years, respectively. Preparing teachers to teach online has not been acknowledged in their standards for education colleges (NCATE, 2008). Twenty-first century learning is mentioned in the NCATE standards, but it is not in regard to K-12 online learning. Instead, what is emphasized is the preparation for teachers to work with 21st century learning. The only time "online" teaching and learning are mentioned is when it has to do with those who are educating teachers to ensure they use "multimedia tools, digital resources, and distance learning systems" in their teaching (NCATE, 2008, p. 52).

Unfortunately, similar findings were found when the authors examined the teacher preparatory standards of the Teacher Education Accreditation Council (TEAC, 2010). Professional organizations have taken the lead in providing standards for teacher preparation programs to follow. These organizations and their respective standards include the International Society for Technology in Education's (ISTE) *National Educational Technology Standards for Teachers* (NETS*T) (ISTE, 2008); Southern Regional Education Board's (SREB) *Essential Principles for High-quality Online Teaching* (SREB, 2006); National Education Association's (NEA) *Guide to Teaching Online Courses* (NEA, 2006); and International Association for K12 Online Learning's (iNACOL) *National Standards for Quality Online Teaching* (iNACOL, 2008).

These standards do not solely concentrate on preparing teachers for online learning; they also talk about technology integration in general and apply to the spectrum of K-12 online learning programs, whether they be 100% online, blended, hybrid or somewhere in between. The standards exhibit some overlap; however, they maintain unique qualities (Kennedy, 2010a). While these organizations might not have control over teacher education programs like the accreditation councils do, they tend to have an effect on policy.

Adding Theory to Practice: Situated Cognition and Pedagogical Content Knowledge

Situated cognition, in which learning requires a contextualized, authentic setting with the participant engaged in direct interaction and reflection within the environment (Brown et al., 1989), can be seen as a rationale for engaging in field experiences within a teacher education program. Situated cognition values practical, hands-on experience as a primary mechanism of learning. Being in an authentic teaching setting allows preservice teachers to apply their pedagogical content knowledge acquired during the course of their program. Shulman developed pedagogical content knowledge (PCK) to describe the relationship between content knowledge, the amount and organization of knowledge of a particular subject matter; and pedagogical knowledge, knowledge related to how to teach various content. PCK includes "the most useful forms of representation of those ideas, the most powerful analogies, illustrations, examples, explanations, and demonstrations—in a word, the ways of representing and formulating the subject that make it comprehensible to others" (1986, p. 9).

To improve preservice teachers' PCK, an important aspect of situated cognition is the cognitive apprenticeship, which "supports learning in a domain by enabling students to acquire, develop, and use cognitive tools in authentic domain activity" (Brown et al., 1989, p. 39). Through a cognitive apprenticeship, preservice teachers directly watch what happens in the classroom, model the practice of their mentor teacher, and identify and reflect on the ideas they learn, including addressing any related misconceptions. These are important skills to become effective teachers. Not only should teachers know the concepts of what they are teaching, but also the potential pitfalls to which students frequently fall victim, depending on the preconceptions they have developed based on their ages and backgrounds, which is a part of PCK. According to Shulman, "If those preconceptions are misconceptions, which they so often are, teachers need knowledge of strategies most likely to be fruitful in reorganizing the understanding of learners, because those learners are unlikely to appear before them as blank slates" (1986, pp. 9-10). Mentor teachers encourage the development of PCK in preservice teachers by making expert tacit knowledge explicit, modeling effective teaching strategies, providing scaffolded support during instruction, and offering specific feedback for improvement (Collins, Brown & Newman, 1989). This apprenticeship is vitally important for the "…transfer of what is presumably learned in teacher education programs to actual classroom practice…"(Moore, 2003, p. 32).

The concept of PCK is particularly relevant to online teaching because it sheds light on what teachers should know and be able to do within the context of the virtual learning environment. Because there is a shift to a "knowledge building" approach to learning, the focus in online teaching necessarily becomes more centered around how the course is structured, with special emphasis on the teaching materials that are used. The teacher in the virtual classroom needs to be overtly aware of the common misconceptions centered around the particular topic within the content they are teaching so that these can be addressed as part of the class materials. Online educators also need to be cognizant of the importance of encouraging and teaching specific self-regulated behaviors to their students to ensure every possible chance for success. Many strategies for teaching self-regulated behaviors relate specifically to Shulman's (1986) notion of PCK in that they involve the use of cognitive strategies such as modeling, analogies, and metaphors to aid in understanding the content-related material. This involves the teacher's ability to translate and contextualize information to improve students' understanding and motivation for learning. In order to be able to create such materials and implement these types of strategies, future online teachers need to have not only an excellent grasp of their given content area but also an appreciation of how technology and the online environment affect the content and the pedagogy of what they are attempting to teach (Archambault, 2011). This approaches the articulation of TPACK, an understanding of the complexity of relationships among students, teachers, content, technologies, practices, and tools (Koehler & Mishra, 2005).

To learn to apply TPACK in the online classroom, preservice teachers must be provided with an authentic learning environment in which their cognitive apprenticeship can be situated. This needs to take place in an online, Web-based setting so that the apprenticeship can occur together with mentorship from an expert online teacher who is able to make visible all strategies, techniques, and approaches to teaching and who is not constrained by the confines of four walls or traditional school hours. The preservice teacher in this context can observe how the mentor teacher is able to engage and motivate students from a distance, implementing and capitalizing on the affordances of new technology-related tools. This could include using such tools to monitor students' progress using real-time data as well as manage the volume of email sent on a daily basis. Especially in the virtual environment, through the cognitive apprenticeship, the preservice teacher must confront his/her beliefs about the role of the teacher, and how this role might be transformed by virtue of being online. In order to gain exposure to the differences in blended and online teaching, preservice teachers should have the opportunity to engage in a field experience that is set in a virtual context and uses the principles of situated cognition and the development of TPACK as theoretical guidelines. A handful of teacher education programs in the United States are moving in this direction, as is described in the next section.

Virtual School Field Experiences: The Models

In 2007, the Iowa State University was awarded a Fund for the Improvement of Post Secondary Education (FIPSE) grant to start the TEGIVS project, which stood for Teacher Education Goes Into Virtual Schooling (Davis, Roblyer, Charania, Ferdig, Harms, Compton, & Cho, 2007). During the fall 2007 semester, the project piloted a virtual school field experience in which two preservice teachers were paired with one virtual school teacher at Iowa Learning Online (ILO) (Compton, Davis, & Mackey, 2009). The ILO teacher provided the two interns with a guided walkthrough of the virtual school environment. The interns were allowed to interact with the K-12 students. In addition to the field experience itself, the interns were required to report back to a one-credit course at ISU where they had to reflect on their experiences in a journal, answer discussion questions in a forum, and participate in research interviews. As a result, the researchers found that the preservice teachers came away from the experience with a newfound understanding and a set of informed theories about K-12 online learning (Compton et al., 2009).

Following in Iowa State's footsteps, the University of Central Florida, University of South Florida, and University of Florida all partnered with the Florida Virtual School starting in 2009 to offer their preservice teachers virtual school field experiences. Each program was set up a little different from the other, depending on the amount of time allotted for the experience in the program. The length of the experiences spanned from four weeks to eight weeks where the UCF and USF experiences catered to undergraduate-level preservice teachers, and the UF experience focused on graduate-level preservice teachers. As of this publication, research has been conducted on the University of Florida cohort (Kennedy, 2010b) but not on the other programs. In addition to this research, the authors conducted a national survey (Kennedy & Archambault, 2012) of teacher education programs in 2011 to explore what types of virtual school field experiences existed. These models will be more fully described in an iNACOL research brief (Kennedy & Archambault, in preparation). Table 1 describes the key elements of the models of virtual school field experiences that were reported in the survey.

Table 1. Models of Virtual School Field Experiences

Location of Teacher Education Program	Description of Virtual School Field Experience
Florida 1	Preservice teachers complete 14 weeks of internship. Cooperating teachers must have at least three years of teaching experience and state-documented clinical education training. Preservice teachers must pass all general and core courses with a grade of "C" or above to participate in the field experience and have demonstrated knowledge of Florida Educator Accomplished Practices at "Competent" or above. Preservice teachers are required to be fingerprinted, approved by the advisor of the practicum, assigned a coordinator, and have a completed application for the internship.

Florida 2	Preservice teachers are placed with cooperating teachers at a state-level virtual school. Experiences are four weeks in length and associated with a graduate-level, university-based course. The structure of the experience is mostly determined by the virtual school with a small amount of input from the university. Preservice teachers and cooperating teachers meet face-to-face for an orientation before the practicum starts. Preservice teachers must be specializing in educational technology to take part in the virtual school field experience. Preservice teachers shadow the cooperating teacher to learn about the content management system (CMS). Preservice teachers are required to reflect on their experiences throughout the practicum. Cooperating teacher is required to have clinical education training to serve as a mentor.
Florida 3	Teacher education program partners with a state-level virtual school. Preservice teachers choose a junior or senior-level virtual school field experience. Junior-level internships are seven weeks in traditional schools and the other seven weeks in a virtual school. Senior interns complete a 16-week internship in a virtual school. Cooperating teachers must be teaching students in the state-led virtual school and are required to have knowledge related to their content area, online learning, as well as academic, technological, and socio-emotional skills. Program provides preservice teachers training and professional development that is related to K-12 online learning. Preservice teachers reflect on their experience throughout the semester and complete specific coursework related to K-12 online learning. Preservice teachers are also tracked by log-in data and observed by their university coordinator.
Florida 4	Not all preservice teachers are able to participate in virtual school field experiences. Program has been piloting with physical education (PE) courses in which preservice teachers are assigned to a virtual school field experience for seven weeks while they assist in teaching high school students required PE health and fitness courses. Preservice teachers assist with the development of online content, create lesson activities, assess student learning, and communicate with parents and students. A small group of school counselors learn about K-12 online learning through required course training modules. Virtual school identifies cooperating teachers to participate. University instructor pairs the cooperating teacher with preservice teachers. Preservice teachers are required to document their experiences via ongoing reflections.
South Dakota 1	Program partners with a school that is not completely virtual. Virtual school offers individual online courses through a statewide network to schools that do not have a family and consumer sciences program. One online course is offered via the virtual school. Preservice teachers who are student teaching in that school teach the course to students at other sites using a Web-based course platform. Preservice teachers must have some technological skills for setting up the course feed. Preservice teachers observe by cooperating teachers at the school. Preservice teachers journal their reflections during the practicum. Program reported that their state does have a virtual high school, but preservice teachers have not worked with it yet. Program faculty are currently considering the inclusion of online course development for preservice teachers.
South Dakota 2	Preservice teachers assist in teaching state and private vendor courses that are offered online. Field experiences are optional to the teacher education candidate. Preservice teachers are given opportunities to volunteer to assist in the K-12 online learning courses. Preservice teachers must log their activity during the virtual school experiences.
North Dakota	Only one student has worked in a virtual school thus far. It was a voluntary experience, completed in addition to a face-to-face practicum. Preservice teacher taught two hours per day at the virtual school. Preservice teacher was observed by a cooperating teacher. Program has educational technology endorsement resulting in a minor in technology.

Implications

Within the models of virtual school field experience, situated cognition offers preservice teachers the ability to learn how to teach online within a contextualized, authentic setting in which they can experience a cognitive apprenticeship (Brown, Collins & Duguid, 1989). Through this experience, future online educators can directly observe what happens in the virtual classroom, model the practice of an expert teacher in this field, and identify and reflect on the ideas they learn. Implementing the tenets of situated cognition, preservice teachers within the predominant models, which are currently underway in Florida, assist with the development of online content, create lesson activities, assess student learning, and communicate with parents and students in online environments. They also observe their cooperating teachers at the virtual school and journal during the field experience to reflect on their learning.

To design effective virtual school field experiences, effective partnerships between teacher education programs and virtual schools need to be established and fostered. Often, virtual schools are more than willing to host teacher candidates but do not know whom to approach within teacher education programs (Kennedy & Archambault, 2012). Because this type of experience should be a part of a course within a preparation program, it behooves faculty in higher education to reach out to virtual school personnel in order to situate learning opportunities for future teachers. Ideally, it would be helpful if the virtual school field experience could span a normal class-length of 16 weeks. This would not only allow for ample time to immerse the pre-service teacher in the new learning environment, but it will also offer a greater amount of time for engaging in a cognitive apprenticeship, with meaningful mentor-mentee activities.

During the first weeks of the virtual school practicum, the instructor should concentrate on helping the pre-service teachers reflect on their past online learning experiences to give pre-service teachers a chance to unpack their beliefs, deconstruct their experiences, and reflect on their past online learning experiences. The field experience itself should be designed in a blended format. The blended format would be especially helpful for students who have not taken an online course before. The course should start out with at least a four-week introduction to K-12 online learning. This introduction would need to include relevant literature and reports regarding K-12 online learning. Especially important to include would be Keeping Pace (Watson et al., 2011), which would provide a broad overview of the current state of K-12 online learning and also introduce various business models of virtual schools.

During the first four weeks, learning for the pre-service teachers should be designed similar to the way in which the K-12 virtual school courses are designed. This would allow the pre-service teachers to experience firsthand what the K-12 virtual students experience. The remaining 12 to 13 weeks should be devoted to the development of the relationship between the supervisor teacher and the pre-service teacher, and dedicated to the pre-service teacher's discovery of what it is like to be a virtual school teacher. Possible activities include grading, facilitating discussions, participating in synchronous work via web conferencing software, engaging in virtual school professional development opportunities, learning about academic integrity, and understanding time management.

As discussed, there are currently only a handful of teacher education programs currently venturing to offer a field experience in a virtual setting. Because the educational system is expanding to include virtual and blended forms of learning, as well as embrace notions of competency-based instruction whereby students are required to demonstrate mastery to progress in the curriculum, teacher education programs need to adapt to prepare future educators for new learning environments. To work toward this vision, teacher education programs would benefit from creating relevant course work and practica, designed to be contextualized and set within an authentic online setting so that preservice teachers can engage in direct interaction and reflection in this new environment. Future teachers need to be able to acquire an understanding of the complexity of relationships among students, teachers, methods, content, and emerging technologies, and then be able to apply this both in face-to-face as well as in online settings. This notion of situating learning within the online environment is important as we progress into the 21st century and prepare future generations for developing and interacting in online teaching and learning environments.

References

Aiken, I. P., & Day, B. D. (1999). Early field experiences in preservice teacher education: Research and student perspectives. *Action in Teacher Education, 21*(3), 7-12.

Alabama State Board of Education. (2008). Alabama Administrative Code (AAC) Rule 290-3-1-.02(12) for Online Courses. Retrieved from http://www.adph.org/tpts/assets/schoolpolicy.pdf

Allen, D. W., & Eve, A. W. (1968). Microteaching. *Theory into Practice, 7*(5), 181-185.

Archambault, L. (2011). The Practitioner's Perspective on Teacher Education: Preparing for the K-12 Online Classroom. *Journal of Technology and Teacher Education, 19*(1), 73-91.

Ballantyne, R., & Hansford, B. (1995). Mentoring beginning teachers: A qualitative analysis of process and outcomes. *Educational Review, 47*(3), 297-308.

Beijaard, D., Verloop, N., & Vermunt, J. D. (2000). Teachers' perceptions of professional identity: An exploratory study from a personal knowledge perspective. *Teacher and Teacher Education, 16*(7), 749-764.

Bonner, J. (9 Sept 2011). Idaho to take comment on online education rule. *Idaho Statesmen.* Retrieved from http://www.idahostatesman.com/2011/09/28/1819141/idaho-to-take-comment-on-online.html#storylink=misearch#ixzz1aUOreKCU

Borrowman, M. (1956). *The liberal and technical in teacher education.* New York: Teachers College Press.

Brown, J., Collins, A. & Duguid, P. (1989). Situated Cognition and the Culture of Learning, *Educational Researcher, 18*, 32-42.

Buck, G., Morsink, C., Griffin, C, Hines, T., & Lenk, L. (1992). Preservice training: The role of field-based experiences in the preparation of effective special educators. *Teacher Education and Special Education, 15*(2), 108-123.

Cattley, G. (2007). Emergence of professional identity for the preservice teacher. *International Education Journal, 8*(2), 337-347.

Collins, A., Brown, J.S., & Newman, S.E. (1989). Cognitive apprenticeship: Teaching the crafts of reading, writing, and mathematics. In L. Resnick (Ed.), Knowledge, learning and instruction: Essays in honor of Robert Glaser (453-494). Hillsdale, NJ: Erlbaum.

Compton, L., Davis, N. E., & Mackey, J. (2009). Field experience in virtual schooling - To be there virtually. *Journal of Technology and Teacher Education, 17*(4), 459-477.

Connecticut State Board of Education. (2010). Senate Bill No. 438 Public Act No. 10-111: An Act concerning education reform in Connecticut. Retrieved from www.cga.ct.gov/2010/ACT/Pa/pdf/2010PA-00111-R00SB-00438-PA.pdf

Davis, N. E., Roblyer, M. D., Charania, A., Ferdig, R. E., Harms, C., Compton, L., & Cho, M. (2007). Illustrating the "virtual" in virtual schooling: Challenges and strategies for creating real tools to prepare virtual teachers. *The Internet and Higher Education, 10*(1), 27-39.

Florida Senate. (2011). H.B. 7197. Retrieved from http://www.flsenate.gov/Session/Bill/2011/7197

Gardner, H., & Henry, M. A. (1968). Designing effective internships in teacher education. *Journal of Teacher Education, 19*(2), 177-186.

Harlin, R. P. (1999). Developing future professionals: Influences of literacy coursework and field experiences. *Reading Research and Instruction, 38*(4), 351-370.

Hatton, N., & Smith, D. (1995). Reflection in teacher education: Towards definition and implementation. *Teaching and Teacher Education, 11*(1), 33-49.

Indiana schools chief backs online class requirement. (2011). *Evansville Courier & Press.* Retrieved from http://www.courierpress.com/news/2011/sep/13/indiana-schools-chief-backs-online-class-requireme/

International Association for K-12 Online Learning (iNACOL). (2008). *National Standards for Quality Online Teaching.* Retrieved from http://www.inacol.org/resources/nationalstandards/NACOL%20Standards%20Quality%20Online%20Teaching.pdf

International Society for Technology in Education (ISTE). (2008). *National Educational Technology Standards (NETS*T) and Performance Indicators for Teachers.* Retrieved from http://www.iste.org/Content/NavigationMenu/NETS/ForTeachers/2008Standards/NETS_for_Teachers_2008.htm

Joyce, B., Yarger, S. J., Howey, K., Harbeck, K., & Kluwin, T. (1977). Reflection on preservice education: Impressions from the national survey. *Journal of Teacher Education, 28*(5), 14-37.

Kennedy, K. (2010a). Cross-reference of online teaching standards and the development of quality teachers for 21st century learning environments. *Distance Learning: A Magazine for Leaders, 7*(2), 21-28.

Kennedy, K. (2010b). *The essence of the virtual school practicum: A phenomenological study of pre-service teachers' experience in a virtual school.* Unpublished dissertation. University of Florida, Gainesville, FL.

Kennedy, K., & Archambault, L. (2012). Offering pre-service teachers field experiences in K-12 online learning: A national survey of teacher education programs. *Journal of Teacher Education.* doi: 10.1177/0022487111433651

Kennedy, K., & Archambault, L. (in progress). Models of field experiences in virtual school settings. Vienna, VA: International Association for K-12 Online Learning.

Koehler, M. J. & Mishra, P. (2005). What happens when teachers design educational technology? The development of technological pedagogical content knowledge. *Journal of Educational Computing Research, 32*(2), 131-152.

Koran, M. L., Snow, R. E., & McDonald, F. J. (1971). Teacher aptitude and observational learning of a teaching skill. *Journal of Educational Psychology, 62*(3), 219-228.

Michigan Department of Education (DOE). (2006). 380.1278a: Requirements for high school diploma. Retrieved from http://www.legislature.mi.gov/%28S%28ma5r4zj5k4qijni2virldx45%29%29/mileg.aspx?page=GetObject&objectname=mcl-380-1278a

Moore, C. (1979). National survey queries early clinical experiences. *ATE Newsletter, 12*, 3.

Moore, R. (2003). Reexamining the field experiences of preservice teachers. *Journal of Teacher Education, 54*(1), pp. 31-42.

National Council for Accreditation of Teacher Education (NCATE). (2008). *NCATE Standards 2008.* Retrieved from http://www.ncate.org/documents/standards/NCATEStandards2008.pdf

NCATE. (2007). *About NCATE.* Retrieved from http://www.ncate.org/public/aboutNCATE.asp

NCATE. (2002). Professional standards for the accreditation of schools, colleges, and departments of education. Washington, D.C.

National Education Association. (2006). *NEA Guide to Teaching Online Courses.* Retrieved from http://www.nea.org/home/30103.htm

New Mexico Public Education Department (NM PED). (2007). SB209/HB201. Retrieved from www.nmlegis.gov/.../SB0209%20%20Cyber%20Academy%20Act.pdf

Shulman, L. (1986). Paradigms and research programs in the study of teaching: A contemporary perspective. In M. C. Wittrock (Ed.), *Handbook of research on teaching* (3rd ed., pp. 3-36). New York: MacMillan.

Southern Regional Educational Board. (2006). *SREB essential principles of high-quality online teaching: Guidelines for evaluating K-12 online teachers.* Retrieved from http://www.sreb.org/programs/edtech/pubs/PDF/Essential_Principles.pdf

Teacher Education Accreditation Council. (2010). Goals and Principles. Retrieved from http://www.teac.org/accreditation/goals-principles/

Walkington, J. (2005). Becoming a teacher: Encouraging development of teacher identity through reflective practice. *Asia-Pacific Journal of Teacher Education, 33*(1), 53-64.

Watson, J., Murin, A., Vashaw, L., Gemin, B., & Rapp, C. (2011). *Keeping Pace with K–12 Online Learning: An Annual Review of Policy and Practice.* Evergreen, CO: Evergreen Education Group.

Wiggins, R. A., Follo, E. J., & Eberly, M. B. (2007). The impact of a field immersion program on preservice teachers' attitudes toward teaching in culturally diverse classrooms. *Teaching and Teacher Education, 23*(5), 653-663.

Wiggins, R. A., & Follo, E. J. (1999). Development of knowledge, attitudes, and commitment to teach diverse student populations. *Journal of Teacher Education, 50*(2), 94-105.

Zeichner, K. M. (1984). The ecology of field experience: Toward an understanding of the role of field experiences in teacher development. Paper presented at the Annual Meeting of the *Association of Teacher Educators*, New Orleans.

New Technology Tools for Science Teachers to Consider: A Case Study of an Online Biology Lab

Gregory MacKinnon, PhD
School of Education
Acadia University
Canada
gregory.mackinnon@acadiau.ca

Eric Alcorn, MSc
Trevor Avery, PhD
Department of Biology
Acadia University
Canada

Abstract: Science teachers have a compounding number of technological tools they might access for the classroom. This case study of an online biology lab considers the potential for three such technologies to supplement or replace traditional approaches. In response to increasing demands on laboratory space, online biology lab activities were prepared within a constructivist pedagogical framework. Three specific technologies were embedded and investigated with a sample of ~200 students. Using a mixed-method action research approach, the relative impact of virtual reality models, animations and simulations was sampled. Surveys, interviews and focus groups established that 1) while face-to-face laboratories were preferred by students, most felt it was acceptable that 30% of their labs be online and 2) within the online laboratories, virtual reality models were the least favored by comparison to animations and simulations. In addition, it was found that at the 95% confidence level, there was no significant difference in the laboratory scores between students who did online versions of the labs and those that face-to-face versions of the same laboratories. This is a promising finding in that an educational problem of limited space has been solved through technology by a means that doesn't seem to compromise the learning of students.

Introduction

The preponderance of new technological tools for learning places a tremendous responsibility on educators and particularly teacher educators to analytically investigate the impact of these new tools on the nature of learning. While online teaching potentially offers unlimited access to education, Postman (1993) warns us that efficiency of teaching should not be the focus but instead the quality of learning. Teacher educators have a role in promoting a critical stance to new technologies as it relates to both their own pre-service trainees and campus–wide educators employing technology. The following study attempts to define productive online technologies within the context of biology laboratories. While the setting of this particular case is an introductory biology course at a small liberal arts college, it has direct implications with respect to the use of similar technologies by science teachers in high school classrooms. Specifically, the instructor (his class being studied by the educational researcher), has chosen to develop a group of laboratories that include animations, simulations and virtual reality models (hereafter object VRs). In this action research, the instructor's aim was to improve the education in his course while responding to the increasing demands for laboratory space; hence a consideration of online versions of his laboratories. These constraints served as the backdrop for making informed choices about how the biology laboratory course would be offered. The researcher, a science education professor, served to design and undertake the research using surveys, student and instructor interviews and focus groups. Within an emerging understanding of the multi-tasking capabilities of the neo-millennial student (Dede, 2005) and their associated digital literacies, it was also important to ask the question whether we are prepared to abandon non-productive technologies and embrace those technologies that empower learning. Research studies such as this have the potential to go beyond the "technoromantic" aura (Benyon & Mackay, 1989) of seemingly promising technologies and establish a confidence that in fact educational objectives and outcomes need to be the centre of any teaching and learning investigation.

Context of the Study

This action research was undertaken by a biology lab instructor (in his classroom) and an educational researcher; i.e. a professor of teacher education acting in the capacity of non-participant observer as defined by Patton (1992). The study was done in a primarily undergraduate liberal arts university of approximately 3000 students and 250 faculty members. While the study took place in a college setting, it arguably has generalizability to public school science classrooms especially in light of resource shortages that challenge school systems to be creative in their delivery of courses.

The sample consisted of a population of 206 students in a first year biology laboratory course. Of six laboratories typically introduced, three were modified for online delivery. Students were assigned specific groups and laboratory schedules so as to enable the instructor to monitor which laboratory versions students attempted. Since students did not complete any laboratory in both formats, only qualitative comparisons could be made between distinct groups.

The role of experienced teacher educators in providing professional development for instructors in higher education cannot be understated. The instructor in this study had no formal teacher training and therefore he benefitted from the pedagogical guidance of the educational researcher (a teacher and faculty member in teacher education) in the study in several ways. First, the instructor was adhering to outdated laboratory approaches that simply reaffirmed theory. Based on interview feedback, the process of rethinking the laboratories within a constructivist framework (Brooks & Brooks, 1993) was a novel process for the instructor and changed his fundamental view of the nature of science and how we should teach it (Hart, Mulhall, Berry, Loughran & Gunstone, 2000). The instructor was involved in a research literacy process. Over the course of the action research, the instructor learned how to properly establish a research protocol such that his investigation outcomes could be injected back into his teaching. Through conversations between educational researcher and instructor, it has become clear that this action research relationship has been a most valuable professional development opportunity for the instructor that necessarily changes the way he now approaches the teaching and learning process. The positive outcomes of this collaborative effort underline the potential for teacher educators to have broader impact on university and college faculty in terms of promoting better teaching and the scholarship of teaching and learning.

Modifying the Laboratories

The courseware management system Moodle® was used to offer all the online laboratory resources. The core curriculum areas of the labs included two tasks regarding taxonomy and one task involving gene technology and PCR (polymerase chain reaction).

The first taxonomy lab was exclusively in the online format and accordingly all students completed the lab independently and electronically outside the classroom setting. This lab relied primarily on textual descriptions, matrices and taxonomic diagrams situated in a format based on constructivist learning principles (Brooks & Brooks, 1993).

The second taxonomy lab involved having students classify a variety of turtles. In the face-to-face (hereafter Ftf) version of the lab, students worked from a hardcopy lab description with full access to actual preserved specimens of turtles. The online version of the lab included a lab description (as electronic file) and a specialized technology referred to as "object VR". An object VR (acronym for virtual reality) is a three-dimensional rendering of a real object. In the online environment, students can pass their mouse over the object both rotating it several directions and enlarging it so as to provide clear inspection of such details as color, size and texture. An example of an object VR used for the taxonomy lab on the turtles is shown in Figure 1 and was created using Object2VR® software.

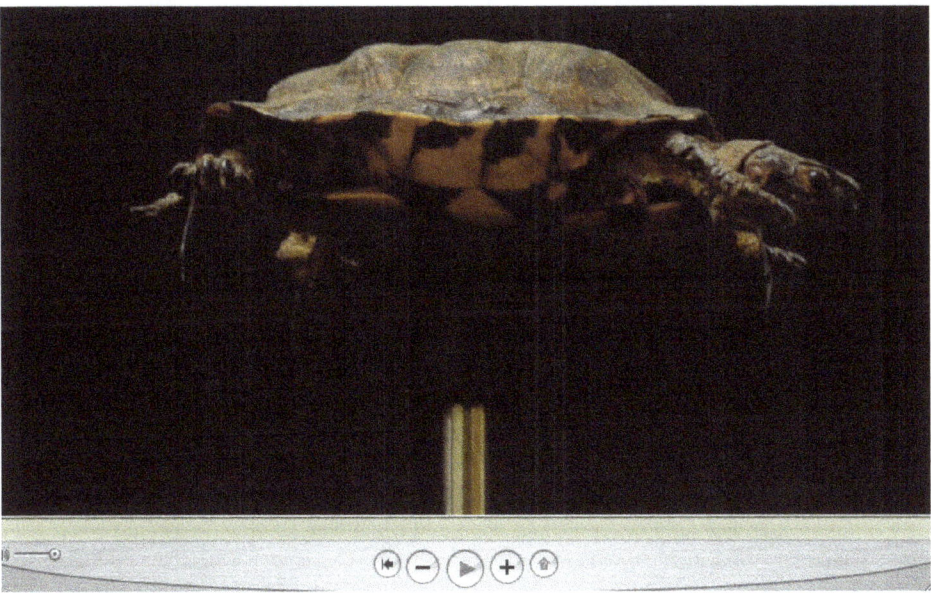

Figure 1. Screen capture of a wood turtle (*Glyptemys insculpta*) object VR.

The laboratory on gene technology and PCR was created in both online and Ftf formats. In a scheduled scheme, students were assigned which experience they would undertake. This lab made use of an electronic lab simulation (Figure 2) created within the software ILab®. Finally web-based animations of transcription (e.g. http://www.gene-quantification.de/Transcription.mov) and translation were incorporated.

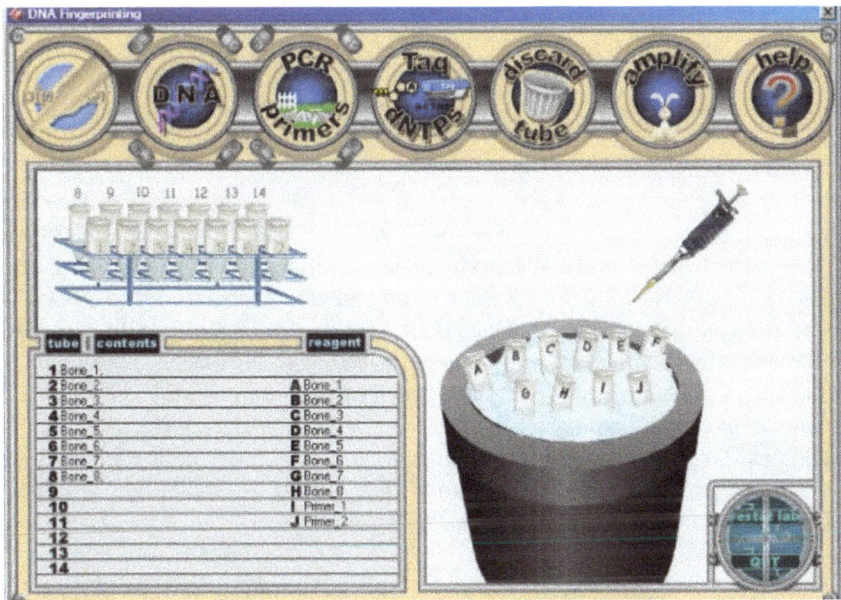

Figure 2. An ILab® simulation on DNA fingerprinting.

Research Methodology

An electronic survey was designed to obtain quantitative information regarding students': 1) comfort level with standard computer technology, 2) relative ease of accessing resources for the online labs, 3) relative ease of following the instructions to complete the online labs, 4) need and access to instructor support to complete online labs, 5) interaction with peers in completing labs and 6) attitude towards using online learning aids (e.g. simulations, videos, object VRs etc.) The survey was field-tested with 3 randomly invited first–year biology students to identify and remove ambiguity and inconsistencies in the presentation of questions. A total of 175 students gave permission to be contacted by email regarding participation in the electronic survey. Of that group, 98 students chose to complete the survey. The sample included 75 females and 23 males with 72 members (of the 98 total) being enrolled in a Bachelor of Science program. Further, 90 students from the sample identified their last course as a second level high school Biology course and 89 members of the sample suggested they made over 71% in that course.

The survey results were collected and analyzed for emergent trends. Based on these trends, a standardized open-ended interview schedule was developed (Patton, 2002) and field-tested with three randomly invited students from the sample. In this way, the interview schedule was proof-read to improve clarity for the student recipients. From the sample, ten students (5 female, 5 male) were invited to participate in a 30 minute audio-recorded interview. The foci of the interviews were 1) to corroborate trends in the 6 aforementioned survey areas and 2) to unearth rationale for perceived trends. The interviews were transcribed and coded (Auerbach & Silverstein, 2003) in an iterative process which incorporated the earlier survey results. A preliminary analysis was completed and peer debriefing (Lincoln & Guba, 1985) was employed to lend reproducibility (i.e. while a single researcher may interpret and code empirical data with an inherent bias, a peer assessment of the same data ensures that conclusions have fundamental basis).

Two focus groups (Kreuger, 1994) of five students were invited to respond to the intermediate results. In this process, the research results were both corroborated and contextualized to remove outlier results and spurious opinions. Several informal interviews were conducted with the instructor. Instructor interviews centered around 1) perceived student satisfaction/frustration with laboratories, 2) technical support issues, 3) student-instructor online interaction and 4) quality of supplemental lab textual materials.

Results

The results of the study are discussed below as a summary of data collected which included grades analysis, surveys, interviews, participant observation/field notes, member checks via focus groups, peer debriefing and instructor interviews.

In this study (n=206), some students completed laboratories online while others completed them face-to-face. By reference to laboratory grades, two determinations were made. First it was found that, at a 95% confidence limit, there was no significant difference in the overall grade of those students who completed laboratories online and those that didn't (means 74.19/74.58, variance 198.19/166.97). Predictably, for the each of the individual laboratories that was offered in both formats, a statistical analysis showed that, at a 95% confidence limit, there was no significant difference in the grades between those that completed the laboratory online and those that completed it face-to-face. These findings would suggest that the online versions of the laboratory neither improve student performance nor impede it. Given that a primary motive of creating the online format was to contend with growing classroom space demands, these results show promise with regard to supplementing traditional laboratories with online versions. But how many online laboratories would students prefer and what are the difficulties they experience in the online environment that could be fine-tuned? The qualitative component of this research was useful in addressing these questions and others.

Surveys established that students' were highly confident in the use of standard office software such as word processing, databases, spreadsheets, email and internet searches. In addition, the materials were posted to a Moodle® site the operation of which, was part of their experience as well. It was corroborated in interviews that students experienced little frustration with accessing their lab materials online or operating multimedia (e.g. animations, video clips, object VR) that supplemented the text-based lab instructions. It was therefore presumed that any overall negativity associated with the lab format had negligible connection with technical difficulties.

While materials access was not a concern, discussion of the nature of the interaction mode with the materials brought about some interesting reflections by students. The Ftf lab instructions were not identical to the online version of the instructions. Students were unanimous in expressing dismay that it was laborious to filter through the seemingly endless online instructions in order to arrive at the practical task at hand. They felt that a more direct set of instructions may help. For instance they suggested bulleted lists numbered steps and highlighted terms as ways of improving readability of the lab directions. When pressed to explain this difference, students in focus groups alluded to scanning a hardcopy lab handout for key concepts/instructions; something that was much more visually difficult to do than scrolling a computer screen. Interviews revealed that students would benefit from electronic "frequently-asked-question" (FAQ) files both to assist in ambiguous procedural points but also to address misconceptions. These discussions quickly drew attention to the issue of instructor access.

The labs were supplemented with regular scheduled tutorials such that students could ask questions. While these were deemed helpful, students were quick to point out that the time advantage afforded by the online format to complete the lab in a convenient period was lost due to the lack of immediate feedback from an instructor. In fact students suggested that even though they could get relatively quick feedback from their instructor by email, the lack of "just-in-time" feedback as they were attempting the lab caused them to take much longer to complete it.

In both Ftf and online lab formats, students were tasked to address the lab individually even though collaboration was not discouraged. In surveys and interviews it was clear that students tended to work together on lab problems more in the Ftf format. With the proliferation of social media, one might predict that students would find it easy to problem-solve together however this sample of students cited scheduling issues as a deterrent to "solving together" whereas the more formalized Ftf lab period forced them all to be in a collaborative space. In focus groups, the social construction of knowledge was pursued further to uncover two related issues. Students suggested that they would attempt labs individually and then set aside their unanswered questions for either a tutorial or asking a peer by email. By their own admission, this sometimes led to plagiarism of previously submitted lab reports (i.e. in other course sections).

It is worth noting that the online lab format (through a multiple choice component) allowed for students to do several electronic resubmissions with instant feedback on incorrect answers. Students in interviews suggested that this "mastery learning" approach had them reconsidering incorrect answers in a way that would rarely occur in an Ftf setting where upon receiving the marked lab back, they would normally be scanning the incorrect answers and beginning the next lab. This multiple attempt approach also allowed them to revisit the lab when they undertook study for a required lab examination.

In interviews and focus groups students were asked to comment on the relative impact of the technologies used within the labs. Students felt that the simulations and videos offered excellent support for the learning in two particular ways 1) a self-paced explanation of the PCR process and 2) an interpretation/analysis of a real electrophoresis sample. In both cases they suggested that value was in the fact they could view the resources repeatedly as they needed.

The object VR technology was not rated as highly in utility on the survey. Further investigation of this finding established some interesting trends amongst interviewees. Students were unanimous in saying that 1) the technology was easy to use and 2) the technology was clear enough to observe details in the turtle anatomy. Given that most of the student sample was enrolled in a Bachelor of Science program (>70%, n=98), it was not surprising that students preferred a hands-on laboratory approach rather than the flexibility to simply rotate and enlarge an online specimen. One focus group paraphrased this by saying "when you hold an object in your hands there is more sensory input than simply observing; texture and the tactile experience is important; doing lab work is one of the exciting aspects of studying science." While a very few students found the visual access through object VR to be adequate for the lab task, the majority of students in interviews were self-identified kinesthetic learners (Gardner, 1993) and preferred to physically interact with the model specimens. Finally, one focus group identified the importance of providing very succinct instructions for using the object VR within the context of the lab queries.

Students in this sample were moderately aware of the primary rationale for employing online labs in their context (i.e. to reduce the demand on resources and lab space). In interviews students were very understanding of the access that online labs could potentially provide in web courses however their choice to attend a "physical university space" framed their overwhelming preference for Ftf labs as opposed to online versions. As noted before, within the used technologies students saw the most promise in simulations and descriptive videos with the object VRs being the least popular technology. Given the noted learning preferences,, the survey made it clear that students would tolerate or prefer no more than two out of six schedule labs be in the online format.

When pressed to describe inherent differences in the nature of learning students were quick to note that their grades were very similar in both formats so this was not an issue of contention. Survey, interviews and focus groups indicated that students felt their learning of the biology content and process skills of science were not compromised by doing the lab in an online format. In interviews, students repeatedly mentioned the advantage of flexibility to complete the online labs within their own schedule. When asked to weigh this factor, the same students qualified this assertion by saying "it wasn't a big enough factor to swing my preference for a hands-on lab experience". Students liked working together and suggested that both formats allowed for peer support and collaboration but that online interactions were much less efficient because student meetings (electronic or otherwise) were difficult to coordinate. In interviews and focus groups students frequently remarked that they appreciated the fact that their instructor strived to investigate how technology could make the laboratory better. Said one focus group "we didn't agree with using technology for every lab, but some worked really well and we think its great that we are at least trying different approaches; the instructor should get credit for at least trying new technologies, the critique of which ones work best is important for us to take part in."

The instructor was interviewed at various junctures of the research to ascertain particular challenges and perceptions of impact. From the beginning the instructor was aware that the VR objects could be enhanced by adding more photographic data to improve overall fluidity of movement in the turtle objects. Creating the VR objects was found to be both time-consuming and tedious yet the finish product was thought to a useful tool that could be utilized in various laboratory contexts. Offering laboratories in both online and Ftf formats was found to require good scheduling skills and the online version in particularly presumed significant email contact with students to support student queries at a distance. According to the instructor, creating laboratory instructions for students in the online format was surprisingly more difficult (i.e. much more detailed) than the Ftf version where lab assistants could readily answer questions and elaborate on technique. Statistical analysis/comparison did not reveal any trends (or correlations) in student attitude or performance by comparison to gender or ethnicity.

Conclusions

The above research has shown that the online versions of a particular group of laboratories seem to have no affect on the student's performance as evidenced by student grades. This suggests that the technologies employed do not have a detrimental effect on students learning. Qualitative feedback suggests that students prefer the tactile face-to-face laboratory over the online versions. Nonetheless, if pressed because of resource constraints, they would prefer no more than 30% online content in their introductory biology lab course. In normal circumstances then, one might abandoned these technologies for lack of demonstrative relative advantage over traditional approaches. However, one of the instructor's aims was to investigate whether online learning could mitigate the problem of limited laboratory space. Given the performance results and students' predisposition to moderate levels of online lab experiences, it seems reasonable to suggest that online experiences of this description may "free up" laboratory time for more decidedly hands-on activities. Of the technologies incorporated in the online labs, students clearly found the object VR to be the least useful primarily because, by comparison "to hands-on approaches" it was quite cumbersome. By contrast the animations and simulations were found to be particularly instructive. It is worth noting that further research may establish that there are additional benefits of the online laboratory that have not been uncovered to date. Within the data set, there was no evidence of gender or cultural correlations with performance or predisposition to the technology.

While this is a unique sample, curriculum and context, the research has provided an instructor with direction in terms of modifying instructional approaches. This research reaffirms (Wong, Marcus, Ayres, Smith, Cooper, Paas, & Sweller, 2009) the power of animations to assist learning given that they can be repeatedly played by students anywhere anytime. The simulation allows students to interact and make choices in a virtual laboratory and as such moves away from passive learning. The initial response of the instructor to a critique of the object VR was to improve the resolution and fluidity of the virtual object (turtle) by creating an improved model. Arguably this may be a moot point if science students in fact simply prefer to hold models in their hands, manipulate and make observations. Perhaps it is the nature of the scientifically-oriented student to flourish in the face-to-face laboratory setting?

References

Auerbach, C. F., & Silverstein, L. B. (2003). *Qualitative data: An introduction to coding and analysis*. New York: New York University.
Benyon, J., & Mackay, H. (1989). Information technology in education: Towards a critical perspective. *Journal of Educational Policy.* 4(3), 245-257.
Brooks, J. G., & Brooks, M. G. (1993). *The case for constructivist classrooms*. Alexandria, VA: Association for Supervision and Curriculum Development.
Dede, C. (2005). Planning for neomillenial learning styles: Implications for investments in technology and faculty. In . D. Oblinger & J. Oblinger (Eds.) *Educating the net generation*. Boulder, CO: EDUCAUSE
Gardner, H. (1993). *Frames of mind: The theory of multiple intelligences*. New York, NY: Basic.
Hart, C., Mulhall, P., Berry, A., Loughran, J. & Gunstone, R. (2000). What is the purpose of this experiment? or Can students learning something form doing experiments? *Journal of Research in Science Teaching 37*(7), 655-675.
Krueger, R. A. (1994). *Focus groups: A practical guide for applied research* (2nd ed.). London: Sage.
Lincoln, Y. & Guba, E. (1985). Naturalistic inquiry. London: Sage
Patton, M. (2002). *Qualitative research and Evaluation 3rd ed*. Thousand Oaks, CA: Sage.
Postman, N. (1993). *Technopoly: The surrender of culture to technology*. New York, NY: Vantage Books.
Wong, A., Marcus, N., Ayres, P., Smith, L., Cooper, G., Paas, F. & Sweller, J. (2009). Instructional animations can be superior to statics when learning human motor skills. *Computers in Human Behavior.* March, 339-347.

Acknowledgement

The authors acknowledge the contribution of Dr. Trevor Avery to the conception of the VR objects as a potential tool in the teaching of his introductory biology course.

The Virtual Boat: Design Team Issues in the Development of a Virtual Simulations for High School Science

Teresa Franklin
franklit@ohio.edu

Sertac Ozercan
so277107@ohio.edu

Chang Liu
liuc@ohio.edu

Nathan Andre
Ohio University
USA
na203602@ohio.edu

Abstract: This paper examines the design process when computer science programmers, non-programmers (engineers) and preservice teachers work as a team to design a 3-D virtual simulation called the Virtual Boat. The challenges of *design* and *team* are discussed to provide insights into game design and the teamwork often required for grant projects to be successful. The Virtual Boat is part of a National Science Foundation GK-12 grant called the Boat of Knowledge in the Science Classroom. The work of the game design team presents challenges when diverse groups are responsible for the design and implementation of the simulation in high school classrooms. A qualitative research approach was used to describe the phenomenon of the Virtual Boat team as it collaborated in the building of a 3-D virtual environment for learning.

Introduction

Game design typically includes large corporations or businesses with teams of artists, programmers, psychologists, marketing specialists and educators. Emerging wireless and mobile technologies bring new opportunities for learners to be more intensely connected by extending learning communities to include friends, teachers, mentors, parents, and others. These technologies support virtual worlds that can augment the learning by providing learning spaces that simulate real-world environments in which learning objects, challenges, and social engagement can occur.

Virtual worlds are multi-user computer programs that use advanced computer graphics, multimedia and broadband networking. Virtual worlds are able to simulate the real world on computer screens using 2-D and 3-D representations. The user engages in virtual worlds with an animated representation called an avatar. Since emerging, virtual worlds have drawn the attention of educators as tools to potentially foster and facilitate distant learning, collaborative learning, and immersive learning in both K-12 and higher education. (Choi 2010; Hew & Cheung 2010; Collins, Bently, & Conto 2008; Styliani, Fotis, Kostas, & Petros 2009). Virtual worlds have been applied to diverse disciplines such as cultural studies (Ligorio & Van der Meijden 2008), the arts (Lu 2009), health and environment (Cooper, Carroll, Liu, Chelberg, & Franklin 2009), education (Childress & Braswell 2006), commerce (Erlenkötter, Kühnle, Miu, Sommer, & Reiners 2008) and science (Turkay 2010). Virtual world building tools vary from commercial products (e.g. Unity 3D, Second Life, Active Worlds, Open Croquet) to self-developed environments (Jackson, Taylor & Winn 1999). With these virtual world technologies, teachers can present lectures and have students discuss remotely, saving transportation fees and commuting time for students while interacting with students inside a virtual classroom. Students can conduct experiments using virtual instruments in virtual labs which decrease investments in lab instruments. Virtual worlds provide places for educational activities such as group thinking and gallery walks to examine research completed and shared by experts.

The Boat-of-Knowledge in the Science Classroom

The Boat-of-Knowledge in the Science Classroom (BOK) sought to create awareness of water quality and environmental issues in the Ohio River Valley by engaging high school science classroom teachers and preservice teachers in game design to enhance communication skills of science and engineering graduate assistants (called fellows) at a large Midwestern University in the Appalachian region of Ohio. Over an 18-month period, nine graduate fellows worked with nine high school science teachers to conduct experiments on a research vessel along the Ohio River from Marietta to Gallipolis, Ohio. Instructional products related to these experiments were disseminated to preservice teachers and high school science classrooms including inquiry lesson activities designed using the 5E Learning Cycle. An online Virtual Boat was constructed to support these materials. The BOK project sought to enhance teaching, communication and presentation skills through interactions with high school teachers, preservice teachers and graduate students using hands-on activities from the river boat to science classrooms. The 5E Learning Cycle (engage, explore, explain, elaborate, and evaluate) provided an inquiry-based structure for lesson design. Preservice teachers reviewed the Virtual Boat activities and the 5E Learning Cycle lesson plans. The interaction of preservice teachers, high school teachers and fellows facilitated a deep understanding of the possible uses of virtual environments in science classrooms.

Three groups made up the design team developing the Virtual Boat. The first group included civil engineering fellows who worked in BOK science classrooms 10 hours per week. The second group was made up of computer science master's degree students who worked as graduate assistants (GAs) on the BOK program. A final group of high school science teachers and preservice teachers from the college of education completed the team.

The Unity software platform was used to develop the Virtual Boat. Unity is a multi-platform development tool, supporting Windows, Mac, and iOS. Unity allows web deployment making it platform-independent and convenient to access with a computer typically found in classrooms (Wendel et al. 2010). Unity includes a powerful and customizable editor (Unity 2010) supporting batch mode which allows building from command line. Developers can use the Unity integrated development environment (IDE) to create game objects, and can associate scripts using JavaScript or C# to control the properties and behaviors of these objects.

This research sought to explore the challenges of working as a team to build a virtual world for use in high school science classrooms. The research questions guiding the work presented in this paper are as follows:

1. *How are the meanings and structures of the lived experiences of the Virtual Boat design team members and teachers who use the simulation in their classrooms described by the design team?*
2. *From the perspective of usability and development, how are experiences noted by teachers, preservice teachers, project directors and the design team members guiding the work of building the Virtual Boat?*

The Study

The methodological approach to this research was a single case study design. A case study allows an in-depth investigation of contextual and phenomenological conditions. Case studies focus on the *how, what,* and *why* questions and are a useful tool for probing into a contemporary, complicated phenomenon of the real world. Case studies embrace a multi-dimensional approach to analyze data through the use of multiple sources of evidence (Yin 2009). A combination of qualitative and quantitative methods is often found in case study design (Flyvbjerg 2011). Creswell (2007) posited that single case design is advantageous in the expression of individual and small group behavioral changes. Lundervold and Belwood (2000) noted that single-case designs are most used in practice settings.

This study used case study methodology, involving both quantitative and qualitative approaches, to examine how a team of designers for the Virtual Boat, negotiated the organization, tasks, skill levels, personalities and project management to facilitate working together to create a virtual learning space. This case study examined the experiences of members of the Virtual Boat design team as they developed the Virtual Boat for use by preservice teachers and in-service teachers.

Data collection included 1) interviews/discussions with the design team, 2) bi-weekly progress reports and meetings concerning the design and development process, 3) team member's contributions, 4) emails concerning the work of the design team, 5) preservice and in-service teacher review of the Virtual Boat and 5E Learning Cycle lesson plans and 6) presentations of the Virtual Boat and its progress over the course of the 9 months of work completed thus far. A usability survey and game play comments were collected from an August professional development session with the fellows and the teachers. Preservice and high school teacher interviews concerning the use of the boat in the classroom, interviews with and observations of the project directors and fellows were also conducted and provided a rich data set for the research.

Findings

The work of the virtual boat design team began in June 2010. The team was composed masters students in civil engineering and computer science. One education faculty member and an instructional technology doctoral student with preservice teachers as reviewers of game and lesson plan design for implementing the Virtual Boat.

Research Question 1

How are the meanings and structures of the lived experiences of the Virtual Boat design team members and teachers who use the simulation in their classrooms described by the design team?

As fellows described their game development experiences, they often presented the game design work as secondary to the classroom experiences while the graduate assistants (GAs) described the game design work as far superior to the work of the fellows in their classrooms. Fellows wanted more organizational structure added to the game design process in a similar way that the teachers they were working with imposed structure on their classrooms. GAs believed that the high school students playing the game should impose the organizational structure on the game. This conflict was understandable considering that the GAs had no classroom experience and little insight into how students might behave in a classroom environment when playing games. The preservice teachers offered insight to both groups through their review of the lesson plan alignment to the activities in the game and their review of the content knowledge to be taught by the game. These reviews brought the separation over organizational structure into focus for both groups. Over time, the members developed organizational structures to support the work of the design team. Team Member [5] stated,

> The Virtual Boat team works together by having weekly meetings between the civil engineering students and the computer science students, as well as at least one professor (Drs. X and Y and Z). At these meetings, new ideas are formulated and incorporated into the game. Each person on the team is given a new task each week to complete before the next meeting. At the meeting, the group sits down and looks through each task and issue to see if they were completed or resolved. New ways of expansion are also discussed such as how the game can be used in the form of a lesson plan.

The fellows detailed how the game should work, what elements should be in the game and provide data, sound clips and in-game questions, content maps and coordinates of the river trip. The fellows often questioned the GAs with statements such as "This is not a game I would play?;" "Do you think this will keep the kids playing?;" and "The game does not seem to show what the kids see when they travel on the real boat. Wouldn't it be better if it were more realistic?" The GAs countered with statements similar such as, "The kids are not very sophisticated players, this will be good for them;" "There is not that much time to play in class, this will work;" and "It is not easy to program what you want. I do not think we have time to do this." An interesting contrast in the data emerged with the discussion by the GAs about how to make the game fit in a K-12 class time frame as well as the lack of respect for the students' abilities to play games with any sophistication. The preservice teachers became angry with comments on students' ability to play the game in the classroom and offered examples of other games often played by high school students. One preservice teacher [11] noted, "This game should help all students learn, not just the smart ones or those that have played games before."

Another member noted "that the leadership did not always agree and then things had to be removed and then recreated at times, thus adding to the work of the team." In further discussion, it became apparent that the engineering faculty were the real drivers of the game design and less input was being considered from other student groups. Below is a sampling of comments from fellows and GAs.

- They [engineering faculty] have no idea what high school students find compelling.
- They seem to think that making the VB compelling would be best accomplished by mimicking the real boat as closely as possible.
- I feel like this is a very bad idea, since in concept the boat trip is very dull.
- The only thing that makes it exciting is the fact that the students get out of school to go ride on a boat (something they likely do either very infrequently or have never done).
- I feel the VB should more closely resemble games from social networking sites (e.g. the games on Facebook).

The preservice teachers provided similar comments: "Farmville is fun. I think the fellow that suggested the FB is correct. Make the game so that it is on the web and shared with team play so students can challenge each other in finding out why the water quality is poor." Another common experience presented by all members of the design team was [Team Member 3]:

> I think the main barrier is making the game an educational asset and/or teaching tool while at the same time making the game a "game". It is hard to maintain the "fun" factor when educational information is being incorporated into it....The gaming industry has made the technological leaps and bounds that allow full interaction of kids in the game. From motion sensors to online multiplayer games, the gaming industry has years of research and experience to develop some of the most intriguing and somewhat addictive games.

One member [5] of the team noted "It might be helpful if the [Faculty names] spent some time observing in the high school classrooms...They might be surprised – I was shocked at the differences between high school and college students for quite some time when I first started visiting ... and its only been about 5 years since I was in high school myself."

In sum, the Virtual Boat team described their experiences as often dull, but at the same time compelling for a number of reasons.

- The games require very little initial investment, and can be picked up or put down as free time permits.
- The games reward player effort by using persistent characters and milestone rewards.
- The game allows passive interactions with friend's characters, allowing them to feel connected without the requirement of being online at the same time.

Research Question 2

From the perspective of usability and development, how are experiences noted by preservice teachers, teachers, project directors and the design team members guiding the work of the design team?

The preservice teachers and the teachers were very interested in the Virtual Boat. One BOK teacher suggested, "The Virtual Boat provides me an opportunity to continue in the grant when the funding is over. I can use it in my classes even when the boat is no longer available and this will be 'real' to the students. This is the world they know – this virtual world. I have no experience but I think they will really like the game play." A second teacher provided a *homework* explanation, "The students will do this at home if I just let them play for a few minutes to make sure everyone can find the web site and then how to move around in the world. They will go home and learn at home."

The preservice teachers were very engaged in trying to understand how the game actually worked from a content perspective. Their comments centered on the step by step process it would take to implement in the classroom. Such comments included, "I can see my future students using such a game for water quality. This would make it easy to study this content in the middle of the winter when the class can't go to a river or stream to test water. The students could practice in the Virtual Boat and then when the weather is good; go to a water source for hands-on testing." However, several preservice teachers noted the amount of time it takes to work with computers and the game. "What if the game crashes?" A preservice teacher noted in response to the question, "I have now wasted my class time on making the computer work not on the content."

The usability survey presented to the BOK teachers, preservice teachers, fellows, GAs and project directors provided interesting insights into how the game might be perceived when played and possible issues that could occur when used in the classroom. Comments from the BOK teachers were typically concerned with the authenticity of the game in comparison to the real BOK experience. The first examination of the Virtual Boat *before teachers had the opportunity to actually play the game* produced these comments:

- I liked the real data incorporated into the game; I also liked the idea of using technology -- the students would love it!!
- Graphics are very good, real world application virtually.
- Real application without actually being there.
- It is a good introduction for the testing on the boat. Could use this to get students ready to do the tests once on the river in the real boat.
- Liked the multiple processes of dropping datasonde and then checking talk on laptop.
- Check the spelling of words in the game. I found several spelling errors.
- The artwork is very good and is fairly realistic to the boat and river.
- Need to be sure the site does not crash with 25 users – and will this be multiplayer?

However, when the fellows, GAs, teachers and project directors played the game during the professional development after 9 months of design work, the comments concerning the actual *playing of the game* included:

- I was extremely frustrated because I could not navigate well. I kept running into the grass and having to start over!
- Navigating the curves in the river. Stopping boating. This is hard.
- I had trouble starting. I am video game challenged.
- Trouble finding a laptop that will work with the game.
- Unable to move the character. Didn't get check-mark after performance task. Fell off boat. Boat got stuck easily. Started walking underwater after I fell off the boat. Should probably not let students fall off the boat into the water.
- I had trouble getting the character in the water at the testing center.
- I couldn't get the datasonde in the water at certain location.
- The objectives started going out of order or repeating. The arrow also would not indicate the next location even through the current location was completed.
- It would nice if the river banks contained similar trees, plants, etc. as well as the landmarks we pass on the trip so these could be discussed in class with all students.

The game play by the project directors and teachers left the fellows and GAs quite frustrated and within about fifteen minutes one design Team Member [4] noted. "The teachers and project directors totally messed up the play in a few minutes! I could not believe they could have so much trouble. I hope this is not how it will be in the classroom."

When the game was played with the preservice teachers as part of their 5E Learning Cycle lesson plan review, the focus of the comments centered on the following:

- This boat is really hard to drive.
- The boat should bounce back to the middle of the river when it hits a bank so that students do not waste time on getting the boat off the bank. Actually, I never got off the bank!
- Objectives are clear but the little clock is so close to them on the screen, it is distracting.
- The content in the Virtual Boat matches pretty well the data that needs to be collected in the lesson.
- Students will like the avatars, they are cute. Mine has pink hair.
- I found out I could walk underwater and I think the game should have fish to identify for those of us that fall off the boat. (Something that should probably be fixed!)

- I am not sure the equipment looks real enough for the students to identify it from what they used on the real boat trip.
- This game is hard and I think students will get frustrated with the boat. Once they are at the fish kill site, it is easy but they may give up before they ever get there.

The preservice teachers while frustrated at times seemed to take the issues of the game in stride focusing rather on the use of the game and lessons and the philosophical issue of game play in the classroom.

Discussion and Conclusions

While this paper presents only a small window into the data collected from the Virtual Boat design team's challenges, the very perceptions of those comprising the team: novice programmers (civil engineering fellows), intermediate programmers (computer science GAs) and preservice and BOK teachers may be part of the difficulty. Each group had a perception of how school works created in part from their own school experiences. The original philosophy of bringing together these different groups with different perceptions presented challenges given the nature of the work the different experiences and concerns of each group. The disconnection between the team members and project leaders and the differences in game design and game play experience among team members hindered the progress of the Virtual Boat. It may have been that roles need to be more clearly identified for all members including the project faculty.

The design team attended a large number of meetings leaving little time for actual work on the Virtual Boat. Time was also limited given that project members attended college classes, worked on their thesis research and had to complete out of class assignments. The addition of the preservice teachers to the mix complicated the process at times as the preservice teachers were not readily available to help in the critique and game play due to classroom observation requirements. A better method for obtaining the critiques from the preservice teachers is being explored. One option being considered to seek gameplay feedback from preservice teachers given that they are often just a few years removed from high school.

Preservice teachers and the BOK teachers needed to be more assertive in providing feedback to the BOK design team. Observations suggested that preservice teachers and BOK teachers did not wish to cause problems by voicing concerns which in turn might have delayed finding solutions to problems in the design and lesson plans. Preservice teachers and the BOK teachers often made excuses for the work of the design team. Both the preservice and BOK teachers needed to use better assessment techniques and critical evaluation when working with the design team products in much the same way that would be expected in the classroom. This would have provided greater direction to the project.

BOK Project leaders needed to meet and identify a vision for the project so that the project was moving in one direction and the work was less scattered in nature. The work of the Virtual Boat needs to be streamlined going forward and the design team needs to honor the voices of all participants including those that are not computer programmers. One suggestion by both the preservice and fellows was to use a *Facebook-like* game design that would be recognizable to students. This statement by Team Member [5] may be at the heart of the problem, "The Virtual Boat project desperately needs a visionary – someone that knows what direction we are going and how to assign tasks to each person to move the project in that direction. Right now if feels like the project lacks direction." Couple this with the concern of Preservice Teacher [12] who said, "I don't think the Virtual Boat will be able to replace the real boat at any point, [the] Virtual Boat cannot simply replace that experience. I think it should be designed as a supplementary learning tool with educational and fun games rather than imitating the real boat for students that cannot go on the trip." Many of the BOK teachers echoed the same sentiment when they became frustrated with the game play during usability testing.

The Virtual Boat may be on the verge of becoming a sinking ship without simulating the learning experiences that the BOK project had hoped to accomplish. This would be disappointing as the work of the real-world boat in collecting water quality data and exposing students to the Ohio River has been viewed by the teachers and high school students as a great experience. By acting on lessons learned from this research, we are confident the project will move forward to bring water quality testing information into a virtual environment for many more learners to experience.

Acknowledgement

The authors of the paper wish to express their sincere thanks for the opportunity to participate in the Boat of Knowledge project (NSF 0947813). This paper reflects the research of the members of the Boat of Knowledge project and does not necessarily represent the work of the National Science Foundation or their expressed beliefs. The researchers wish to also thank the members of the design team, the non-design team fellows and GAs, preservice teachers and high school teachers as well as members of the project leadership.

References

Choi, H. (2010). Social learning through the avatar in the virtual world: The effect of experience type and personality type on achievement motivation. Proceedings of *Society for Information Technology & Teacher Education International Conference 2010*, Austin, TX. 1866-1873.

Childress, M. D., & Braswell, R. (2006). Using massively multiplayer online role-playing games for online learning. *Distance Education, 27*(2), 187-196. doi:10.1080/01587910600789522

Collins, S., Bently, K., & Conto, A. D. (2008). Virtual worlds in education. *EDUCAUSE Evolving Technologies Committee*. Retrieved from http://net.educause.edu/ir/library/pdf/DEC0801.pdf

Cooper, T., Carroll, S., Liu, C., Chelberg, D., & Franklin, T. (2009). Using the virtual world of second life to create educational games for real world middle school science classrooms. Proceedings of *World Conference on Educational Multimedia, Hypermedia and Telecommunications 2009*, Chesapeake, VA. 2124-2133.

Creswell, J. W. (2007). *Qualitative inquiry & research design: Choosing among five approaches*. London, England: Sage Publications.

Erlenkötter, A., Kühnle, C., Miu, H., Sommer, F., & Reiners, T. (2008). Enhancing the class curriculum with virtual world use cases for production and logistics. Proceedings of *World Conference on E-Learning in Corporate, Government, Healthcare, and Higher Education 2008*, 789-798.

Flyvbjerg, B. (2011). Case Study. In Denzin, N. K., & Lincoln, Y. S. (Ed.), *The SAGE handbook of qualitative research* (pp. 301-316). Thousand Oaks, CA: Sage Publications.

Hew, K. F., & Cheung, W. S. (2010). Use of three-dimensional (3-D) immersive virtual worlds in K-12 and higher education settings: A review of the research. *British Journal of Educational Technology, 41*(1), 33-55. doi:10.1111/j.1467-8535.2008.00900.x

Jackson, R. L., Taylor, W., & Winn, W. (1999). Peer collaboration and virtual environments: A preliminary investigation of multi-participant virtual reality applied in science education. Proceedings of the *1999 ACM Symposium on Applied Computing - SAC '99*, 121-125. doi:10.1145/298151.298219

Ligorio, M., & Van der Meijden, H. (2008). Teacher guidelines for cross-national virtual communities in primary education. *Journal of Computer Assisted Learning, 24*(1), 11-25. doi:10.1111/j.1365-2729.2007.00240.x

Lu, L. (2009). Teaching and learning in 3D virtual worlds: Seven art teachers' adventures in Second Life. Proceedings of *Society for Information Technology & Teacher Education International Conference 2009*, Chesapeake, VA. 445-451.

Lundervold. D. A., & Belwood. M. F. (2000). The best kept secret in counseling: Single-case (N = 1) experimental designs. *Journal of Counseling & Development, 78*, 92-102.

Styliani, S., Fotis, L., Kostas, K., & Petros, P. (2009). Virtual museums, a survey and some issues for consideration. *Journal of Cultural Heritage, 10*(4), 520-528. doi:10.1016/j.culher.2009.03.003

Turkay, S. (2010). Student engagement and attitude change towards science when learning with a virtual world based curriculum: A case study. Proceedings of *World Conference on Educational Multimedia, Hypermedia and Telecommunications 2010*, 248-257.

Unity: Features - deployment. Retrieved November 21, 2010, from http://unity3d.com/unity/features/deployment

Wendel, V., Babarinow, M., Hörl, T., Kolmogorov, S., Göbel, S., & Steinmetz, R. (2010). Woodment: Web-based collaborative multiplayer serious game. *Transactions on Edutainment IV, Lecture Notes in Computer Science, Volume 6250/2010*, 68-78. doi: 10.1007/978-3-642-14484-4_7

Yin, R. K. (2009). *Case study research: Design and methods* (4th ed.). Los Angeles, CA: Sage Publications.

Effective Use of Online Quizzes in Science Courses

William Stowe
wstowe@kilgore.edu

Lin Lin
University of North Texas
USA
lin.lin@unt.edu

Abstract: This study investigated ways to effectively incorporate online quizzes in college biology courses. A total of 151 college students participated in this experimental study. They took the online quizzes, lecture exams, and surveys. The online quizzes required the students to answer all the quiz questions correctly before earning quiz credits. Students who scored 10 out of 10 on every quiz achieved the mastery level. For comparison, the lecture exams were composed with half of the material from the online quizzes and the other half from material not in the online quizzes. Student surveys compared the students with online quiz mastery (Group 2) and those without mastery (Group 1). The results showed that the students with mastery scores used the required 30 minute delay between quiz attempts to review quiz feedback, learn the course content, and consequently, increased their lecture exam scores.

Introduction

The purpose of this study was to investigate ways to effectively incorporate online quizzes in college biology courses. Instructors today have access to innovative tools to help students connect their learning to course content beyond the physical walls of a classroom. One way to get students to read the course content is to use online quizzes before class. Online quizzes can be created by the instructor, or they can be supplied to the instructor by the textbook publisher. The online quizzes can be downloaded into the campus course management system (CMS) for students to access outside of class. To increase student interaction with the course content and exam scores, online quizzes have been incorporated into science courses such as biology.

Homework and Quiz Assignments in Preparing Students for Science Courses

One of the most common reasons instructors assign reading homework is to get students to read and understand course material (Ryan, 2006; Johnson and Kiviniemi, 2009). However, studies have shown that students often do not do homework or prepare for lectures beforehand (Sappington, Kinsey, and Munsayac, 2002). Students read very little to prepare for class, even with reading assignments. This problem is common in biology: homework is, to a large degree, underutilized in biology classes. Wood (2009) argued that to innovate teaching in undergraduate biology, instructors should not only ask students to complete homework but also provide students with formative assessment on their homework before class. The online quizzes would provide a channel for instructors to provide students with formative assessment on their homework before class. In addition, the online quizzes could allow students unlimited attempts to answer all the questions correctly. This type of exercise, although appearing to be rote-learning at the beginning, will help students become familiar with the basic biological terminology necessary to effectively participate in class discussions.

It is difficult to motivate students to read the required text before entering the class, except just before exams, where studies show that student reading increases (Burchfield and Sappington, 2000; Clump, Bauer, and Bradley, 2004). Meanwhile, studies with reading-based-homework assignments have found that quizzes or worksheets with extensive teacher feedback increase both reading the textbook and preparation for class (Ryan, 2006). Regular pre-lecture quizzes have been shown to increase class preparation and in class questions from students (Narloch, Garbin, and Turnage 2006; Marcell 2008; Dobson, 2008). Studies have also shown that online pre-lecture quizzes increase exam scores (Dobson, 2008; Hadsell, 2009; Johnson & Kiviniemi 2009).

The Study

This study used the CMS to deliver the online quizzes to college students enrolled in biology and environmental courses at a community college. The online quizzes covered the assigned readings. Students were provided immediate feedback on missed questions. This feedback helped students learn from their mistakes (Brothen & Wambach, 2001; Ryan, 2006; Johnson & Kiviniemi, 2009). Credit for passing an online quiz was awarded only when all of the questions selected randomly from a question bank were answered correctly in a limited amount of time (Brothen and Wambach, 2004; Hadsell, 2009; Johnson & Kiviniemi, 2009). Time limits on Internet quizzes reduced the student's ability to use their textbooks to look up the answers as they work through the quiz. (Hadsell, 2009; Marcell, 2008).

According to Muchovej (2009), voluntary quizzes for extra credit lacked significant participation. In order to increase student participation, the online quiz scores were part of the course grade. This was consistent with other studies that placed a grade on the online quizzes (Narloch et al. 2006; Dobson, 2008; Dantas & Kemm, 2008; Johnson & Kiviniemi, 2009). To determine the effectiveness of online quizzes, students were required to take in-class exams (Johnson & Kiviniemi, 2009). Half of the material on the exams was from the material with an online quiz, and the other half of the exam was from material without an online quiz for comparison. The purpose of the study was to find out if mastery of the online quizzes may help improve students' exam scores in the biology courses, and why.

METHODS

Participants

The participants (n=151) in the study were students taking biology and environmental science courses at a community college in the U.S.. None of the participants were science majors. The study was explained to the participants, and participation was voluntary. The online lecture material for this course was also uploaded in the CMS. Students were provided instructions on how to take the quizzes.

The Study Procedures

Practice Quiz. During the first face-to-face meetings, the instructor explained how to log into CMS. After the instructor covered the quiz instructions with the class, a short practice quiz was demonstrated. The questions on this practice quiz covered the quiz instructions. Brothen and Wambach (2006) recommended practice quizzes.

Online Quizzes and Achieving the Mastery Level of the Quizzes. The first online quiz was made available to the students during the first week of the semester, and the students continued to take quizzes throughout the semester until the week before the final exams. The quizzes covered only the assigned reading. The quizzes were not optional because the objective was to encourage all the students to take the quizzes and to increase exam scores. The questions came from a randomized bank of questions to reduce the chance of students memorizing the questions. Questions selected were not the same as the questions on the exams. The quizzes accounted for less than 20% of the total grade in the courses. Quiz credit was earned for answering all ten questions of the quiz correctly. Successfully completing all ten questions was considered necessary for students to master the assigned material. Students that scored 10 out of 10 on every quiz were deemed to have achieved the mastery level.

The 30 Minutes Time Delay between Quiz Attempts. Before each quiz, there was a reminder about the ten-minute time limit. Students were told that they must answer all ten questions correctly in order to earn credit for the quiz. When a student missed a question or failed to answer all of the questions in ten minutes, the CMS prevented the student from taking another quiz until a minimum of 30 minutes had passed. The CMS feedback instructed the student to reread the material and take another quiz. The time delay between quizzes was to encourage the student to study the material, and to discourage students from continuously taking the quizzes in order to get all of the questions correct by guessing the answers. There were no limits on the number of attempts allowed for a quiz. The reasoning behind allowing unlimited quiz attempts was to increase student preparation and exam scores by reading and mastering the material on the quizzes. It is hoped that the students would be motivated to reread the material in order to answer all ten questions on each quiz correctly and thus to achieve the mastery level and receive the grade credit.

Exams. Four noncumulative lecture exams were taken in classrooms while two exams were taken online. Each exam consisted of 100 multiple-choice questions. None of the questions on the quizzes appeared verbatim on the exam. Half of the questions on the exam were from the material covered by the quizzes for that section. The other half of the exam questions were from the material not covered on the quizzes. The results on the exam questions from the quiz material were compared to those of questions from material covered without quizzes.

RESULTS

The Impact of Achieving the Mastery Level in Online Quizzes

The study divided the students into two groups based on whether they achieved the mastery level of all the online quizzes, that is, whether they answered all the questions correctly in all their online quizzes. Students who did not achieve the mastery level of all the online quizzes were grouped into Group 1 while those who achieved the mastery level of all the online quizzes were grouped into Group 2. ANOVA ($F (1,147) = 27.477$, $p = .000$, $g = 0.9$, $d = 0.91$) was used to compare the two groups' lecture test averages. The analysis indicated a significant difference between the exam averages with Group 2 ($M = 82.77$) and exam averages Group 1 ($M = 72.97$). Both the Hedges g and Cohen's d indicated that the mastery scores on the online quizzes had a large effect on the exam scores (see Table 1 ANOVA of the lecture test averages and quiz mastery). Table 1 below provides a summary of the results:

Table 1

ANOVA of the lecture test averages and quiz mastery

Descriptives								
Mastery	N	Mean	Std. Deviation	Std. Error	95% Confidence Interval for Mean		Minimum	Maximum
					Lower Bound	Upper Bound		
Group 1 No	97	72.97	11.163	1.133	70.72	75.22	38	96
Group 2 Yes	52	82.77	10.320	1.431	79.90	85.64	51	103
Total	149	76.39	11.811	.968	74.48	78.30	38	103
ANOVA								
		Sum of Squares	df		Mean Square	F	Sig.	
Between Groups		3251.285	1		3251.285	27.477	<.001	
Within Groups		17394.138	147		118.327			
Total		20645.423	148					

The Impact of the Thirty Minutes Delay between Quiz Attempts

The students were asked to fill out a survey online. The survey consisted of demographic questions and a 5-point Likert scale questionnaire (1 = disagree strongly and 5 = strongly agree). The purpose of the survey was to determine students' opinions about using online quizzes in preparing them for the lectures and exams. The survey asked the students if they used the 30 minutes between attempts to review the feedback on the missed questions. Comparison of the Group 2 ($M = 4.02$) and Group 1 ($M = 3.53$), indicated Group 1 (the non-mastery group) reported ANOVA ($F(1,116) = 6.439$, $p=.013$), that they did not use the feedback to study. They did not use the required 30 minute delay between attempts to review the feedback from missed questions or study the course content. Group 2 (the mastery group) did use the required delay to review feedback from the missed questions and to study in order to earn credit for the quiz. Furthermore, the survey asked the students if their lack of reading affected their grade. Comparison of Group 2 ($M = 2.62$) and Group 1 ($M = 3.17$), indicated that Group 1 reported ANOVA ($F (1,115) = 5.378$, $p = .022$) that their grades were affected by a lack of reading.

Comparison of Exam Scores with and without Prior Online Quizzes

The exam performance on the lecture quizzes could be due to the "Good Student" explanation discussed by Johnson and Kiviniemi (2009). According to Johnson and Kiviniemi (2009), the hard working "Good Student" student will score high on both the quizzes and the exams. This is because a "Good Student" will read and study for the exams with or without a quiz. Accordingly, the online quizzes should not have an effect on the exam scores. If the online quizzes were actually effective at increasing reading comprehension, then students would do significantly better on the part of the exams that were covered in the online quizzes. To test if the "Good Student" explanation also worked in this study, half of the questions on the exams came from materials covered in the online quizzes and the other half came from the assigned chapter readings not covered in the online quizzes.

When the students were asked if they studied before attempting the quiz; the analysis indicated there was not a significant difference between the two groups. Additionally, there were 1616 missed questions on the half of the exam without the online quizzes, and 1202 missed questions on the half of the exams with the online quizzes as shown in the following figure (Figure 1):

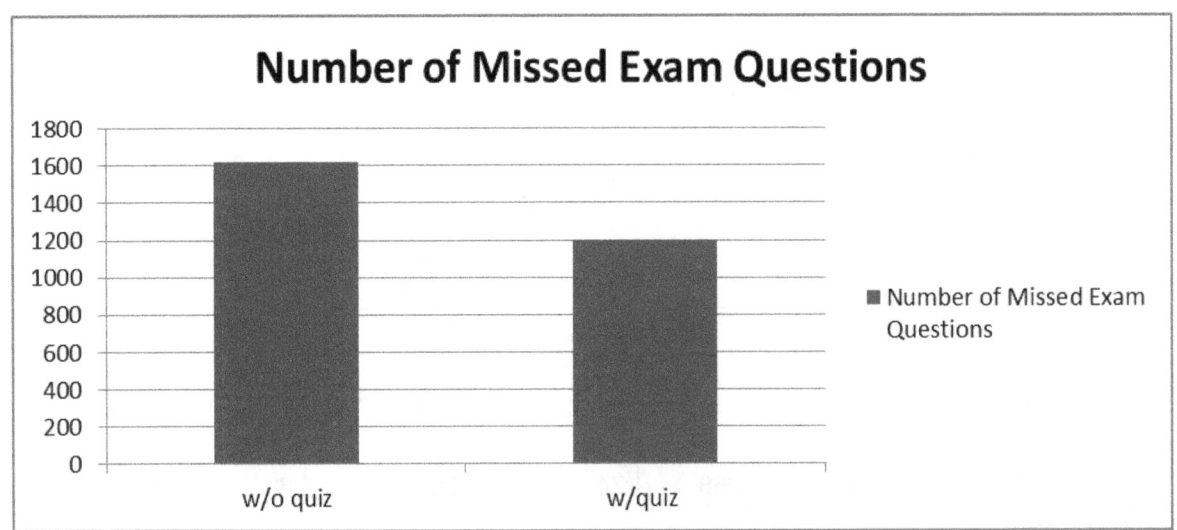

Figure 1: The number of missed exam questions not covered in online quizzes compared to the number of missed exam questions covered in online quizzes

The 26% fewer missed questions on the half of the exams with the online quizzes indicates that some of the student did use the online quizzes to learn the material on the exams. The comparison of the number of missed questions on the exams from the Group 2 students indicated that these students in the study missed fewer questions on average ($M=9.54$) in the exams that were covered in the online quizzes than questions on average ($M=12.83$) in the exams that were not covered in the online quizzes. However the analysis of the exams that had questions not covered on the quiz indicated that Group 2 (M=36.1) were "Good Students" that scored high on both parts of the exam as compared to Group 1 (M=51.7). This indicates that online quizzes had a limited effect on the students that would have read and studied for the exam anyway, and the online quizzes did not help improve the exam scores for Group 1.

CONCLUSION

The study indicated that it is an effective method to encourage some of the students to take online quizzes and to achieve the mastery level in their online quizzes (i.e., to receive credits by answering all the online quizzes correctly). One important factor that makes the method effective is to require a 30 minute delay between quiz attempts to encourage review of the quiz feedback and course content. The online quizzes helped the students to prepare for their course content outside the classroom setting. The students with a mastery score on all of the online quizzes used the required 30 minute delay between attempts to review the quiz feedback and course content. The recommendation for instructors using online quizzes is to implement a 30 minute delay between attempts to create a study time for the student to read the feedback, locate the material related to the missed questions, and reread that material before attempting the quiz again. One issue of concern that emerges from the study was that student in Group 1 did not take advantage of the online quizzes or the 30 minute delay between attempts to study. Given that students in Group 1 were the ones who most needed to study more (as opposed to those in Group 2. Determining the reason why these students did not use the 30 minute delay between attempts to study are possible subjects for future study.

References

Brothen, T., & Wambach, C. (2001). Effective Student Use of Computerized Quizzes. *Teaching of Psychology*, 28, 292-294.
Brothen, T., & Wambach, C. (2004). The Value of Time Limits on Internet Quizzes. *Teaching of Psychology*, 31, 62-64.
Brothen, T., & Wambach, C. (2006). The Value of Practice Quizzes on Developmental Students. *Research & Teaching in Developmental Education*, 22, 42-50.
Burchfield, C. & Sappington, J. (2000). Compliance With Required Reading Assignments. *Teaching of Psychology*, 27, 58-60.
Clump, M., Bauer, H., & Bradley, C. (2004). The Extent to Which Psychology Students Read Textbooks: A Multiple Class Analysis of Reading Across the Psychology Curriculum. *Journal of Instructional Psychology*, 31, 227-232.
Dantas, A., & Kemm, R. (2008). A Blended Approach to Active Learning in a Physiology Laboratory-based Subject Facilitated by an E-Learning Component. *Advances in Physiology Education*, 32, 65-75.
Dobson, J. (2008). The use of Formative Online Quizzes to Enhance Class Preparation and Scores on Summative Exams. *Advance in Physiology Education*, 32, 297-302.
Hadsell, L. (2009). The Effect of Quiz Timing on Exam Performance. *Journal of Education For Business*, 84, 135 – 140.
Johnson, B., & Kiviniemi, M. (2009). The effect of Online Chapters Quizzes on Exam Performance in an Undergraduate Social Psychology Course. *Teaching of Psychology*, 36, 33-37.
Marcell, M. (2008). Effectiveness of Regular Online Quizzing in Increasing Class Participation and Preparation. *International Journal for the Scholarship of Teaching and Learning*, 2, 1-9.
Muchovej, J.J. (2009). Online Quizzes as a Study Tool for Biology for Non-Science Majors. Education, 130, 133-140.
Narloch, R., Garbin, C., & Turnage, K. (2006). Benefits of Prelecture Quizzes. *Teaching of Psychology*, 33, 109-112.
Ryan, T. (2006). Motivating Novice Students to Read Their Textbooks. *Journal of Instructional Psychology*, 33, 135-140.
Sappington, J., Kinsey, K., & Munsayac, K. (2002). Two Studies of Reading Compliance Among College Students. *Teaching of Psychology*, 29, 272-274.
Wood, W. (2009). Innovations in Teaching Undergraduate Biology and Why We Need Them. *Annual Review of Cell & Developmental Biology*, 25, 93-112.

Using Technology in Training Elementary Mathematics Teachers, The Development of TPACK Knowledge

Beth Bos
bb33@txstate.edu

Kathryn S. Lee
Texas State University-San Marcos
USA
kl10@txstate.edu

Abstract: This study examined the effects of a problem-based Elementary Mathematics Specialist (EMMT) Program on mathematical, technological, and pedagogical knowledge (TPACK). A questionnaire adapted from Schmidt, Baran, Thompson, Mishra, Koehler, and Shin (2009) was used with a matched pair t-test for pre- and post-test data. The results revealed statistical significant gains with good effect sizes. The data shows that growth in TPACK knowledge flourished in this content-based program emphasizing technology, critical thinking, problem solving, creativity, and cognitive development.

Introduction

U.S. Department of Commerce statistics show that "education is dead last in technology use…education is the least technology-intensive enterprise in a ranking of technology use among 55 U.S. industry sectors" (Vockley, 2008, p. 2). From this data we can understand why weaving technology into teaching of mathematics has become a national focal point for elementary mathematics teachers (Association of Mathematics Teacher Educators, 2006; National Council of Teachers of Mathematics, 2000). The purpose of this study was to examine the results of the Survey of Preservice Teachers' Knowledge of Teaching and Technology (TPACK Survey) (Schmidt et al., 2009) to determine its value with inservice teachers and to explore the relationships between TPACK domains with inservice teachers when taught from a 21st century framework that included creativity and innovation, critical thinking and problem solving, and communication and collaboration. The inservice teacher program targeted elementary mathematics specialists training and was based on cognitively guided instruction, Hill and Ball's (2004) model of knowledge structures, and the integration of technology.

Significance of Study

For more than 20 years, national advisory groups have voiced ongoing concerns that practicing elementary school teachers are not adequately prepared to meet the demands for increasing student achievement in mathematics (National Council of Teachers of Mathematics, 2000; National Mathematics Advisory Panel, 2008; National Research Council, 2002). Most elementary teachers are generalists; that is, they study and teach all core subjects, rarely developing in-depth knowledge and expertise with regard to teaching elementary mathematics. Wu (2009) observed, "The fact that many elementary teachers lack the knowledge to teach mathematics with coherence, precision, and reasoning is a systemic problem with grave consequences" (p.14).

Hill and Ball (2004) suggested that teaching elementary mathematics requires a specialized knowledge of mathematics-- an applied mathematical knowledge unique to the work of teaching. Additionally, research supports the claim that effective teaching entails knowledge of mathematics above and beyond what a mathematically literate adult learns in grade school, a liberal arts program, or even a career in another mathematically-intense profession such as accounting or engineering (Ball, Hill, & Bass, 2005). Many schools across the nation have responded by using experienced teachers, or teachers with mathematics experience to serve as specialists and coaches working with elementary teachers to improve practice. Unfortunately, there has been no uniform training targeting these teachers that specifically addresses the demands of an elementary math specialist (EMS). As part of the Core Standards State Standards Initiative several mathematics educators are realizing that not only EMS professionals but also all elementary teachers need inventive, quality, research-based training to meet the challenges to improve teacher efficacy and student academic scores (Campbell & Malkus, 2011; Fennell, 2006). Research on the effectiveness of EMS professionals is growing (McGatha, 2008; Gerretson, Bosnick, & Schofield, 2008; Kenny & Faunce, 2004; Sailors, 2010).

Despite best efforts to improve student achievement in mathematics, there remains a profound gap between the knowledge and skills most students learn in school and the knowledge and skills they need in typical 21st century communities and workplaces. Today's education system faces irrelevance unless we bridge the gap between how students live and how they learn. We now have scientific insight about the cognitive processes of learning, effective teaching strategies for engaging students in learning, and motivating student to achieve. The Partnership for 21st Century Skills (P21) combines what we know about cognitive processes and the changing needs of the 21st century into a Framework for 21st Century Learning (P21, 2009). This initiative stresses the importance of core subjects and focuses on learning innovation, information, media, and technology skills. In fact, learning skills relevant for life and work in the 21st century are essential to successfully navigating increasingly complex life and work environments. These skills include creativity and innovation, critical thinking and problem solving, communication and collaboration, and use of technology. The 21st century skills are also the missing components in the traditional elementary math classroom. Teachers unsure of mathematical connections fail to let their students explore and create their own algorithms as they make sense of the mathematics. Ideally, teachers with increased knowledge (and confidence imparting such knowledge) will encourage critical and innovative thinking thereby facilitating students to arrive at the fundamental building blocks of mathematics. By integrating 21st century skills within the ***EMMT,*** Elementary Master Mathematics Teacher program our goal meets the needs of this generation's elementary students.

What we know about digital technology for instructional purposes is that adequate *pedagogical integration* of such technologies is a major factor for success. Without pedagogical integration, the benefit of using technology will not reach its potential in maximizing teaching and learning (Conlon & Simpson, 2003; Cuban, Kirkpatrick, & Peck, 2001). Additionally, in order to pedagogically integrate a technology, teachers must first perceive and understand the affordances of the specific technology and then relate them to their classroom goals during lesson planning (Angeli & Valanides, 2009). In other words, the challenge for the mathematical teacher to leverage technology affordances (e.g., of digital tools) in their classroom begins with *cognitively* integrating these affordances with their knowledge of specific mathematical tasks and instructional guidance. Technology affordances that teachers construct or activate are important for planning use of technology in class within a problem-based instructional learning model. Problem-based instruction creates an atmosphere for reasoning and critical thinking and teamed with technology can be very powerful (Donnelly, 2010). Because most elementary teachers are generalists with little mathematical training there is a growing need for adequately trained elementary mathematical teachers. This study examined the integration of technology into a specialist program—the Elementary Master Math Teacher (EMMT) program using a rigorous 21st Century approach focused on cognitive development.

Theoretical Model

A theoretical model proven useful with preservice teachers in understanding the relationship between technology, pedagogy and mathematical content, known as TPACK, served as the theoretical framework for this study. This model was based on Shulman's (1986) theory of Pedagogical Content Knowledge (PCK) but was designed to support effective technology integration into classroom teaching practices. Consequently, the model includes technology knowledge (TK), pedagogical knowledge (PK), content knowledge (CK), and overlapping relationships of pedagogy and mathematical knowledge (PCK), technology and pedagogy (TPK), and technology and mathematical knowledge (TCK) (Mishra & Koehler, 2006). For the purpose of this study the focus was on the relationships between mathematical knowledge (CK), pedagogical knowledge (PK), technological knowledge (TK) and the bridge between technological and pedagogical knowledge (TPK).

Within the TPACK framework one can successfully leverage the affordance of technology for teaching and learning technological with pedagogical and content-specific characteristics. A number of studies support technological pedagogical content knowledge (TPCK) as a whole leading to a more integrative view and its beneficial effects for teaching with technology (Angeli & Valanides, 2009; Koehler, Mishra, & Yahya, 2007). However, the interplay between the different aspects of teachers' knowledge on a cognitive level remains an unresolved theoretical and empirical issue. Do teachers need to be instructed to construct a unique body of TPCK knowledge (*transformative view*) or is it sufficient to train the separate aspects and assume spontaneous integration on the spot (*integrative view*; Angeli & Valanides, 2009)? Assessing the TPCK components and empirically differentiating between them are still in their early stages (Archambault & Barnett, 2010). Although it may be easy to distinguish between content knowledge and pedagogical knowledge, technology knowledge is more difficult to distinguish as mathematical or pedagogical (Krauss et al., 2008).

Program Design

The elementary master math teacher (EMMT) program studied was designed according to Association of Mathematics Teacher Educators (AMTE) Elementary Mathematic Specialists Standards where content and pedagogy standards are described separately but are taught together along with technology. The graduate courses focus on a comprehensive understanding of mathematical principles and technological skills that include (a) multiple representations (embodiment of concepts), (b) justifications, (c) technological math objects, (d) manipulatives (transformational play), and (e) project-based learning (synthesizing). The courses emphasize communication, critical thinking and problem-solving using interpersonal and self-directional skills. Participants develop wiki-based and problem-based instructional units with lesson plans, concept maps, calendars, YouTube videos, Jing videos, and other 2.0 web technologies. Participants demonstrated application of the course and unit concepts by instructing their students using the principles that they were taught in the course and posting their student products on the wiki. Notable differences were apparent when comparing the traditionally taught class content with the innovative course content offered within this project.

In applying the TPACK model, the content was elementary mathematics; the pedagogy was problem-based inquiry with cognitive-guided instruction. Application of technology within an instructional unit, such as using Web 2.0 technologies, wikis, animoto, voicethread, blabberize, blogs, jings, etc. blended the content, pedagogy, and technology into a meaningful product. For instructional purposes Adobe Connect was used as a medium for the inservice teachers' instruction, collaboration, and production. The inservice teacher students met at a given time online at a given url address. Adobe Connect was used to collaborate on concepts and projects and for basic instruction. Two- thirds of the treatment classes used Adobe Connect as the primary instructional media. The program structure was an integrated approach to TPACK.

Method

A pretest posttest study was conducted based on a convenient sample consisting of practicing teachers enrolled in an elementary masters program at a major university in Central Texas. The study was built around the following questions:

1) How do *inservice* teachers trained using TPACK theory compare with *preservice* teachers with similar training when tested with the TPACK survey?
2) What significant changes, if any, occur in TPACK survey scores for inservice teachers entering the EMMT program (pretest) and completing the program (posttest)?
3) What patterns emerge in comparing the TPACK survey scores for inservice teachers entering the EMMT program (pretest) and completing the program (posttest)?

Participants

The population studied included 30 practicing teachers enrolled in a masters degree program with an emphasis on elementary mathematics. The groups' ethnicity was 3% Asian, 10% Black, 27% Hispanic, and 60% White; and gender 7% male, 93% female. A pretest posttest design was used. The TPACK Survey was administered during their first semester of the program and their last semester of the 36-hour program.

The EMMT program included six semesters of problem-based classes where number theory, geometry, measurement, algebra, and probability and statistics are investigated from a practitioner's perspective, but centered around the cognitive development and thought patterns of a child. In each of the theory classes participants were responsible for making a wiki, creating an instructional video, and using a variety of Web 2.0 tools including Jing, Animoto, Vokis, Voicethread and web pages with interactive mathematical activities such as found on Mathplayground.com, NCTM's illuminations, and National Virtual Manipulatives. Classes offered were a combination of structures, including online (using Adobe Connect), on campus (face-to-face), and hybrid. The focus was student-centered and participants used a collaborative learning environment, based on Sakai, an open source learning management system.

Data Sources

The TPACK Survey by Schmidt, Baran, Thompson, Koehler, Shin, and Mishra (2009), with minor modifications, was used to obtain data. Four content-related questions were omitted to focus solely on mathematical content. The test was originally designed for preservice teachers. An effort was made to determine the reliability of study's survey for inservice teachers. The survey included technology knowledge, mathematical knowledge, pedagogy knowledge and technological pedagogical knowledge.

Item response was scored with a Likert scale of 1-5, ranging from 1 strongly disagree to 5 strongly agree. The data was analyzed using SPSS and matched paired t-test. The modified instrument was tested for validity and compared with the original instrument. Additionally, the modified instrument was examined for any predictive factors.

Results

To measure knowledge in the TPACK domains the researcher administered the research instrument twice by way of a Web-based survey at the beginning of the program (pretest) and again at the end of the program (posttest). First, the Cronbach's alpha reliability coefficients based on the average covariance among items in a scale were determined as shown in Table 2.

Internal consistency and reliability of the instrument when used by *inservice* teachers created Cronbach's alpha coefficients for the subscale ranged from .81 to .95 with the exception of .61 for technology pedagogical knowledge (pretest). See Table 2. The TPACK instrument originally designed for preservice teachers reported Cronbach's alpha coefficients for the subscales ranging from .75 to .92. The technological content knowledge (TCK) and pedagogical content knowledge (PCK) were not recorded because the focus was on mathematics only and questions under each subcategory asked for knowledge about other disciplines. Only one question was used for each subcategory. Therefore, because of limited data both subcategories were eliminated from the tested results. The coefficients of reliability (or consistency) indicated good to excellent alpha scores

Table 2. Cronbach's Alpha Values for Survey Subscales on Pretest and Posttest (N=30)

Sub-Scale	# survey items	Pretest	Posttest
Technological Knowledge (TK)	7	.92	.84
Mathematics Content Knowledge (M-CK)	3	.83	.86
Pedagogical Knowledge (PK)	7	.87	.95
Pedagogical Content Knowledge (PCK)	1	-	-
Technological Pedagogical Knowledge (TPK)	5	.61	.81
Technological Content Knowledge (TCK)	1	-	-
Technological Pedagogical Content Knowledge (TPCK)	5	.81	.83

Results of matched-pairs *t*-test yielded a statistically significant improvement ($t(104) = 2.95$ at $p = .004$) with a small effect size for technology knowledge (TK). A positive change for mathematical knowledge (MK) was statistically significant ($t(84) = 2.96$ at $p < .05$) with a medium effect size. Results of matched-pairs *t*-test for pedagogical knowledge (PK) yielded a statistically significant improvement as the result of the intervention, ($t(179) = 14.44$ at $p = .001$) with a high effect size. The mean pretest scores for technology, pedagogy, and mathematical knowledge (TPCK) yielded a statistically significant improvement as a result the intervention with a ($t(179) = 10.20$ at $p = .001$) with a high effect size. The significant *t* scores and effect sizes indicated a noteworthy improvement.

Table 3. Descriptive Statistics for Subscales on Pretest and Posttest (N = 30)

Categories	Inservice Pre M	SD	Post M	SD	d	Inservice Mean Diff	Preservice * Mean Diff	Diff
TK	3.56	.83	3.87	.86	.37	.31	.02	+.29
MK	3.51	.70	4.10	.75	.81	.59	.22	+.37
PK	3.95	.80	4.55	.55	.87	.60	.36	+.24
TPK	3.68	.60	4.38	.61	1.16	.70	.30	+.40
TPCK	3.64	.67	4.39	.57	1.20	.75	.66	+.09

* (Abbitt, 2011)

The difference between the pretest and posttest scores was compared with a similar study (Abbitt, 2011) that used the TPACK survey but with *preservice* teachers. The results found the *inservice* teachers experienced greater growth than the *preservice* teachers on all of the subscales as shown in Table 3. With the increase in scores of the core knowledge strands of TPACK, there is hope that *inservice* teachers can benefit from a robust mathematical program that uses problem-based learning, cognitive-guided instruction, technology affordances, and transformative skills.

Based on the high t-score and effect size of PK of the matched-paired t-test, an analysis of data first evaluated the bivariate relationships between PK and the TPACK subscales using a Pearson Product-Moment correlation. The researcher calculated a correlation coefficient between the subscale score measuring pedagogical knowledge about technology integration and each of the TPACK subscales for the pretest and posttest data. The bivariate relationship among the variables measured on the pretest showed one medium significant positive correlation between pedagogical knowledge and the subscale measurement of perceived TPCK ($r = .324$ $p < .05$) as shown in Table 4. An analysis of bivariate relationships among the same variables using posttest data revealed stronger positive relationships ($r = .574$, $p < .001$), M-CK ($r = .530, p < .001$), TPK ($r = .407, p < .001$), and TK ($r = .317, p < .001$).

Table 4. Bivariate Correlation Coefficients for TPACK Subscales PK about Technology Integration (N=30)

	Pretest r	r^2	Post test r	r^2
TK	.098	.010	.317**	.100
M-CK	.203	.041	.530**	.281
TPK	.010	.001	.407**	.166
TPCK	.324*	.105	.574**	.329

*p<.05 **p < .001

Following the analysis of bivariate relationships, the researcher conducted a multiple regression analysis using only significant domains to determine the degree to which ratings of perceived knowledge in the pedagogical knowledge (PK) domain had contributed to TPACK domains. However r^2, coefficient of determination, was .43, lower than hoped as shown in Table 6. Compared to pretest multiple regression analysis that showed $r^2 = .11$ there was a notable increase as show in Table 5. Still it would need to be higher before it would lead us to believe that pedagogical knowledge is a predictive variable. Yet, we see the strong role it plays in TPACK domains.

Table 5. Regression of Pedagogical Knowledge on Perceived Knowledge in TRACK Domains Pretest

Variable	B	SE	t	sr	95%CI
TPCK	.34	.12	.32	2.42	.324	(.11, .57)

$r^2 = .11$

Table 6. Regression of Pedagogical Knowledge on Perceived Knowledge in TPACK Domains Posttest

Variable	B	SE	t		sr	95%CI
TK	.06	.06	.10	1.13	.124	(-.05, .17)
M-CK	.20	.06	.30	3.17	.370	(.07, .32)
TPK	.10	.08	.12	1.26	.137	(-.06, .25)
TPCK	.31	.08	.38	4.03	.407	(-.16, .47)

$r^2 = .43$

Limitations

A further examination of the program may reveal other factors such as the instructor influence, maturity of participants, and length of the intervention impacted the data. More testing evidence is needed. Another question to be addressed in future studies is if the same pattern of results occurs with older students.

Discussion

Three issues arose from examining the impact of the program on TPACK scores. First, the research in this study confirmed the findings of Desimone (2011) and Darling-Hammond and McLaughlin (2011) that professional development should be ongoing and intensive. "Professional development needs to be content focused, require active learning, and should be coherent and fit in with other goals within the school environment" (Desimone, 2011, p. 69). "It must be connected to and derived from teachers' work with their students. It must be sustained, ongoing, intensive, and supported by modeling, coaching, and the collective solving of specific problems of practice" (Darling-Hammond & McLaughlin, 2011, p. 82). Teacher professional development is undergoing a paradigmatic shift that suggests the benefits of an intensive and sustained training program similar to the university-school district partnership addressed in this study.

Second, the importance of pedagogy as defined by Shulman (1986) and as interpreted by Ball, Thames, and Phelps (2008) has a very important role in the integration of technology into mathematics. A teacher must understand the pedagogy behind the content before the integration of technology can be successfully implemented. This suggests that teaching the technology apart from the curricular area is ineffectual in teaching content. For example, when teaching division if taught as an algorithm alone and supplemented with practice problems enhanced with technology, the problem lacks the full impact that technology can offer. But input a model (the area model) and enter the values in a scaffold model and learning is more powerful, more exploratory, and more conceptual. Teaching pedagogy shares roles with teaching content and teaching technology.

The third point worth discussing is the importance of TPACK in the teaching of elementary mathematics. Though technology is only briefly mentioned in AMTE Elementary Mathematics Specialist standards (2009), TPACK knowledge structure appears to be very beneficial in training elementary mathematics teachers and should be considered when thinking of core concepts for preparing mathematics teachers to teach to the 21st Century learners.

Conclusion

Where much of the focus has been on studying preservice teachers (Abbitt, 2011; Chai, Koh, & Tsai, 2010; Polly, 2011), inservice teachers need training in TPACK as well. Working daily with students and balancing the demands of testing, managing student behavior, serving as specialists in varying content areas, teachers also need to lay the foundation for STEM field interests for their students' future. They need an in-depth knowledge of mathematics, technology, effective pedagogy, and the unique knowledge of blending the TPACK into a transformative force in their class. This knowledge, and its changing force within the classroom, requires professional development that joins university and local school district expertise. Learning how students learn best with technology, looking at digital technology for affordances that enhance mathematical content, and enabling the use the technology to empower TPACK lends itself to quality teaching and learning.

References

Abbitt, J. C. (2011). A case study investigation of student use of technology tools in a collaborative learning project. *Journal of Technology Integration in the Classroom, 2*(1), 5-14

Angeli, C., & Valanides, N. (2009). Epistemological and methodological issues for the conceptualization, development, and assessment of ICT-TPCK: Advances in technological pedagogical content knowledge (TPCK). *Computers & Education, 52*(1), 154-168.

Archambault, L. M., & Barnett, J. H. (2010). Revisiting technological pedagogical content knowledge: Exploring the TPACK framework. *Computers & Education, 55*(4), 1656-1662.

Association of Mathematics Teacher Educators. (2010). *Standards for elementary mathematics specialists: A reference for teacher credentialing and degree programs.* Retrieved 9/28/11 from http://www.amte.net/sites/all/themes/amte/resources/EMSStandards_Final_Mar2010.pdf.

Ball, D. L., Hill, H. C., & Bass, H. (2005). Knowing mathematics for teaching: Who knows mathematics well enough to teach third grade, and how can we decide? *American Educator, 29,* 14–22.

Ball, D. L., Thames, M., & Phelps, G. (2008). Content knowledge for teaching: What makes it special? *Journal of Teacher Education, 59*(5), 389-407.

Campbell, P. F., & Malkus, N. N. (2011). The impact of elementary mathematics coaches on student achievement. The *Elementary School, 113*(3), 430-544.

Chai, C. S., Koh, J. H. L., & Tsai, C. C. (2010). Facilitating preservice teachers' development of technological, pedagogical, and content knowledge. *Educational Technology & Society, 13* (4), 63–73.

Conlon, T., & Simpson, M. (2003). Silicon Valley versus Silicon Glen: The impact of computers upon teaching and learning: A comparative study. *British Journal of Educational Technology, 34*(2), 137-150.

Cuban, L., Kirkpatrick, H., & Peck, C. (2001). High access and low use of technologies in high school classrooms:
Explaining an apparent paradox. *American Educational Research Journal, 38*(4), 813-834.

Darling-Hammond, L., & McLaughlin, M. W. (2011). Policies that support professional development in an era of reform. *Phi Delta Kappan, 92*(6), 81-92.

Desimone, L. M. (2011). A primer on effective professional development. *Phi Delta Kappan, 92*(6), 68-71.

Donnelly, R. (2010). Harmonizing technology with interaction in blended problem-based learning. *Computers & Education, 54,* 350-359.

Gerretson, H., Bosnick, J., & Schofield, K. (2008). Promising practice: A case for content specialists as the elementary classroom teacher. *The Teacher Educator Journal, 43*(4), 302–14.

Hill, H. C., & Ball, D. L. (2004). Learning mathematics for teaching: Results from California's mathematics professional development institutes. *Journal for Research in Mathematics Education, 35* (5), 330-351.

Kenny, D. T., & Faunce, G. (2004). Effects of academic coaching on elementary and secondary students. *Journal of Educational Research, 98*(2), 115-126.

Koehler, M. J., Mishra, P., & Yahya, K. (2007). Tracing the development of teacher knowledge in a design seminar: Integrating content, pedagogy and technology. *Computers & Education, 49*(3), 740-762.

Krauss, S., Brunner, M., Kunter, M., Baumert, J., Blum, W., Neubrand, M., & et al. (2008). Pedagogical content knowledge and content knowledge of secondary mathematics teachers. *Journal of Educational Psychology, 100*(3), 716-725.

McGatha, M. (2008). Levels of engagement in establishing coaching relationships. *Teacher Development, 12*(2), 139–150.

Mishra, P., & Koehler, M. H. (2006). Technological pedagogical content knowledge: A framework for teacher knowledge. *Teachers College Record, 108*(6), 1017-1054.

National Council of Teachers of Mathematics. (2000). *Principles and standards for school mathematics.* Reston, VA: Author.

National Mathematics Advisory Panel. (2008). *Foundations for success: Final report of the National Mathematics Advisory Panel.* Washington, D. C.: U.S. Department of Education.

National Research Council. (2002). *Scientific research in education.* Washington, DC: National Academy Press.

Partnership for 21st Century Skills (P21). (2009). *Framework for 21st century learning.* Tucson, AZ: P21.

Polly, D. (2011). Examining teachers' enactment of technological pedagogical and content knowledge (TPACK) in their mathematics teaching after technology integration professional development. *Journal of Computers in Mathematics and Science Teaching, 30*(1), 37-59.

Sailors, M. & Shanklin, N. (2010). Introduction: Growing evidence to support coaching in literacy and mathematics. *Elementary School Journal, 111*(1), 106.

Schmidt, D. A., Baran, E., Thompson, A. D., Mishra, P., Koehler, M. J., & Shin, T. S. (2009). Technological pedagogical content knowledge (TPACK), The development and validation of an assessment instrument for preservice teachers. *Journal of Research on Technology in Education, 42*(2), 123-149.

Shulman, L. S. (1986). Those who understand: Knowledge growth in teaching. *Educational Researcher, 15*(2), 4-14.

Vockley, M. (2008). *Maximizing the impact: The pivotal role of technology in a 21st century education system.* Retrieved from http://www.setda.org/web/guest/maximizingimpactreport

Wu, H. H. (2009). What's so sophisticated about elementary mathematics: Plenty—that's why elementary schools need math teachers. *American Educator, 32*(3), 4–14.

Developing Pre-Service Teachers´ Competencies in Using Technologies in the Classroom: An Example From Portugal

Clara Pereira Coutinho
Minho University, Braga, Portugal
ccoutinho@iep.uminho.pt

Abstract: In this paper we present an Information and Communication Technology (ICT) program designed for developing pre-service teachers´ competencies in using technologies in the classroom. Recent research shows that teachers´ familiarity, confidence and skills in integrating technology are dependent on the type of training included in their pre-service education. For one semester 32 pre-service teachers used Web 2.0 tools - blogs, podcasts and Google Sites – to create digital artifacts for classroom use. For data collection several sources of evidence were considered: an electronic questionnaire, an individual written reflection on the learning experience and direct observation. The enthusiasm maintained by the students all over the course, the quality of the artifacts as well as the feedback obtained from direct observation and the online survey, show that participants valued the learning experience with Web 2.0 tools and had a firm intent to integrate the technologies they used in the ICT course in future teaching practices. In this article we describe the ICT program, reflect on the results and discuss guidelines for future research.

Context

In the knowledge-based society, learning is more important than ever. In fact, as stated in a recent report of Cisco Report (2010, p. 1) "All around the world, learning is linked to higher wages, personal fulfilment, better health and longer lives". In fact, as the world becomes more and more global and technological changes accelerates, learning becomes more and more essential and becomes a lifelong activity that cuts across different learning generations and life spheres such as private, public and work (Coutinho & Lisboa, 2011). Learners need to be prepared to use the technology in creative activities that require higher-order skills such as knowing and understanding what it means to live in a digitalized and networked society where information is shared and knowledge collaboratively constructed (Punie & Cabrera, 2006). A new set of skills is essential for any 21st century citizen and a framework for any educational systems that aims to enter the "«learning economy», where the success of individuals, firms, regions and countries will reflect, more than anything else, their ability to learn." (OCDE, 2000, p. 29)

According to Hargreaves (2003) this means a profound change in the traditional standardized curricula that is the same for all students and centred in the approval in final examinations; on the contrary, the priority is the adoption of new standards for educational achievement that prepare students to deal with change and innovation and where the use of ICT is a pre-requisite (NESTA, 2007).

The reform of the European High Education Area (EHEA, more commonly known as the "Bologna Process") that aimed to create a more compatible, competitive and attractive learning space for European citizens and scholars around the world, enhanced "a major change in the teaching process at universities from the knowledge-based to the skills learning-based" (Albino & Armendiz-Inigo, 2010, p. 216).

There is a strong belief that ICT could be the driving force in this change of paradigm in education (Punie & Cabrera, 2006; Coutinho & Alves, 2010), and so, following other European countries, Portuguese policies enhanced integration of ICT in higher education activities. At the same time, huge investments were made in the equipment of non-superior schools with computers and Internet access as well as in the training of teachers for the Learning Society (Coutinho, 2009a; Rocha, Mota & Coutinho, 2011). Regarding teacher education programs, the official legislation recommends the integration of ICT in pedagogical activities and the training of teachers for the use of multiple languages and technological supports in the classroom (Guerra et. al., 2009).

At the Institute of Education of the University of Minho, Braga, Portugal, initial teacher education programs were reorganized considering the need for a "new" context that enhances the preparation of digitally wise teachers (Coutinho, 2009a). A new perspective that sees teacher training as an activity oriented process that considers students to be responsible for their own learning, more focused in the development of very concrete and specific competencies and skills than in the acquisition of theoretical terms and concepts (Coutinho, 2011)

In this paper we present an empirical study that enrolled a group of 32 pre-service teachers who attended the Educational Technology assignment at the University of Minho, Braga, Portugal. After a brief review of literature on the controversial topic of the relationship established between teachers and technologies, we present the course structure, the activities carried out in the classes as well as the evaluation of the whole process. We finish presenting some guidelines for the design of an initial teacher education program that is adapted to the needs of a global society but aims not only to attain changes in teachers´ attitudes and perceptions of ICT educational value, but also that facilitates the effective integration of ICT in teachers´ classroom routines.

Teachers, ICT and Training

The relationship of teachers with ICT is neither simple nor linear. Silva (2005, p. 48) analyzes the fundamentalism of the two extremist positions that oppose, on the one hand, technophobes, who consider ICT tools of evil influence by its "destructive effects on education and customs" and, on the other hand, the technoholics, who view ICT as means for "accelerating the diffusion of efficient education, culture and science". Gil (2001) revisits the issue, contextualizing an historical evolution repeated over time that reveals two opposite positions of technophobic or hypercritical attitudes such as Socrates' when he rejects writing, or the rejection of television and film in the 60's, and more recently, the rejection of computers at school. The opposite is also criticized because it reflects an unreasonable attitude of belief in the miraculous power of ICT, as if its use by the teacher in the classroom would provide a solution to the problems of teaching and learning (Gil, 2001).

In the intermediate position stand all of us who believe that ICT can induce qualitative changes in education if they are used as cognitive tools that engage students in learning and that facilitate critical thinking inducing significant and lasting learning (Jonassen, 2007). Therefore, although important, it is not enough to equip schools, we need to seduce teachers to adhere to the information, knowledge and learning society (Coutinho, 2009; Coutinho & Alves, 2010).

According to Coutinho (2009), the innovative nature of pedagogical practices using ICT, if not accompanied by training that can lead to practical and reflexive activities on teachers, couldn't, by itself, bring great changes in the teaching practices of teachers. This idea that there is a clear discrepancy between what is believed to be the potential of ICT and its use in education is advocated by Costa and colleagues (2008) in an extensive review of literature that supports the proposal of a range of possible scenarios for the training of ICT certification to Portuguese teachers. It is essential to create training models that allow teachers to learn and observe new teaching methods with ICT, to share ideas and constrains with colleagues and explore new pedagogies in the classroom (Coutinho, 2009b). This same idea of the importance of sharing experiences and concerns with peers, i.e., what one might call "culture of collaboration" among teachers, represents a professional development strategy that is beyond personal reflection and independent from external experts and allows teachers to learn from each other by sharing and developing together their multiple skills (Hargreaves, 2003).

In fact, recent studies conducted in Portugal have shown that while teachers today use more ICT in their teaching activity, the type of use that is made is still too narrow in terms of its true potential: ICT are often used to prepare classes but little to direct interaction with students (Fernandes, 2006). On the other hand, research shows that the successful introduction of ICT and Internet in the classroom requires – in addition to the understanding of the teacher to the features of their use – a personal familiarity with this technology (Coutinho, 2010). Regarding the initial training of teachers in ICT, Steketee (2005) identifies four possible approaches:

1. Separate and specialized training courses in the development of computer skills of the teacher;
2. Approaches focused in the training program, where different ways of integrating ICT in pedagogically curriculum are presented;
3. Approaches focused in the teaching subject area in which specific computer programs (software) are integrated into the courses of the training program;
4. Approaches focused in practice, that in the educational component of the training program, trainees design and create digital resources to use in their future teaching practices.

For the four models summarized above, Sanber & Nicholson (2011, p. 229) consider that to develop ICT skills in separate and specialized courses "does not necessarily lead to that future teachers transfer this knowledge to the classroom"; conversely, the development of ICT skill is enhanced if technology training is an integral part of pedagogical training and engage students in learning environments that invite and support the design and development of digital educational content.

However, other skills are required from teachers due to the complexity of today's information and knowledge society. The teacher of today must be able to handle the huge diversity of requirements that information society presents, which requires proactive, interventionist and critical professionals, ready to learn throughout life (Coutinho & Lisboa, 2011). On the other hand, the teacher needs to act less like an expert who applies the knowledge to solve technical problems, and more as a reflective practitioner whose actions and decisions are based on analysis and permanent evaluation of the situations that occur in the classroom. The practice of this teacher is guided by reflection undertaken before, during and after the action. The idea of the teacher as a reflective practitioner is introduced by Schon (1983) which includes the teacher as a professional at school and classroom. For Alarcão (2003), the teacher is not a mere reproducer of ideas and external practices, but a professional with the ability to think, reflect and articulate their practice from their values, beliefs and knowledge, or even as a person who, in professional situations, often uncertain and unforeseen, acts in an intelligent, flexible, situated and reactive way.

Method

The empirical study was developed in school year 2010/11 and enrolled a group of 32 student-teachers who attended a program on Educational Technology (ET) as part a Master in Learning that gives professional qualification to teach in basic and secondary schools. According to the background information collected from individual records 63% were female and 88.5% had ages between 20 and 30 years old. 45% were Biology teachers, 33% Math and 20% Portuguese and Classical Languages. The great majority were novice teachers (88.5%).

ET is a 3 hours/week class that aims to prepare future teachers to integrate technologies as cognitive tools (Jonassen, 2007) into the curriculum. The program, designed according to results of previous research (Coutinho, 2010; Coutinho & Lisboa, 2011) was structured in two complementary parts: a) the conceptual framework that sustains the integration of ICT in the curriculum; b) the hands-on activities where students use technological tools to create digital resources to use in the real classroom. In order to attain the course objectives, students are organised in group of 3-4 according to their their curricular area of teaching and had to read and analyse a selected bibliography, discuss the readings inside the group, develop a collaborative written task using Google Docs and posting it in the group blog. Blogs were visited every week by the instructor and peers that left comments and suggestions. The hands-on activities consisted in the: creation and management of blog as a group e-portfolio; image edition using Gimp; sound edition using Audacity; creation of podcasts as comments to selected Youtube Videos; creation of a WebQuest on a selected topic using the web page editor Google Sites. Digital artifacts were presented to the class for comments and were evaluated both by the instructor and the colleagues in a very democratic fashion.

For data collection several sources of evidence were considered: an electronic questionnaire, an individual written reflection on the course experience and direct observation. The electronic questionnaire was developed considering other survey instruments developed in previous research (Coutinho, 2009a) and aimed to collect data on four different dimensions:

1. Participants personal data (dichotomy/multiple choice): gender, age, curricular area of teaching;
2. Familiarity with Web 2.0 tools/services (multiple choices: I know/I Know but do not use/I use for personal purposes/I use in the classroom).
3. Opinions on the educational potential of the Web 2.0 technologies used in the class activities (Semantic differential scale; open-ended)
4. Individual perceptions on the value of the ICT program for teacher education (5 points Likert Scale of agreement: Total Disagreement/Disagreement/Neither Agree Disagree/Disagreement/Total Agreement).

The questionnaire was submitted to a content validity by two experts who recommended some adjustments. Then it was tested by five novice teachers that didn´t belong to the sample; according to the feedback received two unclear items of the Likert scale were redesigned and one removed (Coutinho, 2011).

Artifacts produced by the groups were assessed considering both technical and pedagogical features. Individual portfolios and direct observation reports were considered to triangulate data.

Results

Digital Artifacts

The 32 participants were grouped in 9 teams according to their curricular area of teaching: 3 groups for Biology, 3 for Math and 3 for Portuguese and Classical Languages. Nine blogs and nine WebQuests were the digital artifacts that resulted from the ICT course activities. In Figures 1, two examples of the group blogs are presented.

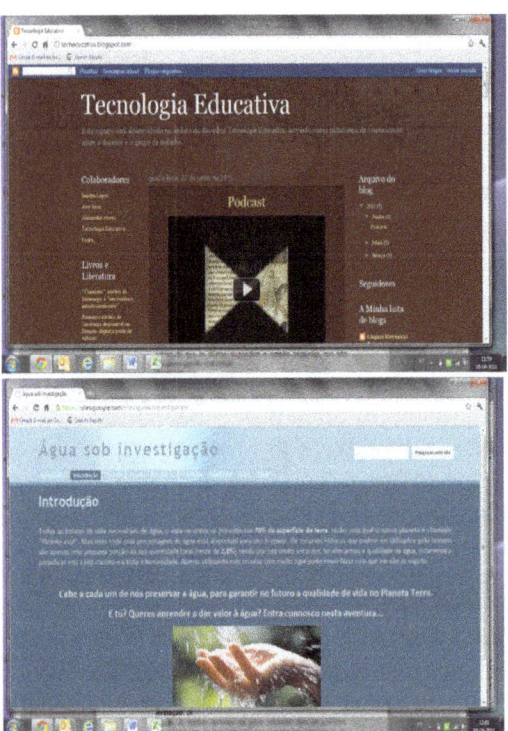

Figure 1 – Examples of blogs created by the groups

The WebQuests were evaluated by the instructor considering both technological and pedagogical features of the digital artifacts. Each group received specific feedback and was encouraged to reformulate the first version of the prototype to a final one that, after a final revision conducted by the instructor, was housed at the Portal of the Portuguese WebQuests in order to be used by other teachers in the schools (www.portalwebquest.net).

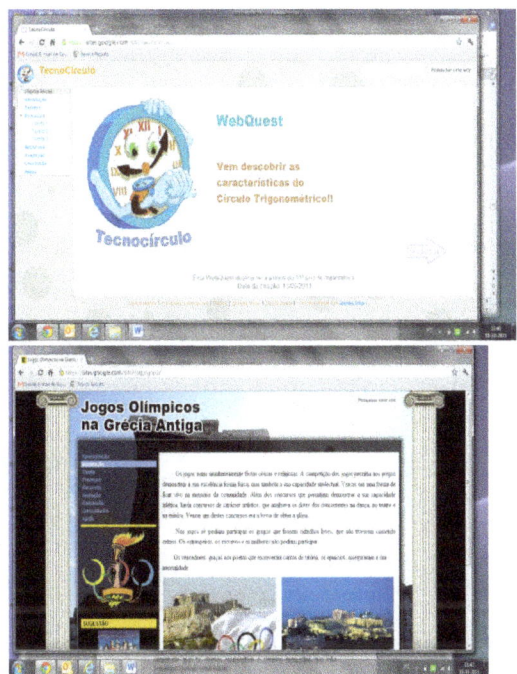

Figure 2 – Examples of WebQuests created by Math and Portuguese Language Students

Online Questionnaire

27 participants (84.4%) completed the final online questionnaire once the classes were over.

Acknowledgement and personal use of Web 2.0 tools

Most participants were already acknowledged with Web 2.0 technologies. Youtube (86.2%) Facebook (78.6%) Hi5 (60.7%), blogs (35.7%), wikis (32%) and Picasa (25%) were the tools student teachers used more for personal purposes; on the opposite, Google Sites, Google Docs were used by 10% of the participants, Flickr by 7.1%, Audacity by 3.8% and Del.ici.ous by 3.7% of the participants.

The educational potential of the Web 2.0 technologies

Students´ opinions on the use of Web 2.0 tools for class work in the ICT course was assessed using a four point differential semantic scale (maximum 4, minimum 1). Results in are presented in Graph 1.

For me, to learn to use Web 2.0 tools in my ICT course was:

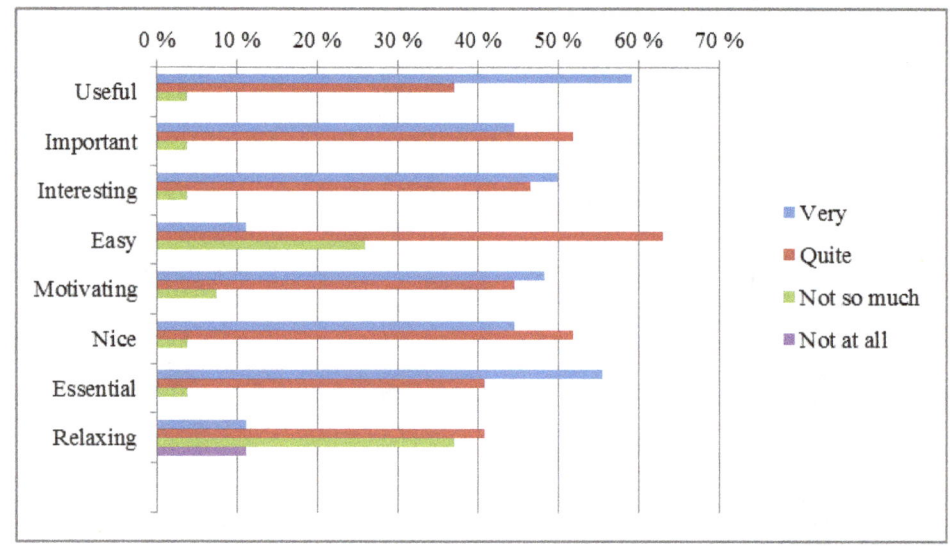

Graph 1 – Perceptions on the use of Web 2.0 tools for class work (N=27)

Data show a positive global perception on the learning experience with Web 2.0 tools reflected on the dominance of the blue and red bars and the corresponding lack of expression of the green and violet ones in most of the eight dimensions considered for the analysis". In fact, the reading of the graph reveals that for most participants to use the Web 2.0 technologies in the ICT course was "very" useful, essential and interesting, "quite" important and nice; only in adjectives easy and relaxing the values of "not so much" and "not at all" had some expression, revealing that some participants felt difficulties in the handling of the tools.

Blogs

The creation and maintenance of a blog for class work was considered easy for all students except for 3. Two already had a Blogger account and managed a personal blog. All agreed that blogs were powerful tools for teaching and learning. When asked on strategies for using the tool in a real classroom, different perspectives were considered by participants. Some examples:

"In my math class I would use the blog as a space for classwork sharing among students. Instead of using the powerpoint to show group work, students create a blog that serves as an e-portfolio to publish exercises, videos, math problems that remain online for the teacher and colleagues to access and leave comments"

"I could have a blog for my class where I could publish useful information such as future class activities, educational resources such as games, puzzles, etc."

"As an individual portfolio"

"For classroom debates and extra-curricular activities"

"As a class diary"

Google Sites to create WebQuest

The activity of creating a WebQuest using Google Sites demanded that students learned to use the software to build a webpage. Seven reported difficulties in using the software, other two reported the limitations it offered in terms of facilities for formatting the text and arranging a successful layout when it included images and video. This is a real constraint of the software reported by other students in previous studies (Coutinho & Bottentuit Junior, 2009b) but as it is free and allows the creation of websites for any web user we still consider using this software in our teacher education programs.

In fact, all student teachers´ were unanimous saying they intended to use this Web 2.0 software in their future teaching practices: eight said they would use it to create other Webquests; eight said they would build a class website with contents related to their curricular subjects; 3 said it was useful for group work; two for their own students to create webpages; two said they would prefer a different platform, more versatile than GS.

Podcast

Eight participants said it was "difficult" to use the Audacity Software and five said it was "somehow difficult". The rest considered it was easy to create a podcast using the Audacity Software.

Regarding the potential of the tool for future teaching practices, the opinions were divided: 6 said they would not use the tool again, justifying that "I don't believe in the potential of the tool" or "maybe it is interesting for very young children of kindergarten or primary schools but not for elder students"; "for math class it is useless". For the fans of this Web 2.0 software the uses in classroom contexts were varied and diversified: "to enhance student participation in the learning process"; "to stimulate the orality of the most shy in the class", "To share pedagogical experiences", "to create more motivating learning activities", "to develop creativity and critical sense", "To enhance diction and orality, collaborative work and learner´ power of synthesis". "To allow for students who miss the class to be aware of what happened in the classroom".

The value of the ICT program for my teacher education

Ten itens in the format of a 5 point Likert scale of agreement (Total Disagreement - Total Agreement) evaluated the participants´ opinion on the value of the ICT program for their education program. Seven itens were formulated in a positive manner and three in a negative statement in order to avoid answer pattern (Coutinho, 2011). Table 1 presents results obtained.

Items	Total Disagreement	Disagreement	Neither Agree/ Disagree	Agreement	Total Agreement	Weighted Average
To work with Web 2.0 tools was very useful for my teacher education	0%	7.4% (2)	0%	**55.6% (15)**	37% (10)	**4.22**
Globally it was a very rich experience both at personal and professional levels	0%	3.7% (1)	3.7% (1)	44.4% (12)	**48.1% (13)**	**4.59**
It opened new horizons for my future teaching practice	0%	3.7% (1)	7.4% (2)	**55.6% (15)**	33.3% (9)	**4.185**
It was irrelevant for my professional development	**44.4% (12)**	40.7% (11)	7.4% (2)	3.7% (1)	3.7% (1)	**1.4**
I believe I will use these tools in my classroom	0%	0%	14.8% (4)	**70.4% (19)**	14.8% (4)	**4.0**
To use Web 2.0 tools as cognitive tools demands creativity and lots of work for the teacher	0%	0%	7.4% (2)	**48.1% (13)**	44.4% (12)	**4.59**

I don't think I will use web 2.0 tools because it does not fit my curricular area of teaching	37% (10)	**55.6% (15)**	3.7% (1)	3.7% (1)	0%	**1.74**
To use technologies in the classroom helps to prepare more interesting classes for my students	0%	0%	3.7% (1)	**48.1% (13)**	**48.1% (13)**	**4.44**
ICT competencies are essential for a XXI century teacher	0%	0%	3.7 (1)	29.6% (8)	**66.7% (18)**	**4.62**
I don't believe that the technologies will help students to learn more	**55.6% (15)**	29.6% (8)	11.1% (3)	3.7% (1)	0%	**1.51**

Table 1 – The value of the ICT program for teacher education (N=27)

A global analysis of the table show how much students valued the ICT program they just attended: all positive items received high degrees of agreement and the two negative items that evaluated this dimension high levels of disagreement ("It was irrelevant for my professional development", "I don´t think I will use Web 2.0 tools because it is not suitable to my curricular area of teaching" with mean values of 1.4 and 1.74 respectively).

We can also see that the highest values of agreement were pointed to the statements that connect directly the ICT program to their teacher education: "ICT competencies are essential for a XXI century teacher" (4.62); "Globally it was a very rich experience both at personal and professional levels" (mean value of 4.56); "To use technologies in the classroom helps to prepare more interesting classes for my students" (4.44) and "The use of Web 2.0 tools in the ICT program was very useful for my teacher education" (4.22). The intention to integrate the technologies in the future teaching practice is also quite clear "I believe I will use these tools in m y classroom" (mean value 4.0), confirmed by the high negative value evidenced in statement "I don't believe that the technologies will help students to learn more" (mean value 1.51).

Discussion

As teacher educators in a public university we believe traditional educational practices no longer provide prospective teachers with all the necessary skills for preparing students to be responsible citizens of the changing learning society we live.

Web 2.0 technologies offer educators amazing opportunities for creating effective and engaging learning environment for their learners. The learning experience we present in this paper intents to sustain the need for new approaches to ICT pre-service teacher education programs. In fact, our main purpose was to show that if we want teachers to use technologies in the classroom we need to give them the opportunity to use the technologies to create educational resources/ artifacts for classroom. The enthusiasm maintained by students all over the course, the quality of the artifacts developed as well as the feedback obtained on direct observation and the final online survey, shows that participants valued the learning experience with Web 2.0 tools and that they showed a firm intent to integrate the technologies they used in the ICT course in their future teaching practices. In this particular we agree with Steketee (2005) that considers who an ICT program for pre-service teachers must be focused in learning activities that value the practice, allowing trainees to design and create digital resources to use in their future teaching practices. The discussions carried out with the instructor and the colleagues as well as the individual reflection on the digital artifacts created are an opportunity and a challenge for pre-service teachers to try new approaches to the use of ICT in the curriculum.

References

Alarcão, I. (2003). *Professores reflexivos em uma escola reflexiva.* São Paulo: Cortez.

Albino, P. M., & Armendiz-Inigo, J. H. (2010). On the utility of ICT in the european higher education area: The Bologna process and its implications in the innovation of the teaching and learning process. *Technology Enhanced Learning, 73,* 216-222.

Bottentuit, J. B., Jr., Lisbôa, E. S., & Coutinho, C. P. (2011). Google Educacional: Utilizando ferramentas Web 2.0 em sala de aula. *Revista EducaOnline, 5*(1), 17-44. Retrieved from http://hdl.handle.net/1822/12655

Cisco Systems, Inc. (2010). *Learning society.* Retrieved from http://www.cisco.com/web/about/citizenship/socioeconomic/docs/LearningSociety_WhitePaper.pdf.

Costa, F. (Org.) (2008). *Competências TIC. Estudo de implementação* (Vol. 1). Lisboa: GEPE/ME.

Coutinho, C. P. (2009). Challenges for teacher education in the learning society: Case studies of promising practice. In H. H. Yang & S. H. Yuen (Eds.), *Handbook of research and practices in e-learning: Issues and trends.* (chap. 23, pp. 385-401). New York: Information Science Reference - IGI Global. Retrieved from http://hdl.handle.net/1822/9981.

Coutinho, C. P. (2010). Storytelling as a strategy for integrating technologies into the curriculum: An empirical study with post-graduate teachers. In C. Maddux, D. Gibson, & B. Dodge (Eds.). *Research highlights in technology and teacher education 2010* (pp. 87-97). Chesapeake: SITE.

Coutinho, C. P. (2011). TPACK: em busca de um referencial teórico para a formação de professores em tecnologia educativa. *Revista Paidéi@, (2)*4. Retrieved from http://hdl.handle.net/1822/13670

Coutinho, C. P., & Alves, M. (2010). Educação e sociedade da aprendizagem: um olhar sobre o potencial educativo da Internet. *Revista de Formación e Innovación Educativa Universitaria, (3)*4, 206-225. Retrieved from http://hdl.handle.net/1822/11229

Coutinho, C. P., & Lisboa, E. (2011). Sociedade da informação, conhecimento e aprendizagem: Desafios para a educação no século XXI. *Revista de Educação, (18)*1, 5-22.

Coutinho, C. P., & Bottentuit, J. B., Jr. (2009a). Literacy 2.0: Preparing digitally wise teachers. In A. Klucznick-Toro, A. Csépe, & D. Kwiatkowska-Ciotucha (Eds.). *Higher education, partnership and innovation.* (pp. 253-261). Budapeste: Publikon-Publishers/IDResearch Ltd. Retrieved from http://hdl.handle.net/1822/9978

Coutinho, C. P., & Bottentuit, J. B., Jr. (2009b). O Google Sites no processo de ensino e aprendizagem: uma experiência no ensino superior. *Revista Teias, (10)*19, 1-12. Retrieved from http://www.periodicos.proped.pro.br/index.php?journal=revistateias

Fernandes, R. C. M. (2006). *Atitudes dos professores face às TIC e a sua utilização ao nível do ensino secundário.* Master dissertation, University of Lisbon, Lisbon.

Gil, F. (2001). Estratégias de utilização das TIC em contexto educativo: um estudo com professores do ensino secundário. In *Actas do 3º Simpósio Internacional de Informática Educativa* (pp. 441-446). Viseu.

Guerra, C., Moreira, A., & Vieira, R. A. (2009, November). Tecnologia educativa na formação de professores de ensino básico. A análise da unidade curricular. *XI Simpósio Internacional de Informática Educativa.* Coimbra.

Hargreaves, A. (2003). *O ensino na sociedade do conhecimento: A educação na era da insegurança.* Porto: Porto Editora.

Jonassen, D. (2007). *Computadores, ferramentas cognitivas.* Porto: Porto Editora.

NESTA (2007). *Innovation in response to social challenges.* London: NESTA

OCDE (2000). *Knowledge management in the learning society.* Paris: OCDE. Retrieved from http://ocw.metu.edu.tr/file.php/118/Week11/oecd1.pdf

Punie, Y. C., & Cabrera, M. (2006, October). *The future of ICT and learning in the knowledge society.* Report on a DG/JRC-DG/EAC Workshop. EU: Joint Research Center.

Rocha, A., Mota, P., & Coutinho, C. (2011). TPACK: Challenges for teacher education in the 21st century. In M. A. Flores, A. A. Carvalho, S. Fernandes, F. I. Ferreira, T. Vilaça, P. Alves, … D. Pereira, D. (Orgs.), *Proceedings of the 15th Biennial of the International Study Association on Teachers and Teaching (ISATT); Back to the future: legacies, continuities and changes in educational policy, practice and research* (pp. 37-44). Braga: CIEd, University of Minho.

Sanber, S. & Nicholson, M. (2011). Longitudinal study of the relationship between students´ perceptions of their problem solving and ICT skills and their ICT experience as part of their teacher education program. In A. Lauriala, R. Rajala, H. Ruokamo, & O. Ylitapio-Mäntylä (Eds.), *Navigating in educational contexts: Identities and cultures in dialogue.* (pp. 227-241). Rotterdam: Sense Publishers.

Schon, D. (1983). *The reflective practitioner: how professionals think in action.* New York: Basic Books, Inc.

Silva, B. (2005). Ecologias da comunicação e contextos educacionais. *Educação e Cultura Contemporânea(2)*3, 31-51.

Steketee, C. (2005). Integrating ICT as an integral teaching and learning tool into pre-service teacher training courses. *Issues in Educational Research, 15*(10), 101-112.

UNESCO (2008). *ICT competency standards for teachers.* Paris: United Nations Educational, Scientific and Cultural Organization. Retrieved from http://unesdoc.unesco.org/images/0015/001562/156209E.pdf

Using Online Learning Networks to Promote Self-Regulated Learning in Primary Teacher Education

Emmy Vrieling
Iselinge University, the Netherlands
Open University, the Netherlands
emmy.vrieling@ou.nl

Theo Bastiaens
Open University, the Netherlands
FernUniversität in Hagen, Germany
theo.bastiaens@ou.nl

Sjef Stijnen
Open University, the Netherlands
sjef.stijnen@ou.nl

Abstract: Many recent studies have stressed the importance of students' self-regulated learning (SRL) skills for successful learning. Consequently, teacher educators have begun to increase student teachers' SRL opportunities in educational pre-service programs. Although primary teacher educators are aware of the importance of SRL, they often find it difficult to implement opportunities in their teaching. To provide more insight into relevant SRL aspects and support implementation in pre-service teacher education, this study first explores the benefits of online SRL learning networks. The authors then present seven SRL design principles for primary teacher education, and show the results of implementing these principles in non-formal learning contexts. Finally, based on the positive results of the implementation process, the authors describe emerging trends for SRL learning networks to enhance further use in pre-service teacher learning programs. In such educational settings, the SRL design principles can be used as a holistic framework.

Primary Teacher Education and Self-Regulated Learning

Teacher education has traditionally focused on relaying subject knowledge and teaching skills (Kremer-Hayon & Tillema, 1999). However, researchers and practitioners in the field have noticed a consistent decline in transfer from theory to practice (Korthagen, Klaassen, & Russell, 2000). In other words, primary student teachers (i.e., prospective primary teachers) are often not able to apply the knowledge and skills they have learned in their teacher education programs in real classroom contexts.

In response to this problem, many primary teacher educators (teachers of prospective primary teachers) are now working to increase student teachers' self-regulated learning (SRL) opportunities throughout their initial training (Lunenberg & Korthagen, 2003). SRL has shown to foster students' deep and meaningful learning, resulting in significant gains in learning, problem solving, transfer and academic achievement in general (e.g. Nota, Soresi, & Zimmerman, 2004; Sundre & Kitsantas, 2004). To attain such an environment, teacher educators often must adjust their own instructional behavior so that they might enhance students' self-regulation.

In general, SRL is a goal-oriented process, proceeding from a forethought phase and continuing through self-monitoring and self-control to self-reflection (Pintrich, 2000, 2004). The most important aspect of SRL is that students can monitor, control, and regulate their own cognitive actions (Pintrich, 2000; Veenman, Van Hout-Wolters, & Afflerbach, 2006; Zimmerman, 2001), an act commonly referred to as metacognition. By using metacognitive skills, student teachers can become aware of and monitor their progress towards their goals. As a result, students can improve their learning and comprehension, realizing any adaptive changes in their learning (Vermunt & Verloop, 1999).

Defining the Problem

Although primary teacher educators understand the importance of the concept of SRL (Kremer-Hayon & Tillema, 1999), they often find it difficult to actually foster it in educational pre-service programs (Korthagen et al., 2000). Since many practicing teacher educators do not have previous experience with SRL, they are still somewhat unprepared for the change and are often worried about their decreasing role as knowledge providers (Kremer-Hayon & Tillema, 1999). In order to improve the implementation of SRL in pre-service education programs, more attention must be focused on the professional development of teacher educators.

Based on the findings of a review study (Vrieling, Bastiaens, & Stijnen, 2010) and two empirical studies (Vrieling et al., 2011a, b), the present analysis provides more insight into relevant SRL design principles and how to best implement them in pre-service teacher education. The research questions are as follows:

1. What is the value of online learning networks for SRL implementation in primary teacher education?
2. Which SRL design principles are distinguished in research literature?
3. In what way are the SRL design principles useful for primary teacher educators?
4. What are emerging trends for online learning networks to support SRL implementation?

In the following sections, the importance of online learning networks for SRL implementation in primary teacher education is introduced first. Then, seven SRL design principles for primary teacher education are outlined, followed by their application in non-formal empirical settings within primary teacher education. Finally, based on the findings of the empirical studies, recommendations to enhance SRL implementation through online learning networks are outlined.

The Value of Online Learning Networks for SRL Implementation in Primary Teacher Education

For successful implementation of an innovative design like SRL, educational developers must be very explicit about the behaviors they expect from teacher educators (Könings, Brand-Gruwel, & van Merriënboer, 2007). Since many teacher educators have little to no previous experience in such an instructional design, they are sometimes ill prepared to fully implement it in their teaching (Könings et al., 2007). Hence, teacher educators play a crucial role in the interpretation of SRL design and its translation into educational practice.

Similarly, Vrieling et al. (2011a, b) noted that primary teacher educators need informal SRL trajectories such as online interaction because learning networks are not limited by geography, space, or time. Rather, they can provide experiences for extending learning beyond the classroom walls that can be applied in classroom practice.

To fulfill this need, Laferrière, Lamon, and Chan (2006) indicate that learning networks can enhance lifelong learning for teacher educators. Redmond and Lock (2009) also report on similar online learning networks where student teachers, teacher educators, and practicing teachers discussed current issues such as SRL. Their research shows that the participants were involved in meaningful conversations that provided rich understanding of teaching practice by creating transfers between theories, experiences and realities of teaching in contemporary contexts. Thus, professional learning networks strongly influence teachers' professional roles, can lead to changes in their classroom activities, and consequently can have positive effects on students' learning progress (Lieberman & Wood, 2003).

In general, more focus is now being placed upon social aspects that influence learning and professional development (Brown & Duguid, 2001), as well as the spontaneous and informal learning processes in the development of social capital (Wenger, Trayner, & De Laat, 2011). Rapid technological developments enable this social knowledge construction in educational practice (Brown & Duguid, 2001; Lieberman & Wood, 2003). Technology can promote the building of learning networks, where people with common interests work and learn together although they may be separated by time and location (Shoffner, 2009). Technologies such as email, discussion boards, and weblogs provide opportunities for learning networks, in which teacher educators can reflect on practice with colleagues, share expertise, and build a common understanding of new instructional SRL approaches for classroom practice.

Based on an international literature study, Villegas-Reimers (2003) concludes that network learning is an important way for teachers to professionalize, because it joins teachers with different classroom experiences and a common desire to work on challenges and questions in social learning settings. In the development of social learning, Wenger et al. (2011) distinguish "communities" from "networks." Communities (or learning teams) can be defined as "groups of people that work together cohesively toward a common goal" (Dechant, Marsick, & Kasl, 1991, p.1). In such communities, the learning partnership creates an identity around a common agenda or area for learning. The term "network" refers to a set of connections among people. Networks using information technology can optimize the connectivity among teachers. Strengthening existing connections, enabling new connections and getting a speedy response can increase the extent and density of the network. The interplay between community and network processes thus enhances social learning.

Design Principles for a Successful Implementation of Self-Regulated Learning

To provide more insight into relevant SRL aspects during teaching, Vrieling et al. (2010) formulated seven SRL design principles for primary teacher education that can play an important role in increasing student teachers' SRL opportunities in educational pre-service programs.

The first principle suggests that teacher educators should create a sufficient knowledge base for their students. Teacher educators cannot expect their students to immediately regulate their learning all by themselves. As experts in the relevant subject-matter domain, the teacher educator must make this domain more accessible to student teachers (Bolhuis & Voeten, 2001).

To do this, teacher educators should integrate the necessary metacognitive skills and content matter into their teaching, comprising the second design principle. As part of the third principle, this integration should be modeled upon the following four regulatory skill levels (Schunk & Zimmerman, 2007):

- Level 1. Observation: Learners can induce the major features of the skill from watching someone model learning or performing.
- Level 2. Emulation: The learner, with assistance from the group, imitates the model's performance.
- Level 3. Self-control: The learner independently performs under structured conditions.
- Level 4. Self-regulation: The learner shows an adaptive use of skills across changing personal and environmental conditions.

In the fourth principle, control of the learning processes should gradually transfer from teacher to student ("scaffolding"). To ensure successful knowledge building, teacher educators must provide considerable guidance to students (Kirschner, Sweller, & Clark, 2006). In this way, student teachers gain sufficient prior knowledge to be able to internally guide them. Only then should the guidance of the teacher educator begin to decrease.

The fifth principle moves past successful knowledge building to encompass knowledge of the conditional factors that can foster or hinder successful implementation. This ensures that teacher educators are adequately prepared for their job, that they use suitable (digital) learning materials, to relay to their students a solid understanding of the significance of SRL and to create an appropriate school context and culture. Student teachers stress the importance for all teacher educators to use any learning materials (e.g. an electronic learning environment) in the same way (Vrieling et al., 2010). In line with the findings of Sim and Hew (2010) in higher education settings, student teachers note that reflective learning in electronic environments requires clear technological instructions and sufficient time to be appreciated and adopted in student teachers' learning.

The sixth principle stresses the engagement of student teachers in collaborative (digital) learning environments. Student collaboration facilitates the development of SRL (Wigfield, Hoa, & Klauda, 2007). When students have collaborative projects to complete, they make special effort to contribute significantly to the group. Also, encouraging students to consult with peers can lead them to utilize their classmates as knowledge resources. To instill such an environment, teacher educators should ensure positive interdependence in the group, provide clear instructions to student teachers, and provide adequate feedback on their working process.

Finally, the seventh SRL design principle explores the relevant aspects of the learning task (i.e., assignments student teachers have to accomplish).

- *Goal setting:* Academic goals are important variables for student teachers because they serve as self-defining reference points that determine the next processes of SRL, such as planning, executing, and monitoring (Schunk & Ertmer, 2000).
- *Prior knowledge activation:* This enables student teachers to understand the task and its goals, to recognize the required knowledge for performing it, and to distinguish the several characteristics and their prediction of performance (Eilam & Aharon, 2003).
- *Metacognitive knowledge activation:* This includes the activation of knowledge about cognitive tasks and cognitive strategies in the SRL forethought phase (Pintrich, 2000, 2004).
- *Metacognitive awareness and monitoring of cognition:* As a core component within information processing models of self-regulation (e.g. Nietfeld, Cao, & Osborne, 2006), it is important for student teachers to develop thinking activities to decide on learning contexts, to exert control over their processing and affective activities and to steer the course and outcomes of their learning (Vermunt & Verloop, 1999).
- In the SRL self-reflection phase, Pintrich (2000, 2004) distinguishes two cognitive key processes.
    a. The first process involves learners' *"judgments" and evaluations of their performance of the task*. Students can learn to make judgments about the way their work relates to the criteria.
    b. The second concerns students' *"attributions" for performance*. Attributions are beliefs concerning the causes of outcomes (Butler, 2002). Teacher educators can facilitate effective self-regulation by providing attribution feedback to students that indicates factors students can control, such as effort and strategy use (Schunk, 2007).
- *Task value activation:* This process encompasses perceptions of the relevance, utility and importance of the task (Pintrich, 2000).
- *Time management:* This important component of SRL (Dembo & Eaton, 2000) may involve making schedules for studying and allocating time for different activities.

Application of the SRL Design Principles in Primary Teacher Education

Vrieling et al. (2011a, b) successfully applied the SRL design principles in non-formal teacher education learning settings. In such settings, there is an explicit learning intention, but the participants do not receive a formal certificate after completion of the course of learning. Vrieling et al. (2011a, b) measured the dynamics of student teachers' use of metacognitive learning strategies and motivation for learning in environments with increased SRL opportunities. The research was conducted in educational theory courses containing lectures and moments of guidance. In total, 14 teacher educators and 387 first- and second-year student teachers of seven primary teacher education institutes in the Netherlands participated. During one semester, teacher educators participated in training courses and tutorial conversations aimed at increasing student teachers' SRL opportunities in the curriculum.

The researchers in these empirical studies used a mixed methods pre- and post-test design. They developed a questionnaire to collect quantitative data regarding student teachers' motivation for learning and use of metacognitive learning strategies. They used semi-structured interviews and tutorial conversations to track qualitative data on teacher educators and student teachers.

Their results demonstrated that the SRL design principles provide more insight for primary teacher educators into relevant SRL aspects and can help guide further implementation. Furthermore, the studies showed that student teachers' use of metacognitive learning strategies increased significantly during one semester in learning environments with increased SRL opportunities. This indicates that teacher educators can play a major role in developing student teachers' use of metacognitive learning strategies by increasing student teachers' SRL opportunities. In addition, qualitative analyses identified student teachers' need for more explicit metacognitive strategy instruction. These findings corresponded with the recommendations of Veenman et al. (2006) and Vrieling et al. (2010), indicating the necessity for primary teacher educators to explicitly model metacognitive learning strategies to student teachers.

Although student teachers' motivation for learning correlated significantly positive with SRL opportunities and SRL was shown to be a significant positive predictor of the motivation score, the increase of student teachers' motivation for learning appeared not to be significant during that one semester. One potential reason for the absence of motivation may be that the temporal interval was too brief for the effects to be detected. However, the increase of student teachers' expectancy, a component within the motivation scale, was shown to be significant. The expectancy scale includes control belief and self-efficacy for learning and performance (e.g. "I think that I will get good grades for this course."). Student teachers indicated appreciation of the increased SRL opportunities in the curriculum. Nevertheless, they also stressed the importance for teacher educators to provide an adequate knowledge base to avoid uncertainty. For example, student teachers like to know the criteria for judging their work in advance. Therefore, teacher educators are advised to focus on knowledge building in the domain, including both metacognitive skills and content matter (Vrieling et al., 2010).

In general, Vrieling et al. (2011a, b) revealed that the level of SRL opportunities in pre-service teacher learning environments is a strong predictor of primary student teachers' use of metacognitive learning strategies and enhances student teachers´ motivation for learning, both important for their academic career.

Exploring SRL design principles in Online Learning Networks

Networked learning is increasingly considered as a powerful way to stimulate and facilitate teachers' professional development in educational settings (Lieberman & Wood, 2003). In such learning and knowledge-building communities, teachers interact with peers, students, information and recourses by studying authentic problems (Laferrière et al., 2006). However, informal learning networks only result in innovative communities of practice if they are successfully facilitated. To enhance networked learning in the start-up phase, Hanraets, Hulsebosch, and de Laat (2011) distinguish five recommendations that are very similar to those of the SRL design principles:

- Facilitators must demonstrate a facilitating role instead of a directing role.
- Participants must feel responsible for their network activity (i.e., shared ownership).
- Participants must possess sufficient networking skills.
- Face-to-face and online interactions need to be combined.
- Support from management and direct supervisors is necessary.

Zooming in on the third recommendation concerning networking skills, Laferrière et al. (2006) illustrated that internet-based technologies support teachers' opportunities for reflective and collaborative learning. However, teachers and school managers are often not trained to develop competencies for networked learning such as reflective dialogues. Moreover, the culture in educational settings is often not conducive to learning networks. Since the effects of online learning vary depending on the self-regulation of learning by participating teacher educators (Laferrière et al., 2006), participants must be coached intensively, for example, in the use of technology. Thus, in line with the recommendations of the SRL design principles, the transition from guided learning to SRL should be a gradual process ("scaffolding") in web-supported learning networks for professional development.

In such networks, teacher educators can gain more practice modeling metacognitive skills to their student because explicit training of metacognitive learning strategies tends to be rare in primary student teachers' classrooms (Vrieling et al., 2011a, b). These findings echo the results of Kistner et al. (2010), who conclude that a great amount of strategy teaching occurs in an implicit way because teacher educators often find it difficult to serve as a role model. Teacher educators are absolutely willing to invest effort in the instruction of metacognition within their lessons, but they need the "tools" for implementing metacognition as an integral part of their lessons and for making students aware of their metacognitive activities and the usefulness of those activities (Veenman et al., 2006).

The empirical studies of Vrieling et al. (2011a, b) also showed that teacher educators can improve their students' learning tasks (the seventh SRL design principle) by utilizing real-life problems that require the integrated use of knowledge, skills, and attitudes. The four-component instructional design (4c-id) model (Van Merriënboer & Kirschner, 2007) can be applied during this exercise in learning networks. In the 4c-id model, student teachers start with relative simple but realistic situations that contain all essential aspects of the complex task, and then gradually receive more complex authentic assignments characteristic for their professional situation. This improves the transfer between theory and practice.

The gradual shift in control over learning processes from teacher to student (or "scaffolding"), as stressed by Vrieling et al. (2010), offers a final example for further exploration of SRL design principles in online learning networks. In most primary teacher education programs, there exists a gap between SRL opportunities in the second and the third years (Vrieling et al., 2011a, b). In the first two years--the major phase--educational programs are mainly teacher centered. From the start of the third year, student teachers are often asked to self-regulate their learning by applying all they learned in self-chosen specializations, resulting in their graduation paper. In learning networks, the SRL design principles can be further utilized to enable primary teacher educators to implement SRL opportunities in their teaching, gradually moving from teacher to student regulation of the learning process.

In summary, qualitative analyses of the empirical studies showed teacher educators' need to further develop the SRL design principles for application in classroom practice. By creating online learning networks, teacher educators can be better equipped to elaborate the SRL principles. In addition, in line with the "knowledge building" and "scaffolding" principles, online learning networks should be gradually developed.

Discussion

Successful SRL implementation requires explicit instructions about the teaching behaviors expected from teacher educators. Teacher educators sometimes labor under the false assumption that they can invest less time in the guidance of their students, mistakenly expecting them to work more independently than they may be able. Proper SRL development demands adequate guidance and thorough preparation by teacher educators, and they must always consider new ways to elicit goal setting, planning, monitoring, control and reflection by student teachers themselves.

Teacher educators also have to pay attention to individual differences between students, and must provide each student with specific guidance and feedback. They should be flexible enough to share control with their students. Actively involving students in preparing lesson plans, for example, can lead to prior knowledge activation. Overall, the key is to find out what students already know and what they want to learn.

In fact, perhaps the increase of student teachers' SRL opportunities demands even more effort and attention of teacher educators than the regular approach. As noted earlier, the use of informal trajectories such as online learning networks can help support teacher educators' long-term professional development and enhance lifelong learning. As stated by Laferrière et al. (2006), formal training courses in which experts transmit de-contextualized knowledge do not provide deep learning for teachers; effective learning is situated and needs to be grounded in teachers' own practice, experience, and community.

Within their own cultural contexts, teacher educators can create online learning networks where they interact with colleagues, student teachers, information, and resources as they tackle real-life challenges. After proper training in the SRL principles, teacher educators can better utilize these networks to adequately transfer knowledge and ensure it can be put into practice by student teachers. In this way, teacher educators can continue learning within their organizations, an important step towards lifelong learning.

References

Bolhuis, S. & Voeten, M.J.M. (2001). Toward self-directed learning in secondary schools: What do teachers do? *Teaching and Teacher Education, 17,* 837-855.

Brown, J.S., & Duguid, P. (2001). Knowledge and Organization: A social-practice perspective. *Organization Science, 12,* 198-213.

Butler, D.L. (2002). Individualizing instruction in self-regulated learning. *Theory into Practice, 41,* 81-92.

Dechant, K., Marsick, V.J., & Kasl, E. (1991). Towards a model of team learning. *Studies in Continuing Education, 15,* 1-14.

Dembo, M.H., & Eaton, M.J. (2000). Self-regulation of academic learning in middle-level schools. *The Elementary School Journal, 100,* 473-490.

Eilam, B., & Aharon, I. (2003). Students' planning in the process of self-regulated learning. *Contemporary Educational Psychology, 28,* 304-334.

Hanraets, I., Hulsebosch, J, & de Laat, M. (2011). Experiences of pioneers facilitating teacher networks for professional development. *Educational Media International, 48,* 85-99.

Kirschner, P.A., Sweller, J., & Clark, R.E. (2006). Why minimal guidance during instruction does not work: An analysis of the failure of constructivist, discovery, problem-based, experiential, and inquiry-based teaching. *Educational Psychologist, 41,* 75-86.

Kistner, S., Rakoczy, K., Otto, B., Dignath-van Ewijk, Ch., Büttner, G., & Klieme, E. (2010). Promotion of self-regulated learning in classrooms: Investigating frequency, quality, and consequences for student performance. *Metacognition and learning, 5,* 157-172.

Könings, K.D., Brand-Gruwel, S., & van Merriënboer, J.G. (2007). Teachers' perspectives on innovations: implications for educational design. *Teaching and Teacher Education, 23,* 985-997.

Korthagen, F., Klaassen, C., & Russell, T. (2000) New learning in teacher education. In P.R-J. Simons, J. van der Linden, & T, Duffy [eds.], *New learning* (pp. 243-259). Dordrecht: Kluwer Academic Publishers.

Kremer-Hayon, L., & Tillema, H.H. (1999). Self-regulated learning in the context of teacher education. *Teaching and Teacher Education, 15,* 507-522.

Laferrière, T., Lamon, M., & Chan, C.K.K. (2006). Emerging e-trends and models in teacher education and professional development. *Teaching education, 17,* 75-90.

Lieberman, A., & Wood, D.R. (2003). *Inside the National Writing Project: Connecting network learning and classroom teaching.* New York: Teachers College Press.

Lunenberg, M., & Korthagen, F.A.J. (2003). Teacher educators and student-directed learning. *Teaching and Teacher education, 19,* 29-44.

Nietfeld, J.L., Cao, L., & Osborne, J.W. (2006). The effect of distributed monitoring exercises and feedback on performance, monitoring accuracy, and self-efficacy. *Metacognition and Learning, 1,* 159-179.

Nota, L., Soresi, S., & Zimmerman, B.J. (2004). Self-regulation and academic achievement and resilience: A longitudinal study. *International Journal of Educational Research, 41,* 198-215.

Pintrich. (2000). The role of goal orientation in self-regulated learning. In M. Boekaerts, P.R. Pintrich, & M.Zeidner (eds.), *Handbook of self-regulation* (pp. 451-502). San Diego, CA: Academic Press.

Pintrich, P.R. (2004). A conceptual framework for assessing motivation and self-regulated learning in college students. *Educational Psychology Review, 16,* 385-407.

Redmond, P. & Lock, J.V. (2009). Authentic learning across international borders: A Cross institutional online project for pre-service teachers. In C.D. Maddux [ed.], *Research Highlights in Technology and Teacher Education 2009* (pp. 265-273). Society for Information Technology and Teacher Education.

Schunk, D.H. (2007). Attributions as motivators of self-regulated learning. In D. H. Schunk & B.J. Zimmerman [eds.], *Motivation and self-regulated learning* (pp. 245-266). New York: Lawrence Erlbaum Associates.

Schunk, D.H., & Ertmer, P.A. (2000). Self-regulation and academic learning. In M. Boekaerts, P.R. Pintrich, & M. Zeidner (eds.), *Handbook of self-regulation* (pp. 631-649). San Diego, CA: Academic Press.

Schunk, D.H., & Zimmerman, B. (2007). Influencing children's self-efficacy and self-regulation of reading and writing through modelling. *Reading and Writing Quarterly, 23,* 7-25.

Shoffner, M. (2009). Creating a community of support for beginning English teachers. In C.D. Maddux [ed.], *Research Highlights in Technology and Teacher Education 2009* (pp. 311-318). Society for Information Technology and Teacher Education.

Sim, J.W.S., & Hew, K.F. (2010). The use of weblogs in higher education settings: A review of empirical research. *Educational research Review, 5,* 151-163.

Sundre, D.L., & Kitsantas, A. (2004). An exploration of the psychology of the examinee: Can examinee self regulation and test-taking motivation predict consequential and non-consequential test performance? *Contemporary Educational Psychology, 29,* 6-26.

Van Merriënboer, J. J. G., & Kirschner, P. A. (2007). *Ten steps to complex learning.* Mahwah, NJ: Erlbaum.

Veenman, M.V.J., Van Hout-Wolters, B.H.A.M., & Afflerbach, P. (2006). Metacognition and learning: Conceptual and methodological considerations. *Metacognition and learning, 1,* 3-14.

Vermunt, J.D., & Verloop, N. (1999). Congruence and friction between learning and teaching. *Learning and Instruction, 9,* 257-280.

Villegas-Reimers, E. (2003). *Teacher professional development: an international review of the literature.* Paris: UNESCO.

Vrieling, E.M., Bastiaens, T.J., & Stijnen, S. (2010). Process-oriented design principles for promoting self-regulated learning in primary teacher education. *International Journal of Educational Research, 49,* 141-150.

Vrieling, E.M., Bastiaens, T.J., & Stijnen, S. (2011a). *Effects of increased self-regulated learning opportunities on student teachers' motivation and use of metacognitive skills.* Manuscript submitted for publication.

Vrieling, E.M., Bastiaens, T.J., & Stijnen, S. (2011b). *Effects of increased self-regulated learning opportunities on student teachers' motivation and use of metacognitive skills*. Manuscript under revision.

Wenger, E., Trayner, B., & De Laat, M. (2011). *Telling stories about the value of communities and networks: A toolkit*. Heerlen: Ruud de Moor Centrum. Open Universiteit.

Wigfield, A., Hoa, L.W., & Klauda, S.L. (2007). *The role of achievement values in the regulation of achievement behaviours*. In D. H. Schunk, & B.J. Zimmerman [eds.], *Motivation and self-regulated learning* (pp. 169-195). NewYork: Lawrence Erlbaum Associates.

Zimmerman, B.J. (2001). Theories of self-regulated learning and academic achievement: An overview and analysis. In B. J. Zimmerman, & D. H. Schunk [eds.], *Self-regulated learning and academic achievement: Theoretical perspectives* (pp. 1-37). Mahwah, NJ: Lawrence Erlbaum.

Preservice Teachers' Personality, Motives, Motivation, and Attitudes Associated with the Use of Social Network Services: Facebook Case

Oğuzhan Atabek
Department of Computer Education and Instructional Technology
Akdeniz University
Turkey
atabek@metu.edu.tr

Abstract: The paper reports the findings from the quantitative part of an ongoing research study on Turkish preservice teachers who use Facebook (FB). Social network services are increasing in popularity and certain social network services are already being used for educational purposes. Social network services simulate and may even emulate existing social networks on an abstract level and reflect them in the electronic world. The social structures that they rely on are already being studied in regard to the context of learning and education. But the electronic simulations or reflections of existing social structures need further explorations. To investigate the personality, motivation, motives, and attitude factors that influence FB use, 641 preservice teachers who were students of Middle East Technical University (METU) in Turkey were surveyed. Four regression analyses were used to describe the results of the collected data.

Introduction

The movie of the year in 2010 was "The Social Network," which was the last feature film of accomplished American film director David Fincher. Fincher's movie tells the story of Harvard computer science undergrad Mark Zuckerberg who founded FB in 2003. This "provocative" movie delves into "the impetus for invention, the changing face of social interaction and the limits of friendship — the old-fashioned kind and the version linking 500 million Facebook users" (Puig, 2010). According to Hornaday (2010), the movie depicts "a man who changes society through bending an emergent technology to his will." Interestingly, Rickey (2010) defines the movie correctly by stating that "it is the improbably entertaining story of how new media are altering the very nature of courtship and friendship." Wilson (2010) defines the movie as "[a] film that's at once timely and timeless." Apparently, the genius director is credited with a serious portion of the success and popularity of the movie. But the cause of the popularity of the movie and the excitement it generates isn't limited to the people behind it. What makes watching this film "the event of the year" actually is its subject: Facebook. Obviously, being the focal center of it, FB makes a movie a worldwide social event. With this in mind, it is not hard to understand the tremendous impact of FB on society. The world economy informs us about FB, and its impact on the society, as well. World Economic Forum's "The Global Information Technology Report" depicts FB as a major player in the world economy which grew at a brisk pace even in the economic crisis (Dutta et al., 2010, p. 3). It indicates that "social networking and Web 2.0 companies such as Facebook" emerged as the "major segment" of information and communication technologies (ICT) throughout 2008, even while the core subsectors, such as semiconductors have suffered. As a consequence of its economic success, FB leads all online publishers with a 23% share in the market for display ads (Lipsman, 2010).

Computer networks, once considered the "hard side" of computing, are now utilized for helping bring the private lives of individuals to online social networks services. And these social network services (SNS) are increasing in their importance as they become part of many people's daily lives. Being used for many purposes, SNSs can also serve as educational applications. The National School Boards Association, representing 95,000 local school board members across the United States, has released a report on student use of social networking and reported that 59% of students who use social networking say they talk about education related topics (NSBA, 2007, p. 1). More significantly, 50% of those students who use social networking say they talk specifically about schoolwork. Considering those connotations of FB regarding its impact such as: invention, social interaction, changing the face of social interaction, changing society by a technology, altering the nature of interpersonal relationship; one can easily come up with serious questions about "this society changing" and "human nature altering" technology regarding learning, teaching, and education.

SNSs are a relatively new phenomena and related literature is limited. Given the overwhelming popularity of FB, its profound social and cultural impact, and its potential for educational implications, this paper aims to extend the existing literature by reporting the findings from the quantitative part of an ongoing research study on Turkish preservice teachers who use FB. The purpose of the study is to provide scholars and professionals in the field of educational technology and teacher training community with useful information by investigating the nature of FB use among preservice teachers and finding out personality, motives, motivational and attitudinal factors that influence its use.

Background

An SNS is an Internet website that highly invests in social networks. Those services represent and recreate an actual social network among the users of the service on the internet, and add many features that facilitate the relationships of those users. SNS can be defined as "web-based services that allow individuals to (1) construct a public or semi-public profile within a bounded system, (2) articulate a list of other users with whom they share a connection, and (3) view and traverse their list of connections and those made by others within the system" (Boyd & Ellison, 2008, p. 211). A social network (SN), which is a critical concept for FB as for other SNSs, is a social structure that is comprised of individuals who have relationships among each other. An SN is made up of those individuals, their relationships, attributes of those relationships, and properties of those individuals such as personality and motivation.

There are numerous SNSs varying in the number of their users, focus of the site, or the geographical area in which the site is popular. Among many SNSs having millions of users, (FB) is "overwhelmingly more popular" (Kirschner & Karpinski, 2010, p. 1239). It has "more than 800 million active users" and "50% of [its] active users log on to Facebook in any given day" (Facebook, 2012). Even though it has users from every age group; FB "remains primarily a college-age and emerging adult phenomenon" (Kirschner & Karpinski, 2010, p. 1239). As previously highlighted, the Internet defines the nature of SNSs and, thus, Internet makes them accessible "anytime, anywhere." Being almost infinitely accessible, information exchange works extremely well via SNSs. Taking into consideration how previous technologies changed how people communicated, FB has the potential to change how people behave.

Considering it a hypermedia internet application, for FB, therefore, personality is a core concept. Personality may be defined as "important and relatively stable characteristics within a person that account for consistent patterns of behavior" (Ewen, 2003, p.5). Among many others, there is also "The Five Factor Model" (FFM). FFM is a hierarchical organization of personality traits in terms of five basic dimensions: Extraversion, Agreeableness, Conscientiousness, Neuroticism, and Openness to Experience (McCrae & John, 1992, p. 175). FFM is categorized as being in or associated with the "trait theory" of personality (p. 199). Personality traits correlate with technology use. For example Butt and Phillips (2008, p. 348) state that neurotics are "using the Internet to feel part of a group and to escape loneliness" whereas Kraut et al. (2002) report that "Internet use with changes in community involvement was positive for extraverts and negative for introverts" (p. 61). Moreover, Schrammel et al. (2009) state that "interest of using the internet for communication" is high for those "with high levels on neuroticism" (p. 170). When exploring human behavior in internet communication, personality and motivation go hand in hand. On the relationship of personality and motivation Ewen (2003) states that "personality is a comprehensive construct and motivation is a fundamental aspect of behavior ... Therefore, theories of personality are in large part theories of motivation" (p.6). On the other hand, FB is a communication tool and "it is necessary to take into consideration a person's motivation for communication" (Spitzberg, 2006, p. 580).

SNs can have a profound impact on learning experience. Regarding computer science students, Liccardi et al. (2007, pp. 224-226) highlights many roles of SNs in learning experience, especially in the context of "pedagogies of social-cultural theories of learning" (p. 226). They argue that SNs can act as a pedagogical agent with problem-based learning (p. 224) and can be construed as communities of practice (p. 226) and can assist educators with their teaching (p. 225). SNSs are software which builds on SNs. Therefore, the nature of an SNS is inherently interpersonal. This interpersonal nature, according to McKenna et al. (2002) causes "many relationships formed online" to "eventually result in real world contact" (p. 28). They state that SNSs demonstrate an "online-to-offline" trend in the meeting of the people indicating the impact of SNSs on the lives of individuals. The striking point, however, is that, according to Ross et al. (2009), FB "tends to demonstrate opposite progression" (p. 578). The possibility of carrying over the negative aspects of "offline" SNs to the learning environment will always exist; however, FB has the potential to carry all the positive effects of "offline" SNs to an "online" platform.

SN is a key issue for teaching, teachers and, thus, teacher training. Coburn et al. (2010) state that "teachers' [SNs] are an important part of the school improvement puzzle" (p. 33). They argue that the nature and quality of SNs are associated with "a myriad of outcomes that are central to instructional change and school improvement." They indicate that "[SNs] with strong ties can facilitate diffusion of innovation, transfer of complex information, and increased problem solving." Moreover, Daly (2010) states that, SN theory "provides insight into motives of resisters to change, and spheres of social influence" (p. 3). Regarding teaching and SNs, Atteberry et al. (2010) state that SNs "play a key role in understanding the degree of success schools experience in terms of improvements for teachers and students" (p. 73). SNSs can have a positive effect on teacher professional development as well. Baker-Doyle et al (2010) argue that using SNS increases collaboration (p. 119) and "teachers communicate with each other more frequently on the [SNS] during the school year to share resources, request directed help from peers for both curricular and technological instruction, and connect about difficulties experienced in implementation efforts" (p. 124). Therefore, SN and SNSs can play a crucial role in teacher training considering their positive effect on preservice teachers' future jobs regarding implementation, improvement and development of teachers' professions.

The Study

The purpose of the research is to identify and analyze the association of preservice teachers' personality, motives, motivation, and attitudes with the use of SNSs (specifically, FB). To investigate those relationships, four instruments were used to measure psychological constructs and demographics: "NEO Five Factor Inventory," "CMC Motivation Scale," "Facebook Motives Scale," and "Facebook Attitudes Scale." All of the instruments had previously been developed and used for earlier research and were originally developed in the English language. One of the instruments (NEO Five Factor Inventory) was previously translated into Turkish by a Turkish researcher. The other three were translated into Turkish by the author of this paper and tested in a pilot study. In the actual study, only the Turkish versions were used. Because of relative advantages of an online survey compared with paper-based survey, a free (software) and online survey application (Limesurvey) was used to conduct the survey. This research study complies with the Ethical Principles of Psychologists and Code of Conduct set by the American Psychological Association (2010) and ethical standards set by the Research Center for Applied Ethics of METU and the entire study has been reviewed by Human Subjects Ethics Committee of METU.

NEO Five Factor Inventory (NEO-FFI) is a personality scale developed by Robert R. McCrae and Paul T. Costa and first published in 1985. NEO FFI is a shortened (60 item) version of the revised NEO Personality Inventory (NEO PI-R) which consists of 240 items. The scale is based on trait theory of personality and an "operationalization of the Five-Factor Model (FFM), which structures specific traits in terms of five broad factors" (Costa et al., 2001, 322). The scale is designed to "measure the five factors of personality: Neuroticism (N), Extraversion (E), Openness to Experience (O), Agreeableness (A), and Conscientiousness (C). Items in NEO FFI are answered on a 5 point Likert scale, ranging from "strongly agree" (1) to "strongly disagree" (5). It was translated into Turkish by Ersin Ku dil for his doctoral thesis research (Ku dil, 2000, p. 147). Computer Mediated Communication Competence Measure version 5 (CMC competence measure) was developed by Brian H. Spitzberg (Spitzberg, 2006, p. 629). Ross et al. (2009) used three factors of Spitzberg's CMC (Computer Mediated Communication) competence measure in their research: "Motivation," "Knowledge," Efficacy" (p. 580) and reported that only the "motivation" (M) factor was correlated with FB usage (p. 581). Ross et al. (2009) reports that the "reliability for the three domains is acceptable (from a = .73 to a = .90)" (p. 580). Thus, even though only the motivation factor seems to be necessary for this research, just to be cautious, it was decided that three factors of Spitzberg's measure as used by Ross et al. were to be used. The measure consists of 18 items being answered on a 5 point Likert scale, ranging from "not at all true of me" (1) to "very true of me" (5). Facebook Motives Scale was first developed by Pavica Sheldon (2008, p. 44) based on gratification theory. She used 38 items and extracted 6 factors of which the Eigen values are greater than 1.0 and altogether are accounted for 60 percent of the variance. Cronbach's alpha values ranged from 0.75 to 0.90 (p. 47). The items were answered on a 5 point Likert scale, ranging from "not at all" (1) to "exactly" (5). Facebook Attitude Scale was extracted from the Facebook Questionnaire developed by Ross et al (2009, p.580). The questionnaire consists of 28 items and the scale includes an attitudes factor comprising of 7 items. Items are being answered on a 5 point Likert scale, ranging from "strongly agree" (1) to "strongly disagree" (5).

Since this research is aimed to identify and analyze existing relationships among existing variables, correlational research was considered as the appropriate method of investigation. After factor analyses, predictor variables were "attitude towards using FB," "motives to use FB" (Virtual community: V, Relationship maintenance: R, Passing time: P), "motivation to use CMC" (M), "personality" (E, A, C, N, and O). Therefore 10 psychological constructs constituted the set of predictor variables. The criterion variables were demographic information about the use of FB.

The sampling method was convenience sampling. The target population of the study is all the preservice teachers in Turkey. The accessible population is all the preservice teachers who are currently enrolled in the Faculty of Education of METU in Turkey. The sample is the group of individuals who participated in the study and who have a FB account. There are seven undergraduate programs in the Faculty of Education of METU. The total number of the undergraduate students is 1510 and all of them were asked to participate in the study. Of this 1510, 229 were enrolled in the department in which the author of this paper is a research assistant: Computer Education and Instructional Technology (CEIT). Two hundred twenty nine CEIT students were reserved for the pilot study and the remaining 1282 students were asked to participate in the actual study.

Findings

One hundred seventy nine of 229 students participated in the pilot study and 136 of them had a FB account. Only those who have a FB account ($N_{pilot}=136$) could complete the survey (Table 1). In the actual study 780 of 1282 students participated in the study and 641 of them had an FB account ($N_{actual}=641$, Table 1). The actual sample was comprised of 518 female and 123 male students, having an average age of 21.29 years (SD=1.855). For conducting statistical analysis a specific computer software program -IBM SPSS v19.0.0 (www.spss.com)- was used. After the pilot study, all of the instruments except NEO-FFI-TR were revised according to Principal Component Analysis (PCA) results. In the actual study, the revised versions of the instruments were used and after collecting the data, a second PCA with Varimax rotation was conducted. A reliability analysis was conducted for the factor groups and factor variables were constructed by regression coefficients produced by the Factor Analysis procedures of SPSS.

	Gender	Accessible	Responded	Completed	Completion
Pilot		229	179	136	59.34 % of Accessible
	Male (%)		129 (27.9)	96 (70.6)	
	Female (%)		50 (72.1)	40 (29.4)	
Actual		1282	780	641	50 % of Accessible
	Male (%)		160 (20.5)	123 (19.2)	
	Female (%)		620 (79.5)	518 (80.8)	

Table 1. Demographics.

Consistent with previous research (Ross et al., 2009, p. 581) 82.12% of the participants have a FB account. 41.5% had an account for more than 3 years and the majority (60.7%) spends 30 to 180 minutes on FB daily. Another remarkable fact was related to privacy: 85.5% reported that only their friends can see their profiles. To investigate the relationships, 4 regression procedures were conducted by using SPSS. Each regression received 1 dependent variable (demographics regarding FB use) and 10 independent variables. For ordinal dependents (Duration, Intensity), Ordinal Logistic Regression was used whereas a Multinomial Logistic Regression was used for the categorical dependent variable (ProfileSee). The only continuous dependent variable –FriendCount- was assessed in the Multiple Linear Regression (See Table 2 for results summary).

First, an ordinal logistic regression was conducted between predictor variables and Duration (Approximately how long have you had your Facebook profile?) ($\chi^2 = 78.680$, df=10, p<0,001). Neuroticism (Wald=3.940, df=1, p<0.05; exp(B)=1.16), Openness to Experience (Wald=8.461, df=1, p<0.05; exp(B)=1.24), Attitude (Wald=8.052, df=1, p<0.01; exp(B)=1.32), Motivation (Wald=5.787, df=1, p<0.05; exp(B)=1.24) and Passing Time (Wald=9.726, df=1, p<0.05; exp(B)=1.32) predicted the Duration successfully. The results indicate that people didn't rush to FB for finding friends. Interestingly, it started as a means for users who were seeking a way to pass time. Moreover, attitude has the highest effect size (exp(B)=1.32). Results indicate that having motivation and attitude predicts having a FB account earlier.

Second, another ordinal logistic regression was conducted between predictor variables and Intensity (On average, approximately how many minutes per day do you spend on Facebook?) (χ^2 =353.114, df=10, p<0.001). Extraversion (Wald=6.818, df=1, p<0.01; exp(B)=1.22), Neuroticism (Wald=4.108, df=1, p<0.05; exp(B)=1.16), Openness to Experience (Wald=11.884, df=1, p<0.001; exp(B)=1.29), Attitude (Wald=74.614, df=1, p<0.000; exp(B)=2.38), Motivation (Wald=9.760, df=1, p<0.005; exp(B)=1.31), Passing time (Wald=55.633, df=1, p<0.000; exp(B)=2.00) predicted the Intensity. Strikingly, attitude towards FB has the strongest effect size (exp(B)=2.38) followed by Passing time (exp(B)=2.00) indicating that even though there is a significant relationship between personality traits and intensity of FB use, personality is not the main factor influencing its use. So that educational uses of FB or SNSs in general are feasible. Another point is that neurotics and those who are open to experience are both predicting the Duration and Intensity.

Third procedure was a multinomial logistic regression between ProfileSee (Who can see your Facebook profile?) and predictors (χ^2 =60.303, df=30, p<0.001). The model successfully predicted %85.3 of cases. This procedure produced 3 sets of results associated with the levels of the dependent variable. In the second level of ProfileSee (All Networks and Friends), only the motives predicted the change in outcome: Passing Time (Wald=5.904, df=1, p<0.05; exp(B)=0.602), Relationship (Wald=6.542, df=1, p<0.05; exp(B)=0.607), Friendship (Wald=10.362, df=1, p<0.01, exp(B)=1.726). The regression used the first level of the ProfileSee variable (Only my friends) to refer first. Thus, results indicate that motives are important factors regarding the privacy issues. In the third level of ProfileSee (Some networks/all friends) there was no significant prediction. Result shows that the respondents dichotomize their contacts as "Only my friends" and "All Networks and Friends." The last level (I Don't know), had two personality traits and one motive dimension: Neuroticism (Wald=6.793, df=1, p<0.01; exp(B)=1.971), Conscientiousness (Wald=4.097, df=1, p<0.05; exp(B)=0.602), Passing (Wald=5.131, df=1, p<0.05; exp(B)=0.495).

	Duration	Intensity	ProfileSee	FriendCount
Model	χ^2 = 78.680	χ^2 =353.114	χ^2 =60.303	R^2=0.183
Extraversion	-	exp(B)=1.22	-	+0.223
Agreeableness	-	-	-	−0.998
Conscientiousness	-	-	exp(B_3)=0.602	-
Neuroticism	exp(B)=1.16	exp(B)=1.16	exp(B_3)=1.971	-
Openness to Experience	exp(B)=1.24	exp(B)=1.29	-	+0.107
Friendship	-	-	exp(B_2)=1.726	-
Relationship	-	-	exp(B_2)=0.607	+0.102
Passing Time	exp(B)=1.32	exp(B)=2.00	exp(B_2)=0.602 exp(B_3)=0.495	+0.099
Motivation	exp(B)=1.24	exp(B)=1.31	-	-
Attitude	exp(B)=1.32	exp(B)=2.38	-	+0.197

Table 2. Summary of statistical results.

Finally, a multiple linear regression was conducted between FriendCount (Approximately how many friends are on your Facebook Friends List?) and the predictor variables (F(10.622) = 13.921, p <0.001). All independent variables entered in the regression. The standardized regression equation (Y^1= 0.223*E–0.998*N+0.107*O+0.197*A+0.099*P+0.102*R) included 3 personality traits (E, N, O), attitude, and two motive dimensions (P, R). The sample multiple correlation coefficient was 0.428 and approximately 20% of the variance on the number of FB friends is accounted for Extraversion, Neuroticism, Openness to Experience, Attitude towards FB use, Passing Time, and Relationship (R^2=0.183). The results indicate that personality traits are more important predictors of the "social" side of FB followed by attitude towards FB use.

Discussion

The purpose of this paper was to investigate the relationship of personality, motivation, attitude, and motive related factors with FB use. In parallel with previous research (Ross et al., 2009, p. 582) personality traits were associated with FB use. Especially Neuroticism, Extraversion and Openness to Experience yielded significant prediction results in regression analysis. Motive to use FB and attitude towards FB use also are associated with FB use. Extraversion and Neuroticism are influential in the number of friends. While extraverts have a positive relationship with the number of friends, Neurotics have stronger but negative relationship with number of friends. Results also indicate that neurotic and conscientious students tend to have privacy concerns. Contrasting with the findings on the number of friends neurotics tend to use FB more often. Extraverts and those students who are "open to experience" are using FB often too. These results indicate that personality is a major issue regarding the educational uses of FB. The ongoing and future efforts to develop educational modules on or in the FB infrastructure or those teachers who are using or considering to directly using FB for daily educational activities should consider that personality differences highly influence the way students use it.

On the other hand, for some aspects, personality traits are less important than other factors. Results indicate that motive to pass time and attitude towards FB use were more influential on those students who were first and most attracted to FB. Motives and attitudes are more influential on the time spent on FB. This result, actually, is a promising result for scholars, teachers, and developers who are considering SNSs as educational environments. The results on the frequency of using FB indicate that personality doesn't constitute a major problem for teachers and developers since ways for helping students to develop a positive attitude towards SNSs are probable. Another significant finding was that the motives to use FB are highly associated with the privacy concerns of the students. Considering the natural properties of an educational environment, teachers and developers should seriously take the privacy concerns into account. In parallel with previous research (Ross et al., 2009, p. 582; Spitzberg, 2006, p. 639), motivation is highly associated with FB use. All statistical analysis except the one predicting the number of friends revealed high associations of FB use with motivation construct. This is another promising finding regarding the educational uses of SNSs and FB in particular. The findings regarding "motivation to use CMC" and "attitude towards FB use" reveal that, since these factors are subject to improvement, teachers may have a chance to better keep students "in" the learning environment.

The study resulted in important findings regarding teacher training. As previously stated, regarding the teachers, SNSs have the potential to influence the diffusion of innovation, social influence, and receiving help from peers. The results indicate that use of FB correlates with personality traits. Therefore, considering their low profile on SNS environment, especially, neurotic preservice teachers are more likely to fail to benefit from SNSs in their future professions. On the other hand, parameters of use of FB correlate with motives and attitude, as well. Therefore, it should be noted that the nature and quality of SNS coverage in teacher training programs will influence teachers' professional development in the future regarding perceptions, beliefs, and readiness of teachers about SNSs. Finally, emergence of privacy concerns in the implementation of FB indicates that a possible gender difference might emerge in terms of benefits that a teacher may gain from SNSs while working, especially regarding professional development. Considering female individuals' privacy concerns compared to male counterparts, teacher training programs should take into account placing more emphasis on learning to utilize and use of SNSs by female preservice teachers. SNS developers, policy makers, and educational administrators should consider privacy concerns of preservice teachers as well as students while developing and implementing SNS applications.

Further Research

This paper reports the findings from the quantitative part of ongoing research. Qualitatively studying the use of FB is necessary for better understanding the possibility of educational use of FB. SNSs, by definition, are based on and simulate social structures, and cultural differences are even more significant when the learning environments require human-computer interaction. Thus, another important contribution would be investigating the phenomenon by a cross-cultural research design.

References

Atteberry, A., Bryk, A. S. (2010). Centrality, connection, and commitment: The role of social networks in a school-based literacy initiative. In A. J. Daly (Ed.), *Social network theory and educational change* (pp. 51-75). Cambridge, MA, USA: Harvard Education Press.

Baker-Doyle, K. J., Yoon, S. A. (2010). Making expertise transparent: Using technology to strengthen social networks in teacher professional development. In A. J. Daly (Ed.), *Social network theory and educational change* (pp. 115-126). Cambridge, MA, USA: Harvard Education Press.

Boyd, D. M. & Ellison, N. B. (2008). Social network sites: Definition, history and scholarship. *Journal of Computer-Mediated Communication, 13*(1), 210-230.

Butt, S. and Phillips, J. G. (2008). Personality and self reported mobile phone use. *Computers in Human Behavior, 24*(2), 346-360.

Coburn, C. E., Choi, L., Mata, W. (2010). "I would go to her because her mind is math": Network formation in the context of a district-based mathematics reform. In A. J. Daly (Ed.), *Social network theory and educational change* (pp. 33-50). Cambridge, MA, USA: Harvard Education Press.

Daly, A. J. (2010). Mapping the terrain: Social network theory and educational change. In A. J. Daly (Ed.), *Social network theory and educational change* (pp. 1-16). Cambridge, MA, USA: Harvard Education Press.

Dutta, S., Mia, I., Geiger, T., Herrera, E. T. (2010). How networked is the world? Insights from the networked readiness index 2009–2010. In S. Dutta & I. Mia (Eds.), *The global information technology report 2001–2002: Readiness for the networked world*, pp. 3-30. Geneva: World Economic Forum. Retrieved on October 3, 2010 from http://www.weforum.org/en/initiatives/gcp/index.htm

Ewen, R. B. (2003). *An introduction to theories of personality*, (6th ed.). New Jersey, USA: Lawrence Erlbaum Associates.

Facebook. (2012). Statistics. Retrieved on January 19, 2012 from http://www.facebook.com/press/info.php?statistics

Hornaday, A. (2010). The social network: A universal story that's hard not to like. *Washington Post*. Retrieved from http://www.washingtonpost.com/gog/movies/the-social-network,1159821/critic-review.html

Kirschner, P. A. and Karpinski, A. C. (2010). Facebook® and academic performance. *Computers in Human Behavior, 26*(6), 1237-1245.

Kraut, R., Kiesler, S., Boneva, B., Cummings, J., Helgeson, V., & Crawford, A. (2002). Internet paradox revisited. *Journal of Social Issues, 58*, 49–74.

Ku dil, M.E. (2000). Value-socialisation in cultural context: A study with British and Turkish families. (Unpublished doctoral dissertation).University of Sussex at Brighton, United Kingdom.

Liccardi, I., Ounnas, A., Pau, R., Massey, E., Kinnunen, P., Lewthwaite, S., Midy, M., Sarkar, C. (2007). The role of social networks in students' learning experiences. In *ITiCSE-WGR '07: Working group reports on ITiCSE on Innovation and technology in computer science education* (pp. 224-237). New York, NY, USA: ACM.

Lipsman, A. (2010, November 8). U.S. online display advertising market delivers 22 percent increase in impressions vs. year ago. Retrieved November 12th, 2010, from http://www.comscore.com/Press_Events/Press_Releases/2010/11/U.S._Online_Display_Advertising_Market_Delivers_22_Percent_Increase_in_Impressions

McCrae, R. R., John, O. P. (1992). An introduction to the five-factor model and its applications. *Journal of Personality, 60*(2), 175-215.

McKenna, Katelyn Y.A., Green,A. S., & Glenson, Marci E.J.(2002). Relationship formation on the Internet: What's the big attraction? *Journal of Social Issues, 58*(1), 9–31.

National School Boards Association (NSBA). (2007). *Creating and connecting: Research and guidelines on social and educational networking*. Alexandria, VA, USA: NSBA.

Puig, C. (2010). 'Social Network' puts story of Facebook into the big picture. *USA Today*. Retrieved from http://www.usatoday.com/life/movies/reviews/2010-09-30-socialnetwork30_ST_N.htm

Rickey, C. (2010). An engrossing portrait of Facebook and its creators. *The Philadelphia Inquirer*. Retrieved from http://www.philly.com/inquirer/columnists/carrie_rick ey/20101001_An_engrossing_portrait_of_Facebook_and_its_creators.html

Ross, C., Orr, E.S., Sisic, M., Arseneault, J.M., Simmering, M.G., Orr, R.R. (2009). Personality and motivations associated with Facebook use. Computers *in Human Behavior, 25*(2), 578-586.

Schrammel, J., Köffel, C., Tscheligi, M. (2009). Personality traits, usage patterns and information disclosure in online communities. In *Proceedings of the 23rd British HCI Group Annual Conference on People and Computers: Celebrating People and Technology (BCS-HCI '09) (pp. 169-174)*. Swinton, UK: British Computer Society.

Sheldon, P. (2008). Student favorite: Facebook and motives for its use. *Southwestern Journal of Mass Communication, 23*(October), 39-54.

Spitzberg, G. H. (2006). Preliminary development of a model and a measure of computer mediated communication (CMC) competence. *Journal of Computer Mediated Communication, 11*, 629–666.

Wilson, C. (2010). Story of Facebook makes for a top film. *St. Louis Post-Dispatch*. Retrieved from http://www.stltoday.com/entertainment/movies/reviews/article_701b45c5-1757-541c-b102-1d65703ce7fa.html.

InteractiveSchoolWall: A Digital Enriched Learning Environment for Systemic-Constructive Informal Learning Processes

Thomas Winkler
winkler@imis.uni-luebeck.de

Martina Ide
martinaelisa.ide@gmail.com
Institute for Multimedia and Interactive Systems, University of Luebeck,
Germany

Michael Herczeg
Institute for Quality Development of Schools in Schleswig-Holstein
Germany
herczeg@imis.uni-luebeck.de

Abstract: In this paper we reflect on the impact of a novel digitally enriched learning space for teaching and teacher education. For this purpose we present a hypermedia presentation and interaction platform, publicly accessible in the lobby of a secondary school in northern Germany. We show how this learning space digitally extends learning spaces in a new way. Interactive navigation and self-determined networking allow active learning in an informal way, where students, teachers and, indeed, all other people involved in school engage in the presentation and exchange of views. We explain how to meet the pedagogical implications of a presentation and interaction tool, called InteractiveSchoolWall (ISW), with the requirements of *Open Learning*. The ISW consist of multiple multi-touch screens running specific applications, i.e. *Interactive Timeline, Hypervid Player, Semantic Map,* and Media Gallery. The technical construction of the ISW follows the logic of a novel digital network environment (NEMO). This framework allows the cross-wise use of personalized and semantic enriched multimedia objects. Referring to recent systemic-constructivist pedagogical approaches and media-theoretical considerations we reflect on the function and significance of the ISW as a specific multimedia learning environment. A first impression of teachers' reaction to the system is presented. Finally we discuss to what extent the interactive structure of the ISW encourages the reflective handling of complex knowledge, so that teaching models in teacher education and in-service teacher education programs can be enhanced. We envisage that the ISW will open new perspectives in the management and organization of schools, thus improving school development processes.

Introduction

We all live in a world where digital media have developed rapidly, and this exerts a powerful influence on people's lives. But the acceptance of these new media differs widely. Children and young people have grown up with this new world of computers. The enormous technical achievements have become part of students' everyday life and many know how to use them effectively. This is not so for many older people, among them teachers. Older citizens need to learn how to use the advanced technology that is more than just an extension of traditional office technology. This is not only a matter of handling them technically. These new media represent a totally new form of constructing knowledge, of processing reality.

In this paper we want to explain, in what way a web-based hypermedia platform for presentation and interaction at school, the so called *InteractiveSchoolWall* (ISW) (Figure 1),[1] may change the attitude of teachers by means of new ad-

---

[1] The concept of this project and its realization was set up in cooperation between the *Institute for Multimedia and Interactive Systems* of the *University of Luebeck*, the *Institute for Quality Development at Schools in Schleswig-Holstein*, and the Secondary School *Carl-Jacob-Burckhardt Gymnasium.* They are located in northern Germany.

ditional learning space. We will deal with the problems emerging from this medial extension of learning space regarding teachers in school. But also the opportunities for school development provided by the ISW will be discussed. Further on we describe the technical and theoretical context, in which the design of a digitally enriched learning environment is embedded. We emphasize the importance of web-based software and the use of personalized, semantic-annotatable media objects, which can be used on a variety of different hardware with novel physical and spatial interfaces. These are considered in the context of systemic-constructive pedagogies, particularly in their role for the co-construction of knowledge, and the assistance in the symbolic organization of certain areas of experience (Holz, 2008). Regarding media theory, the design of the ISW is based on the thoughts of McLuhan, that media are extensions of man (McLuhan, 1964). deKerckhove extends this theory by saying that the increasing cross-linking by means of digital media effects changes in individuals as well as in society. Humans and digital media form a *dynamic interconnected system* that can be understood as *connected intelligence* (deKerckhove, 1997).

Figure 1: The ISW. Above the multi-touch screen are webcams and below the screens RFID-reader.

Our research on an innovative learning environment is founded on Design-Based Research (Brown, 1992). According to this approach theory and real-world usage are conjoined and of equal importance. Thus theory and applications evolve simultaneously during the design process. In a collaborative design process the implementation of the ISW began in 2010. The applications were developed by a group of students in media computer science in cooperation with the users. The construction of the ISW consists of several multi-touch screens, speakers, web cams with microphones, RFID reader and embedded computers with Internet connectivity, built into a wall in the lobby of the school. There is a platform that provides a place with body-and space-related interfaces and applications that emphasize social and physical activities. This place is freely accessible for all those involved in school and offers playful and interdisciplinary, exploratory, collaborative work and learning.

In a first, very early survey teachers were asked about the combination of subjects they teach, whether they have used the ISW already, how they like the ISW, and whether they want to use the ISW for their work. Because the currently available applications of the ISW are in a still ongoing co-design process, influenced by pedagogical implications, accompanying evaluations are ongoing and will be performed in future. This is and will be done in several stages and at different levels of evaluations with different users: students at school, their parents, teachers, and teachers in education.

New opportunities for learning with digital technology

In the future people may well intercommunicate with their digitally-enriched physical environment not only via keyboard and screen, but with their whole body. Intelligent spaces, digitally enriched everyday objects, mobile devices, as well as body-worn computer systems, such as interactive and intelligent clothing and jewelry will radically change our learning spaces. Also a key role is played by systems across, Internet-based connectivity of applications with specific reference to body and space. In order to realize learning scenarios with this interconnectedness we are developing and implementing a platform called *NEMO* (*Network Environment for Multimedia Objects*). NEMO is a new kind of media repository, which provides the user with access to contextualized, personalized, semantically enriched and device-specific *NEMO Multimedia Objects (NMOs)* (Winkler & Cassens, 2010). These NMOs are containers for metadata and media objects, which consist of media entities like videos, audio files, texts or 3D objects. These media hold different kinds of meta-information like authorship, access rights, content descriptions, semantic annotations, location data, or device-specific information. These data make the NMOs much "richer" than most multimedia data, which allows deducing dependencies between NMOs or retrieving user- and location-related information (Winkler Scharf, 2011).

NEMO Multimedia Objects can be accessed and manipulated from a variety of computing platforms and interaction devices, such as mobile phones, multi-touch tables, desktop computers and of course the ISW. NEMO facilitates the communication and exchange of data between those devices. Users are able to work on the same set of data, while making use of the distinct advantages and capabilities of the current computing device they use. For example, en route, one can survey objects or make small annotations on a mobile device, while at home at the desktop computer, complex and optimized tools can be used on the same object for further processing. As NEMO knows which device and device type it is communicating with, it is able to adjust the content of the NMOs to adjust to the capabilities of the different devices. Multi-touch screens need information about position, rotation and scale of an image, while cellular phones just need basic and low-resolution images. The ISW will get larger sized versions of videos and pictures or more additional information of the same object than mobile devices because of their greater resolution and display size. The digitally enhanced learning environment ISW in context with NEMO can be a powerful informal space for professional education, playful and exploratory learning and working. Most notably, the importance of direct social interaction in groups is promoted. As an exploratory space, the available applications function almost as a kind of new instrument. In communal experience, they allow us to see, survey, orient and interact with the digitally shaped world.

Systemic Constructivist pedagogy in context of a digitally enriched learning environment

Our world, including the world of schools, can no longer be structured deterministically or generally. According to Leo Marx, this is …"*truly an almost a miraculous era. What is before us no one can say, what is upon us no one can hardly realize.*" (Marx, 2010). Nothing is how it seems any longer: reality is not clearly or objectively interpretable. Hence, in the future it is important that students learn to gather knowledge (which is always unique for every individual) from new contexts, and to recognize the underlying knowledge structures. School must evolve to "allow new educational products, such as reconstruction, new construction, deconstruction of knowledge, …for future *applications, contexts and situations.*" (Kösel, 2007) According to Kösel, knowledge differs from information in this way: that information is transformed into personal knowledge through the process of acquisition, judgment and reflection of the viewer in relation to others (for example, through common usage), through contradiction, and through recognition of distinctions; and thus becomes available as a tool for coping with existence. "New and different" structures of awareness, precipitated by today's new forms of identity representation, media aesthetics and body orientation, must be integrated into students' "cognitive toolkit". Nevertheless, teachers react primarily in the confines of their own "cognitive" structures – they cannot see what they have not learned to see. The ability to develop and promote autodidactic competence is strongly influenced by the extent to which educators themselves were able to experience self-directed learning or not. These paradoxes can be observed as the inner self-contradiction of Teacher Education: one argues for new learning culture in forms and methods of the old culture of learning (Arnold, 2007). Teachers themselves need to make statements about the architecture of their learning, to be able to reveal them, to finally have the ability for new designs. For the mediation process in the sense of an "organized knowledge work" it must be asked in what way digitally enriched "metaphors" allow a learning culture, in which learners are able to construct and communicate knowledge, self-determined and socially interactive rich in connotative references. The didactic potentiality of digitally enriched learning environments, as implemented with the ISW, is based on the dynamic knowledge representation, which initiates a highly visual, affected, "intelligent" communication and interaction between learners and computer system. In particular, the exposure to visually represented complexity is essential for the construction of structures of understanding. This culture of learning is motivated and promoted by visualizing the ongoing disciplinary and interdisciplinary debate on "intelligence", i.e. contextually and in semantic relation. Participation and co-construction of knowledge occurs by the connection between cognition and action, due to the appreciation of patterns in which the student learns to ask questions.

Media theory as inspiration for the design of digital enriched learning space

Today the phrases and aphorisms *the global village* and *the medium is the message* by McLuhan are standard terms in our contemporary vocabulary. Media have always expanded our body, but now this is done at a very rapid pace. Through the novel web-based media with new body- and space related interfaces, our culture, and our relation to time and space is changing in a radical way (McLuhan, 1964). Computer systems with which we live almost in symbiosis are understood here as the so far most flexible extension of man, in terms of McLuhan, or as autonomous dialogue partner or agents. The rapidly increasing networking with these changing media effects individuals and society. Humans and digital media form a dynamic, *interconnected system* that can be understood as *connected intelligence*. According to de Kerckhove it is important, that we are involved in the design process on these media, such as neural networks, so they do not design us. Here a major role is played by *open source* and *common media data*, like public domain and free license, which all people are allowed to use (de Kerckhove, 1997).

The InteractiveSchoolWall and current applications

The ISW serves as a platform for presentation and interaction for informal learning. Groups of learners can structure and arrange information, supported by visual aids. Although no systems similar to the ISW exist at school, many applications akin to those found in the ISW have already been developed in other contexts and examined in research. Based on our experience in developing several interactive applications for learning during the last years (Winkler & Ide, 2011; Winkler & Ide, 2010; Winkler & Ide, 2009, Winkler & Ide, 2008) we argue that body- and space related digital learning applications at school can only accomplish sustainable enhancement if they are always present and accessible for all students as well as the teachers. Our solution to this challenge is based on the idea of a physical-dominant user-interface, placed centrally inside the school building. We explain how social co-operation of students can be fostered by placing the InteractiveSchoolWall (ISW) at a vital, physical place at school, on permanent display. The ISW provides new options for co-operative, explorative, informal and in further time game based learning. By means of a multimodal (haptic, acoustic, visual, etc.) and multicodal (images, writing, music, etc.) interface students are able to communicate and interact with the ISW and with each other. The design of the ISW supports various body- and space-related applications, e.g. *timeline*, *hypervid*, *media gallery*, and *semantic map*. In the near future the ISW will be also a place for partial learning with the *Mobile Learning Exploration System* (*Moles*), a place for performances using the webcams imbedded in the ISW, or a place for imploding physical space by communicating and interacting with others at distant places all over the world in real time.

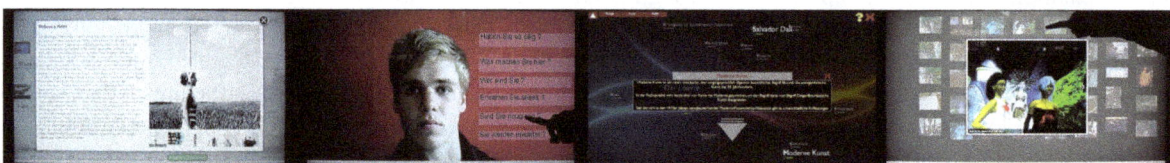

Figure 2: Timeline, Hypervid Player, Semantic Map, Media Gallery.

Timeline

The timeline of the ISW is implemented as an organizational tool in the context of learning. It can visualize the contents of existing courses at school basically in cross-curricular connections. The design of the timeline tool makes complex relationships comprehensible in an intuitive way. The composition of each timeline is designed dynamically. That means, the timeline interface allows you to place content on a specific issue-oriented timeline in a specific way, so that the content and timing relationships are visible between the different subject areas (Figure 2). For the user every single item on the timeline is represented by an icon. An enormous amount of data is hidden behind it, visualized by means of image, text and video. The respective data entries describe information in relation to the time entry, which the viewer can explore by navigating freely. In parallel, contextual linking to other topics, simultaneously a multiple way of looking at things appears, indicating new contents (not previously imagined) to the viewer. The form of data-visualization is essential for the thinking in networked contexts. It helps students to understand specific events in interdisciplinary contexts.

Hypervid Player

Hypervid is a browser-based interactive system for creating, editing, managing and playing hyper video. Due to time jumps within a video hypervid enables to understand a story not as a rigid structure. Instead, while watching, the story can be generated within a specific scope. The hyperstructure is reticulate, associative thinking comparable. The advantage of hyperstructure is that no context-dependent, tree-like classification systems are necessary for systematization or acquisition of terms. The design of hyperstructures implies more than another form of presentation level. It allows you to look at information in their intercorellation with each other in networked contexts, also implies playful thinking, and focused not on monocausal solutions in terms of explicability of objects but uses the potential of navigation of the interaction of the user for a variable set of perspectives. The linked video fragments can be shown by hypervid player in a secured browser (Figure 2). On the one hand, this blocked the ability for users to leave the resulting hypervideo. On the other hand, it increases the degree of immersion, because the hypervideo does not leave the full picture and the video fragments load dynamically inside the player. Also *hypervid* offers the possibility to create groups. Making videos for one specific group accessible and manipulable, groups can communicate with each other. Therefore the systems stay abreast of changes in today's increasingly networked media society and allows for shared learning all over the world.

Semantic Map

The potential of the *semantic map* lies in the possibility to visualize documents of various types of content in their relationship to each other and spatially adjacent (Figure 2). The basis of the interface is that we must act on the assumption of changing organizational forms and ways of thinking in the acquirement of world view, information may no longer be taught sequentially but by fragmentation and linkage (Kuhlen, 1991). By connecting information on similarity principles in meshed complexities, the semantic map organizes and visualizes such multiple perspectives on the world (Bush, 1945; Fleischmann, 2001-2010). It illustrates in what context of a whole and a detail a term can stay, which references and links exist to related content, and in which spatial relationships this can be arranged. Thus, the observer finds it easier to navigate and orientate in wide range of topics than in a traditional online search, where content is distributed without regard to context in various pages. The fact that the viewer behaves actively using the semantic map, selecting individually specific terms, an expanded idea of knowledge as a way of thinking in higher complexities can be promoted.

Media Gallery

Contemporary forms and formats of representation of "self" have changed. Young people increasingly communicate and interact via chat and pictures on internet forums. The media gallery represents in their possibility for presentation of images and videos a surface, in which potentially reflect all facets of school life (Figure 2). Divided into content categories such as projects, working groups, study tours, forums, art, music, theater, sports, etc, it provides almost unlimited space to visualize the variety of school life in image and video for students, teachers, parents, and guests. So that it becomes an important tool of social interaction within the school, which can contribute to identity formation and appreciation. Free navigation and content selection allows investigating individual projects that are always expandable. Depending on the priority of specific projects and priorities within the school work, the presence of content on the ISW can be controlled temporarily, to make an emphasis on the visualization of specific content.

Evaluation results as focus of a new role for teachers in the learning environment at School

Background

This section describes preliminary results of a questionnaire provided to the 67 teachers of the school. The questionnaire was distributed to the teachers in the teachers' room together with envelopes for anonymous return. Participation was voluntary and no incentive was given to the participants. The ISW ran for test purposes for three month. This offered the chance for teachers and students to get in contact with the system. The ISW was in regular service on 7 schooldays when the questionnaire was distributed. Different applications ran on the ISW (timeline, media gallery and hypervid player)[2] and all teachers and students of the school had access to the system and could become acquainted with it. The sample consisted of 18 teachers with two persons excluded due to missing values and lack of demographic information.[3] So the final sample consisted of 16 persons. This small sample size corresponds to a response rate of 24%. The sample

---

2 At this time the semantic map was not running, because of technical enhancements.
3 Teachers who were involved in the developing process of the ISW did not participate in the evaluation.

comprised 9 men and 7 women. The participants' mean age was 44.6 years (SD=9.4) with ages ranging from 31 years to 62 years. The participants taught subjects covering the whole range of subjects of the school (table 1).

Table 1: Teachers' school subjects (N=16). Note: Teachers often belong to more than one category.

Subjects	N	(%)
German, foreign languages, art, music, performance art	11	(68.8%)
history, geography, economics/politics, religion, philosophy	9	(56.3%)
mathematics, biology, chemistry, physics, information technology	3	(18.8%)
sports	3	(18.8%)

Activities and applications

Teachers were asked to report frequencies of different activities concerning the ISW. The activities were reading or viewing information presented by the ISW, the use of applications by the persons themselves, the search for information and a visit to the ISW along with students. Participants specified whether they had performed activities "never", "occasionally" or "often". Because the system was very new, it was not surprising that none of the activities was performed "often". The results indicate that the majority of the respondents had read or viewed information and half of them used, started or quit applications. This might suggest a rather exploratory approach to the system. The distribution of answers is depicted in Figure 3.

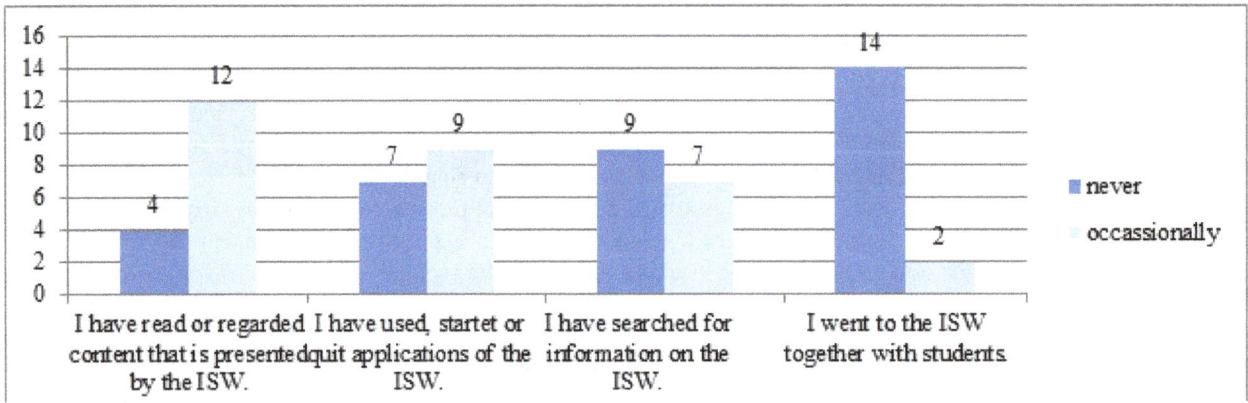

Figure 3: Reported frequencies of activities (N=16).

Further, respondents were asked to report their affinity for the existing applications. Additionally, they were asked if they knew of the applications. The affinity was judged on a 7-point scale (ranging from -3="very bad" to 3="very good"). For this rating it has to be kept in mind, that sample sizes were very small. The applications timeline and media gallery were rated positively by the respondents (Figure 4).

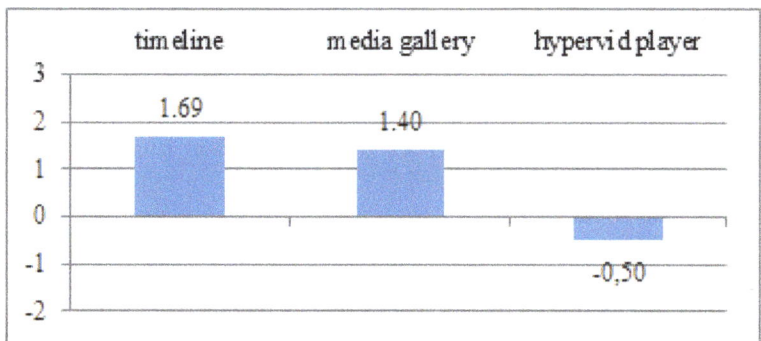

Figure 4: Means of rating the existing applications.

Both means were significant different from the middle of the scale (timeline $t(7)=3.90$, $p<.01$, media gallery $t(9)=3.50$, $p<.01$, hypervid player $t(1)=-0.33$, ns). Only two persons rated their liking for hypervid player, which 12 participants reported not to know. This might be explained by the demonstrative nature of the application during operation time. Table 2 reports upper and lower limits of confidence intervals of the means.

Table 2: Means and confidence intervals of liking for the applications.

	timeline	media gallery	hypervid player
N	8	10	2
Mean	1.69	1.40	-0.50
Standard deviation	1.22	1.26	2.12
Upper limit (95%)	2.71	2.30	18,56
Lower limit (95%)	0.67	0.50	-19,56
N application unknown	6	5	12

Further, teachers were asked whether they intended to use the system in class, e.g. for presenting or searching for information. Seven of the participants declared that they intended to use the ISW in class, whereas one person negated this. Eight participants did not know yet whether they wanted to use the system in class or not.

Finally, the agreement on simple statements on pedagogical issues concerning the ISW were rated by the participants (7-point scale ranging from 1="I do not agree" to 7="I totally agree"). The distributions of answers (Figure 5) as well as mean, standard deviation and median (Table 3) are reported for a simple descriptive inspection.

1. The ISW encourages me to present and work on content.	2. The ISW can support students in learning.
3. The ISW enhances informal learning.	4. The ISW offers special opportunities to the school.

Figure 5: Distribution of answers.

Table 3: Mean, standard deviation and median of the statements.

Statement	Mean (standard deviation)	Median	N
The ISW encourages me to present and work on content.	4.89 (0.92)	5.00	14
The ISW can support students in learning.	6.36 (0.84)	6.50	14
The ISW enhances informal learning.	5.23 (1.01)	5.00	13
The ISW offers special opportunities to the school.	5.21 (1.93)	5.50	14

It has to be taken into account that this data is based on a very basic method. Nevertheless, we want to present a first impression of a sample of teachers' reactions to the system. According to demographic information the participants covered a wide range of the school, but no information is available on representativeness regarding the investigated issues.

Conclusions

Processes of teaching and learning, which are in principle open and not constricted by linear models of mediation, open spaces for independent learning and various forms of appropriation of knowledge. This thinking underlines, that learners can only learn by themselves. But it is necessary to create motivational events for self-directed learning and reflexive use of complex knowledge. In this context the ISW, as a dynamic, enriched digital presentation and form of interaction, extends the existing learning environment in school to this important didactic function: it represents diverse perceptions and scripts by the learners to acquire a picture of world in such a way, that the appropriation and self-learning competences can be strengthened.

The result of the initial evaluation makes clear, that a larger number of teachers surveyed, are observant, cautious, undetermined, or in opposition to changes regarding previously practiced knowledge-oriented ways of teaching. This is reflected in the number of those who have not participated in the evaluation (table 1). Simultaneously, this can also be an expression of an inner, structural uncertainty of the teacher, questioning his role as "facilitator of content" by a systemic-constructivist teaching-learning model, as it is based on the ISW. In contrast to this, the distribution of the responses of those who have participated in the evaluation, a predominantly constructive attitude towards the ISW is shown: in their opinion, the ISW opens special facilities for the school, promotes informal learning of pupils and the teachers feel encouraged, to work with the ISW to present content (table 5).

The first survey shows that in daily contact with the ISW a high affinity for the timeline is identifiable. In comparison, the *Media Gallery* is a little less used (table 3). These responses are interesting, as this visual and auditory form of restructuring and integration of knowledge obviously arouses interest. The *Hypervid Player* requires a high degree of willingness on the part of the teachers to question the usual thinking in linear structures. Currently, the survey suggests that the low affinity for hypervid could be a result even less pronounced form of thinking in hyperstructures. Particularly by divergent scripts of perceptions of teachers and students, it is necessary to initiate systemic-constructivist motivated thinking to design new learning spaces within teacher education and further teacher education. Here are the media more than just technology: As a mediator of learning processes different media unfold options for different kind of thinking about their content, messages, and diverse ways of offerings. It is similar to the ISW, which can improve a new framework and context for teaching - and the school life in general.

In the context of ongoing evaluation, we look to what extent the ISW will open new perspectives in the management and organization of schools. It serves in particular as a place of knowledge construction for learners. In its non-hierarchical structure, the ISW provides a new architecture for knowledge construction. It does not meet the conventional academic structures of learning, but expands them. As an example for teaching models in teacher education and in-service teacher education programs the ISW provides new ways of thinking and learning structures and therefore improves learning and school development processes. The existing training formats referring specifically to ISW applications, e.g. hypervid (Winkler, 2011), are developed on the basis of ongoing evaluation in a way that shows how this learning space digitally extends learning spaces at school in a new way. Interactive navigation and self-determined networking allow active learning in an informal way, where students, teachers and other people that are involved in school are engaged in the presentation and exchange of views.

References

Arnold, R. (2007). *Ich Lerne, also bin ich. Eine systemisch-konstruktivistische Didaktik*. Heidelberg: Carl-Auer.
Bush, V. (1945). *As We May Think*. In: Atlantic Monthly. July 1945, Band 176, Nr.1, S. 101-108.
Brown, A.L. (1992). *Design experiments: Theoretical and methodological challenges in creating complex interventions in classroom settings*. The Journal of the Learning Sciences, 2(2), 141-178.
Deleuze, G. & Guattari, F. (1977). *Rhizom*. Berlin.
Fleischman, M. (2001-2010). *„Netzspannung.org"*, *Media Art Archive & eTeaching Platform*.
Holz, K. L. (2008). *Einführung in die systemische Pädagogik*. Heidelberg, Germany: Carl-Auer.
Kerckhove de, D. (1997). *The Skin of Culture – Investigating the New Electronic Reality*. London: Kogan Page.
Kösel, E. (2007). *Die Modellierung von Lernwelten*. Vol. 2. Die Konstruktion von Wissen – Eine didaktische Epistemologie für die Wissensgesellschaft. SD-Verlag: Bahlingen, Germany.
Kuhlen, R.(1991). *Hypertext. Ein nicht-lineares Medium zwischen Buch und Wissenbank*. Springer, Berlin.
Marx, L. (2010). *Technology-a-hazardous-concept*.
    http://etc.technologyandculture.net/2010/08/technology-a-hazardous-concept/
McLuhan, M. (1964) *Understanding Media: The Extentions of Men*. New York, USA: McGraw Hill.
Winkler, T., Scharf, F., Hahn, C., Herczeg, M. (2011). *Ambient Learning Spaces*. In: Méandez-Villas (Ed.). Education in a Technological World: Communicating Current and Emerging Research and Technological Efforts. ITC's book series No 1. Badajoz, Spain: Formatex.
Winkler T., Ide M., Herczeg M. (2011). *YouTube Annotations: Reflecting Interactive, Web based Hypervideos in Teacher Education*. In Proceedings of the SITE. AACE. 3517-3524.
Winkler T., Cassens J., Abraham M., Herczeg M. (2010). *Die Interactive School Wall – eine be-greifbare Schnittstelle zum Network Environment for Multimedia Objects*. In Schroeder, U (Ed.) Workshop-Proceedings der Tagung Mensch & Computer 2010: Interaktive Kulturen. Berlin: Logos Verlag. 177-178.
Winkler T., Ide M., Herczeg M. (2010). *Teaching Teachers to Teach with Body and Space related Technologies: Programmable Clothing in Performative Teaching Processes*. In Cleborne D. Maddux, David Gibson, B D (Ed.) Research Highlights in Technology and Teacher Education 2010. AACE. 221-228.
Winkler T., Ide M., Herczeg M. (2009). *Connecting Second Life and Real Life: Integrating Mixed-Reality-Technology into Teacher Education*. In R., W, Mc. Ferrin, K, Carlsen, R & Willis, D A (Eds.) Proceedings of SITE 2009. Chesapeake, VA: AACE. 1141-1148.
Winkler T., Ide-Schöning, M., Herczeg M. (2008). *Mobile Co-operative Game-based Learning with Moles: Time Travelers in Medieval Ages*. In McFerrin, K, R., W, Carlsen, R & Willis, D A (Eds.) Proceedings of SITE 2008. Chesapeak, VA: AACE. 3441-3449.

Parents' Influence on Adolescent Children's Media-multitasking Attitudes and Behaviors

Lin Lin, Ed.D.
University of North Texas, U.S.A.
Lin.Lin@unt.edu

Kim Nimon, Ph.D.
University of North Texas, U.S.A.
Kim.Nimon@unt.edu

David Bonner, Ph.D.
University of North Texas, U.S.A.
DMBonner@umhb.edu

Abstract: This study examined mothers' influence on their adolescent (10-14 years old) children's media multitasking attitudes and behaviors. Data analysis was based on 109 mother-adolescent pairs. The paired participants took three surveys including the Media Multitasking Self Efficacy (MMSE), Media Multitasking Attitude (MMA), and Media Multitasking Index (MMI) in addition to demographics. Results showed that the adolescents had more favorable attitudes and active behaviors towards media multitasking than their mothers. This is especially true in attitudes. Additionally, there was a positive relationship in attitudes towards media multitasking between adolescents and their mothers. However, there were no relationships in self efficacy or activities towards media multitasking between adolescents and their mothers. Gender-wise, the girls had more favorable attitudes and active behaviors than boys, but the boys seemed to have a slightly better self efficacy than the girls towards media multitasking. Results from this study offer significant implications for parenting, teaching and learning.

Introduction

We see our students do this all the time: texting or talking on the phone while walking or biking on campus, listening to the lecture in the classroom while chatting with their friends on Facebook, or studying while watching television. When asked how they accomplish what they are supposed to be doing, the typical response is some version of "I multitask!" Media multitasking has captured the attention of both popular media and scholar communities in recent years. Kaiser Family Foundation reported that young people pack a total of 10.45 hours' worth of content into 7.38 hours of media use daily (Rideout, Foehr, and Roberts, 2010). While some scholars are excited about the possible new cognitive and social skills, others are concerned about the lack of focus, attention, or self-regulation related to multitasking.

The propensity our high-school and college-aged students have for juggling multiple lines of input, thought, and response has no doubt been met with skepticism by those who want to see greater focus applied to the most important tasks at hand (Carr, 2010; Jackson, 2008). If our students are wavering in their attention and missing important information while studying, most would agree this presents a potential problem. The purpose of this study was to look into factors that might be connected or even be facilitating young people's attitudes and behaviors towards media multitasking. Specifically, we wanted to investigate parents' influence on their adolescent children's media multitasking attitudes and behaviors.

Media Multitasking Abilities and Generation Differences

One difficult task in research is to determine human beings' capacity for multitasking. Research on aspects of multitasking such as dual tasking, task switching, and sequential actions has revealed that people experience severe interference when tasks are performed simultaneously, and that multitaskers do not retain as much information as they would have, if they had focused on one task (Baddeley, Chincotta, & Adlam, 2001; Burgess, Veithc, De Lacy Costello & Shallice, 2000; Meyer & Kieras, 1997; Monsell, 2003; Poldrack & Foerde, 2007). Various studies also show that multitasking capacity depends on differences in gender, age, experience, cognitive load, tasks involved, automation, and expertise levels (Just et al., 2001; Lin, Robertson, & Lee, 2009; Sohn & Carlson, 2000; Spink & Park, 2005).

Some recent media studies argue that new media have changed the way we retain and process information (Gee, 2003; Prensky, 2001). The Internet, with its non-linear hyperlinks and multimedia, has changed our habits of searching and obtaining information (Lin, 2009). The computer offers many opportunities for media multitasking, both within itself and across other platforms (Foehr, 2006). Computer-based learning environments incorporate text, video, and pictures to load the learner's input channels in a complementary manner and enrich the learner's experiences (Clark & Mayer, 2003). One of the benefits of multi-user virtual environments is the richness and complexity of the information they can display, creating something closer to a real-world environment (Dede, 2003; Dede, Ketelhut, & Reuss, 2003; Nelson, Ketelhut, Clarke, Bowman, & Dede, 2005), utilizing ill-defined learning outcomes and processes (Barab, Thomas, Dodge, Carteaux, & Tuzan, 2005; Jonassen, 1999), and requiring a complex set of interactions (Bruckman, 2000) to increase participant engagement and cognitive processing.

One of the concerns educators have had about these new technologies and technology-rich systems is the possibility that multimedia streams not directly supporting the material could have a distracting effect on the learner and actually impede the intended learning that relates to imbedded reading materials (Nelson & Erlandson, 2008). In a more traditional environment, educators are concerned about the distracting effects background television or discussions with friends via Email or Chat systems can have on a student while studying at home or at school (Jackson, 2008), including with the acceptance of lap-top computers in the classroom (Fried, 2008). This study was conducted in this context to help teachers and teacher educators better understand the complexity of students' learning environments.

Parents' Influences on Adolescents' Attitudes and Behaviors

Children's beliefs, emotions, cognitive abilities, and behaviors are affected by multiple influences at different developmental stages. These influences include inherited temperamental qualities, parental practices and personality, quality of schools attended, relationships with peers, ordinal position in the family, and the historical era in which late childhood and early adolescence are spent (Kagan, 1998). Each of these factors is most effective during particular age periods. Most developmental scientists believe that parental qualities contribute to children's attitudes and behaviors. Oskamp (1977) commented that "a child's attitudes are largely shaped by its own experience with the world, but this is usually accomplished by explicit teaching and implicit modeling of parental attitudes" (p. 126). Hardin and Higgins (1996) present considerable evidence demonstrating that individuals seek, achieve, and are guided by shared reality.

When it comes to media multitasking attitudes and behaviors, Foehr (2006) reported five characteristics contributing to predicting teenagers' media multitasking. They are "gender (with girls tending to multitask with various media more than boys), media exposure, the prominence of television in the household, computer ownership/placement and sensation-seeking personality traits" (Foehr, 2006, p. 9). Since children's media habits are heavily shaped in home environments, it is important to examine the possible connection of media multitasking attitudes and behaviors between the children and their parents. In this study, we investigated media multitasking attitudes and behaviors of adolescents age 10-14 and of their parents. The following research questions guided our investigation:

1. What are media multitasking attitudes and behaviors of adolescents aged 10-14?
2. What are media multitasking attitudes and behaviors of parents of these adolescents?
3. Do parents and their adolescent children have similar attitudes and behaviors towards media multitasking?
4. What is the relationship between parents' and adolescents' media-multitasking attitudes and behaviors?
5. Do adolescent boys and girls aged 10 – 14 have different attitudes and behaviors towards media multitasking?
6. Is there a difference by gender in parents' attitudes and behaviors towards media multitasking?

METHODS AND DATA SOURCE

Procedure and Participants

Participants were recruited from a medical office in the U.S. The location was chosen because it was a logical place to find adolescents with their parents. The participants each signed consent forms and received a thank-you gift of $5 in cash for their participation. A total of 129 families participated in the study, including 118 mothers, 14 fathers, 93 boys, and 51 girls. In order to obtain a cohesive and reliable dataset, we excluded data from 14 families, where only the father completed the survey. Additionally, we excluded five other families based on outlying data. In the case where two or more adolescents of a family completed a survey, only one child was selected in the data. Mother-adolescent pairs with girls were selected when possible since there were fewer girl participants.

Because the data on fathers were removed, the final data analysis was based on 109 mother-adolescent pairs. Consequently, research question 6, which was to examine the difference by gender in parents' attitudes and behaviors, could not be answered in this current study. Across the 109 mother-adolescent pairs, 38% of the adolescents were female. On average mothers were 39 years old and the adolescents were 12 years old. Over half (58%) of the mothers were white, although all races were represented in the participant population. Over half of the mothers (62%) reported a household income below $50,000. Their education level was high, with 62% of the mothers reporting some college background.

Instruments

In addition to demographics, three surveys were filled out by both the mothers and their adolescent children. They were the Media Multitasking Self Efficacy survey (MMSE), the Media Multitasking Attitude (MMA) survey, and the Media Multitasking Index (MMI) survey.

MMSE. The MMSE survey was developed to measure perceptions of one's ability to multitask based on the self-efficacy literature (Bandura, 1986, 1997). The MMSE used five items modified from Jones' (1986) measure. Items were rated on a 7-point scale with 1 indicated strongly disagree and 7 strongly agree. One item was negatively worded and reverse coded, and it caused the MMSE to have poor reliability when tested with the adolescent population. For this reason, the MMSE employed in the remainder of the study consisted of the four positively worded items.

MMA. The MMA survey was adopted using the ten items from the affective subscale of the Computer Attitude Measure (Kay, 1993), a semantic differential instrument originally designed to measure teachers' attitudes towards computers (Kay, 1993; Miyashita & Knezek, 1992; Christensen & Knezek, 2002). The items were measured on a 7-point scale (*extremely, moderately, slightly,* neither, *slightly, moderately, extremely*).

MMI. The MMI was adopted from a recent seminal work by Ophir, Nass and Wagner (2009) and it was designed to measure media multitasking activities including time spent and media involved. The MMI addressed 12 different media forms: print media, television, computer-based video, music, non-music audio, video or computer games, telephone and mobile phone calls, instant messaging on a computer, SMS text messaging, email, web surfing, and other computer-based applications (such as word processing). For each medium, participants reported the total number of hours per week they spent using the medium. In addition, they filled out a media-multitasking matrix, indicating whether, while using this primary medium, they concurrently used each of the other media *Most of the time, Some of the time, A little of the time*, or *Never*. Numeric values were assigned to each of the matrix responses as follows "Most of the time" (= 1), "Some of the time" (= 0.67), "A little of the time" (= 0.33), and "Never" (= 0) (Ophir, Nass & Wagner, 2009). The responses were summed for each primary medium. This resulted in a measure of the mean number of other media used while using each primary medium. The MMI was created by computing a sum across primary media use weighted by the percentage of time spent with each primary medium to account for the different amounts of time spent with each medium. Thus, the index is an indication of the level of media-multitasking the participant is engaged in during a typical media-consumption hour. In the study conducted by Ophir, Nass and Wagner (2009), the MMI produced a relatively normal distribution, with a mean of 4.38 and standard deviation of 1.52. Media multitasking was correlated with total hours of media use, $r(260) = 0.46$, $P < 0.001$.

Analyses

To answer research questions 1 and 2, we computed descriptive statistics on each of the study's measures for the paired sample of adolescents (research question 1) and their mothers (research question 2). To answer research question 3, we conducted paired samples t-test on each of the study's measures. As a measure of practical significance, we computed d_c as defined by Dunlap, Cortina, Vaslow, and Burke (1996, p. 171). To answer research question 4, we conducted bi-variate correlation tests between adolescent and mother responses to each of the study's measure. To answer research question 5, we conducted independent samples t-tests on adolescent responses to each of the study's measures. We computed Cohen's (1988) *d* as a measure of practical significance.

RESULTS

Research questions 1 and 2 respectively considered the media multitasking attitudes and behaviors of adolescents and their mothers. Table 1 presents descriptive statistics on each of the study's measures for mothers and their adolescents. On average, both adolescents and mothers reported more positive attitudes and activities towards media multitasking.

Table 1
Mean (Standard Deviation) of adolescent and mother responses to study measures

	MMSE	MMA	MMI
Adolescent	5.29 (1.40)	5.26 (1.36)	5.36 (3.09)
Mother	5.07 (1.40)	4.67 (1.39)	5.00 (3.09)

Note. αs for adolescent responses to the MMSE and MMA = .933 and .859, respectively.
αs for mother responses to the MMSE and MMA =.960 and .924 respectively.

Research question 3 considered whether mothers and their adolescents had similar attitudes and behaviors toward media multitasking. Across the study's measures, adolescents reported more positive attitudes and behaviors than their mothers. For MMA, the mean difference between mother and adolescent responses was statistically and practically significant (t_c = 3.703, $p < .001$, d_c = .424). In contrast, the mean difference between mother and adolescent responses was not statistically or practically different for the MMSE (t_c = 1.195, $p = .235$, d_c = .153) or the MMI (t_c = .905, $p = .367$, d_c = .121).

Research question 4 considered whether there was a relationship between mothers' and their adolescents' media-multitasking attitudes and behaviors. Correlations demonstrated varying levels of relationships between mother and adolescent responses to the study's measures. The amount of shared variance between mother and adolescent responses to the MMA was statistically and practically significant ($p < .001$, $r = .571$, $r^2 = 32.60\%$). There was no statistically or practically significant relationship between mother and adolescent responses to the MMSE measure ($p = .128$, $r = .150$, $r^2 = 2.25\%$) or the MMI ($p = .294$, $r = .106$, $r^2 = 1.12\%$).

Research question 5 considered whether adolescent boys and girls had similar attitudes and behaviors toward media multitasking. Table 2 presents descriptive statistics on adolescents' response to each of the study's measures by gender. There was a practically significant difference between gender on responses to the MMI (t = -1.774, $p < .079$, d = -.371). Although not statistically significant, boys scored lower on the MMI than girls. No statistically or practically significant difference was found between gender on MMSE ($t = .242$, $p = .809$, $d = .049$) or the MMA ($t = -.601$, $p = .549$, $d_c = -.120$).

Table 2
Mean (Standard Deviation) of adolescent responses to study measures by gender

Group	MMSE	MMA	MMI
Male	5.29 (1.43)	5.16 (1.54)	4.91 (3.09)
Female	5.21 (1.46)	5.33 (1.28)	6.03 (2.95)

Note. αs for male responses to the MMSE and MMA = .946 and .855, respectively.
αs for female responses to the MMSE and MMA = .883 and .871, respectively.

Limitation of the Study

This study was conducted at a pediatrician's office because it was a natural place to find adolescents and their parents together. However, doing so might have created a bias because the families visiting a specific pediatrician's office might be more homogenous than diverse with their social economic status. Over half (58%) of the mothers were white, 62% of the mothers reported a household income below $50,000, and 62% of the mothers reported some college background. The study was further limited by the lack of father participants. Consequently, we were not able to answer one of the original questions. The third limitation was that the study depended on self report of attitudes and behaviors, and that only quantitative data were collected. As a result, we were not able to answer questions that would look more deeply into the how, when, and why of the issues. Future studies need to be conducted to address these issues.

Discussion and Scholarly Significance

The study showed that in general, adolescents (10-14 years old) had more favorable attitudes and active behaviors towards media multitasking than their mothers. This is especially true in attitudes. Additionally, there was a positive relationship in attitudes towards media multitasking between adolescents and their mothers. However, there were no relationships in self efficacy or activities towards media multitasking between adolescents and their mothers. Gender-wise, the girls had more favorable attitudes and active behaviors than boys, but the boys seemed to have a slightly better self efficacy than the girls towards media multitasking.

Some of these findings supported past research. For instance, according to Oskamp (1977), children's attitudes are influenced by their physical environments and parental attitudes. In this study, the adolescents' attitudes towards media multitasking appeared to be influenced by the technological world they live in and by their mothers' attitudes. Foehr (2006) reported that girls tend to multitask more than boys. Our study showed similar results. However, this study also left us with more questions. The fact that the adolescents did not exhibit significantly better self efficacy or more activities than their mothers towards media multitasking seemed to contradict to some literature that the younger generations are multitasking more or better than older generations (Prensky, 2001).

Obviously, more studies are necessary to understand media multitasking attitudes and behaviors of adolescents. As computers and mobile technologies are increasingly integrated into the school classrooms and curricula, teachers and teacher educators need new information on how to take advantage of new technologies while still keeping students on track of their learning goals. It is important for teachers and teacher educators to understand the context, limitations, and recent research on media multitasking among their students. Such studies will help provide insights to ensure that they develop healthily and intellectually. Results from this study offer significant implications for parenting, teaching and learning.

References

Baddeley, A., Chincotta, D., & Adlam, A. (2001). Working memory and the control of action: evidence from task switching. *Journal of Experimental Psychology: General, 130*(4), 641-657.

Bandura, A. (1986). *Social foundations of thought and action: A social cognitive theory.* NJ: Prentice-Hall / Englewood Cliffs.
Bandura, A. (1997). Self-efficacy: The exercise of control. NY: W. H. Freeman.
Barab, S. A., Thomas, M., Dodge, T., Carteaux, R., & Tuzan, H. (2005). Making learning fun: Quest Atlantis, a game without guns. *Educational Technology, Research, and Development,* 53(1): pp. 86-108.
Bruckman, A. (2000). *Uneven achievement in a constructivist learning environment.* Paper presented at the International Conference on Learning Sciences, Ann Arbor, MI.
Burgess, P. W., Veithc, E., De Lacy Costello, A., & Shallice, T. (2000). The cognitive and neuroanatomical correlates of multitasking. *Neurosychologia, 38*(6), 848-863.
Carr, N. (2010). *The Shallows: What the Internet Is Doing to Our Brains.* NYC: W.W. Norton & Company.
Christensen, R., & Knezek, G. (2002). Instruments for Assessing the Impact of Technology in Education. In Assessment/Evaluation in Educational Information Technology, *Computers in the Schools, 18*(2/3/4), 5-25.
Clark, R. C.; Mayer, R. E. (2003). *E-learning and the science of instruction: Proven guidelines for consumers and designers of multimedia learning.* San Francisco: Pfeiffer.
Cohen, J. (1988). *Statistical power analysis for the behavioral sciences* (2nd ed.). Hillsdale, NJ: Erlbaum.
Dede, C. (2003). Multi-user virtual environments. *Educause Review, 38*(3): pp. 60-61.
Dede, C., Ketelhut, D. J., & Reuss, K. (2003). *Motivation, usability, and learning outcomes in a prototype museum-based multi-user virtual environment.* Paper presented at the 5th Int'l Conference of the Learning Sciences.
Dunlap, W. P., Cortina, J. M., Vaslow, J. B., & Burke, M. J. (1996). Meta-analysis of experiments with matched groups or repeated measures. *Psychological Methods, 1,* 170-177.
Foehr, U. G. (2006). *Media multitasking among American youth: Prevalence, predictors and pairings.* Washington, D.C.: The Henry J. Kaiser Family Foundation.
Fried, C. B. (2008). In-class laptop use and its effects on student learning. *Computers & Education,* 50: pp. 906-914.
Gee, J. P. (2003). *What video games have to teach us about learning and literacy.* New York: Palgrave Macmillan.
Hardin, C. D., & Higgins, E. T. (1996). Shared reality: How social verification makes the subjective objective. In R. M. Sorrentino & E. T. Higgins (Eds.), *Handbook of motivation and cognition: Vol. 3. The interpersonal context.* pp. 28–84. New York: Guilford Press.
Kagan, J. (1998). *Three seductive ideas.* Cambridge, MA: Harvard University press.
Kay, R. H. (1993). An exploration of theoretical and practical foundations for assessing attitudes toward computers: The computer attitude measure (CAM). *Computers in Human Behavior, 9,* 371-386.
Jackson, M. (2008). *Distracted: The erosion of attention and the coming dark age.* Amherst, NY: Prometheus Bks.
Jonassen, D. H. (1999). Designing constructivist learning environments. In Reigelugh (Ed.), *Instructional design theories and models: A new paradigm of instructional theory (Vol. 2):* pp. 217-239. Mahwah: Lawrence Erlbaum Associates, Inc.
Jones, G. R. (1986). Socialization tactics, self-efficacy, and newcomers adjustments to organizations. *Academy of Management Journal, 29,* 262–279.
Just, M., et al. (2001). Interdependence of non-overlapping cortical systems in dual cognitive tasks. *Neuroimage, 14,* 417-426
Lin, L. (2009). Breadth-biased versus focused cognitive control in media multitasking behaviors. *Proceedings of the National Academy of Sciences USA* 106: 15521-15522.
Lin, L., Robertson, T., & Lee, J. (2009). Reading performances between novices and experts in different media multitasking environments. *Computers in the Schools, 26:* 3, 169-186.
Meyer, D. E. & Kieras, D. E. (1997). A computational theory of executive cognitive processes and multiple-task performance: Part 1. Basic mechanisms. *Psychological Review, 104,* 3-65.
Miyashita, K., & Knezek, G. A. (1992). The Young Adolescent's Computer Inventory: A Likert scale for assessing attitudes related to computers in instruction. *Journal of Computing in Adolescenthood Education, 3*(1), 63-72.
Monsell, S. (2003). Task switching. *Trends in Cognitive Neuroscience, 7*(3), 134-140.
Nelson, B., & Erlandson, B. E. (2008). Managing cognitive load in educational multi-user virtual environments: reflection on design practice. *Educational Technology, Research, and Development,* Dec. 2008, 56: pp. 619-641.
Nelson, B., Ketelhut, D., Clarke, J., Bowman, C., & Dede, C. (2005). Design-based research strategies for developing a scientific inquiry curriculum in a multi-user virtual environment. *Educational Technology,* 45(1): pp. 21-27.
Ophir, E., Nass, C. I., & Wagner, A. D. (2009). Cognitive control in media multitaskers, *Proceedings of National Academy of Sciences USA* 106:15583–15587.
Oskamp, S. (1977). *Attitudes and opinions.* NJ: Prentice-Hall/Englewood Cliffs.
Poldrack, R. A., & Foerde, K. (2007). Category learning and the memory systems debate. *Neuroscience and Biobehavioral Reviews, 32,* 197-205.
Prensky, M. (2001). *Digital game-based learning.* The McGraw-Hill Companies.
Rideout, V.J., Foehr, U. G., and Roberts, D. F. (2010). *Generation M2 Media in the lives of 8 to 18 year-olds.* Menlo Park, CA: Kaiser Family Foundation.
Sohn, M. H., & Carlson, R. A. (2000). Effects of repetition and foreknowledge in task-set reconfiguration. *Journal of Experimental Psychology: Learning, Memory, and Cognition, 26*(6), 1445-1460.
Spink, A., & Park, M. (2005). Information and non-information multitasking interplay. *Journal of Documentation, 61*(4), 548-554.

Examining the Impact of the Professional Development Model for International Educators on Greek Teachers

Debra R Sprague
dspragu1@gmu.edu

Anastasia Kitsantas
akitsant@gmu.edu

Beverly Shaklee
bshaklee@gmu.edu

Maria Katradis
mkatradi@gmu.edu

George Mason University
USA

Abstract: This paper examined the long-term effects of the Professional Development Model for International Educators (PDMIE). The PDMIE encompasses an academic program, field experiences in diverse secondary schools, cultural exchanges and trips to provide the international educators with a vast array of tools, technologies, and perspectives for introducing and sustaining innovative educational practices upon their return to their home country. Nineteen Greek educators were invited to participate in the project. The professional development program lasted for eight weeks. It was hypothesized that the educators would become engaged in innovative teaching practices such as integrating technology, show higher levels of self-efficacy, and develop pedagogical knowledge, It was also expected that these positive effects will be sustained overtime. Overall these hypotheses were supported.

Introduction

There is increasing research evidence demonstrating that technology integration is largely reliant on the attitudes and beliefs of teachers (Kitsantas, Sprague, Shaklee, 2011; Dunn and Rakes, 2010; Lee & Tsai, 2010; Teo, 2009). Dunn and Rakes (2010), using Bandura's (1986, 1997) social cognitive theory, investigated the influence of teachers' learner-centered beliefs and teacher efficacy on consequence concerns. They found that learner-centered teachers' with greater self-efficacy demonstrated a greater degree of interest on the impact of technology on students' learning. Teo (2009) found that computer technology and attitudes towards computer use is directly related to intentions to use technology in the classroom.

The long-term effect of professional development programs on teachers' self-efficacy and their ability to integrate technology has been explored within the literature (Pearson & Smart, 2011; Watson, 2006). Watson examined the long-term impact of the West Virginia K-12 RuralNet Project, an NSF-funded professional development program designed to help inservice teachers integrate the Internet into the Science and Mathematics curriculum. Teachers completed a survey six years after participating in the project. Watson found that teachers' self-efficacy remained high years later.

Pearson and Smart (2011) followed-up with a group of international educators who participated in a six week intercultural program in the United States (U. S.), one year after their departure to return to their home countries. They found that approximately one-third of the participants are incorporating instructional strategies learned in the U.S. and expressed confidence or high confidence with using technology. However, it should be noted that only nine of the 27 teachers in the Pearson and Smart study completed the online follow-up survey.

Professional Development Model for International Educators (PDMIE)

The creation of our professional development model for international educators (PDMIE) was inspired by a growing consensus concerning how to best support teachers' learning from various international organizations and institutions around the world. Further, it was important that the design of the program also reflect the core values of the College of Education and Human Development (CEHD): innovation, research-based practice, social justice, collaboration and ethical leadership. The model encompassed an academic program, field experience in diverse K-12 schools, cultural exchanges and trips to provide the international educators with a vast array of ideas, tools, technologies, and perspectives for introducing and sustaining innovative educational practices upon their return to their home country.

Founded upon the CEHD's core values, the PDMIE offers international educators opportunities to gain new perspectives, develop advanced skills and enhance their repertoire in new pedagogies. See Figure 1 for the PDMIE. The goals of the PDMIE include: exchanging cross-cultural knowledge and understanding, cultivating effective teaching practices for international and multicultural settings, fostering technology integration in teaching and learning, and developing self-reflective teaching practices.

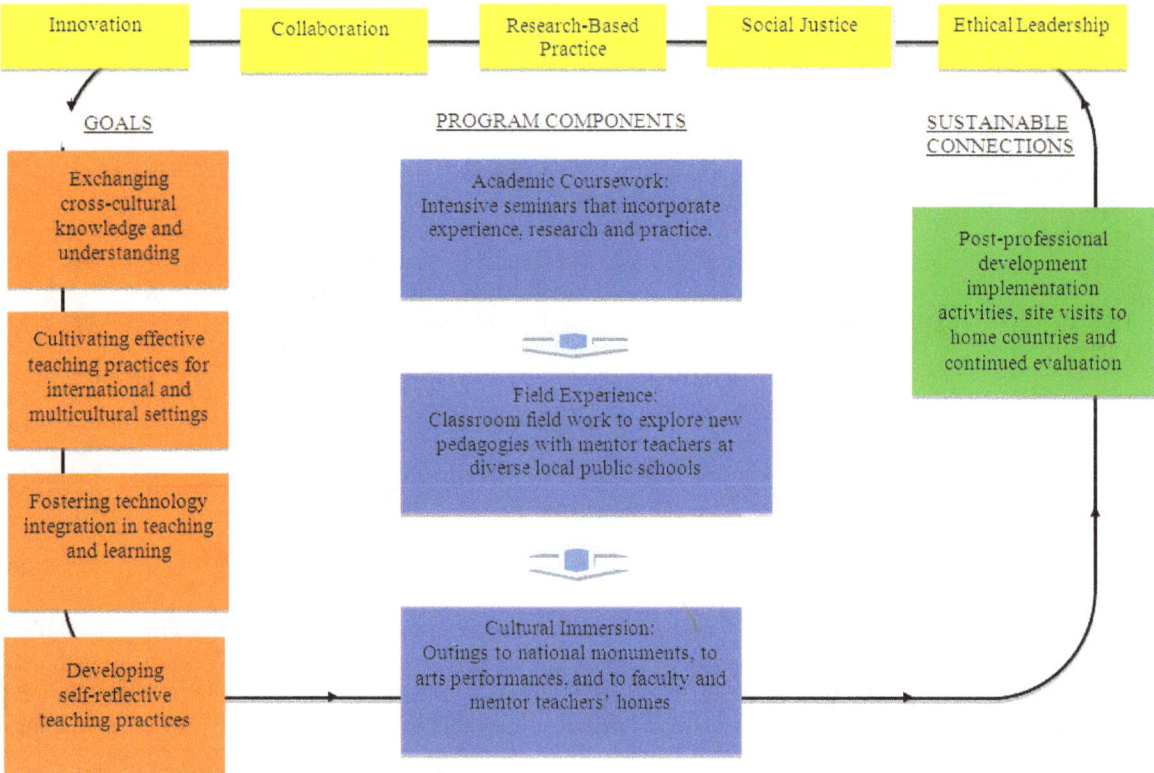

Figure 1. Professional Development Model for International Educators

Kitsantas, et. al. (2011) examined the impact of the Professional Development Model for International Educators Model (PDMIE) on Greek teachers' integration of technology in the classroom. They found that PDMIE had a positive impact on teachers' self-efficacy and knowledge of technology. The teachers in the study not only developed the confidence to use technology, but also the ability to use the technology to support student learning.

The Study

This study examined the long-term effect of the PDMIE on Greek teachers' self-efficacy towards integrating technology in their classrooms, knowledge of teaching and technology, and perspectives about technology and education. Using the PDMIE, the teachers had completed an eight week professional development and cultural exchange project in the US. While in the United States, the participants attended professional development courses at the university, which focused on using technology, teacher reflection, differentiation and assessment, and multiculturalism in the classroom, for a total of 150.5 academic hours. Participants were matched with master host teachers, in one of two local high schools, who taught the same subject they did. Participants completed 56 hours of field experience with their master host teacher.

Upon returning to Greece, the teachers remained in contact with each other and with the PDMIE instructors through e-mail and *Facebook*. Seven months after returning to Greece the teachers and PDMIE instructors met for a two-day follow-up workshop. During the workshop, follow-up surveys were administered to the 19 teachers.

Participants

Nineteen in-service secondary education teachers of the humanities (12 women, 7 men, *M*age = 32.3, age range: 27-40 years) participated in the project. Participants were all Greek citizens (100%) whose primary language was Greek (100%). Participants at the time of the program had at least a Bachelors Degree. Participants' highest earned degrees: 15.7% Bachelor's, 78.9% Master's, 5.2% Doctorate. The humanities in Greece are defined as any subject in school except Mathematics and the Sciences. Participants' subjects ranged from Ancient and Modern Greek to English as a Foreign Language to Music.

Data Collection Instruments

Several instruments were used for the follow-up that included: Survey of Preservice Teachers' Knowledge of Teaching and Technology (PTKTT, adapted from Schmidt et al., 2009), a seven subscale survey assessing teachers' level of self-efficacy regarding technology measured on a five-point Likert scale ranging from 1 (Strongly Disagree) to 5 (Strongly Agree). The seven subscales include: Technology Knowledge (α = .86); Pedagogical Knowledge (α =.87); Pedagogical Content Knowledge (α =.87); Technological Pedagogical Knowledge (α =.93); Technological Content Knowledge (α =.86); and Technological and Pedagogical Content Knowledge (α =.89).

Online Technologies Self-Efficacy Scale (OTSES; Miltiadou & Yu, 2000) assessed participants' self-efficacy beliefs (self-efficacy refers to the degree to which an individual believes he/she can perform a task under specified conditions) and competency in using various online communication technologies. The scale was administered as a four-point Likert scale ranging from 4 (Very Confident) to 1 (Not Confident At All) with 29 (α = .95) items divided into four subscales: Internet Competencies, Synchronous Interactions, Asynchronous Interactions I, and Asynchronous Interactions II.

Technological and Pedagogy Content Knowledge – Web Survey (TPACK, Lee & Tsai, 2010) examines teachers' self-efficacy of technological pedagogy content knowledge with regards to the Web and to assess their attitudes towards online teaching and learning using a 6-point Likert Scale: 1 (Strongly Unconfident) through 6 (Strongly Confident). This survey includes six subscales which include: Web-general seven items (α = .94); Web-communicative four items (α = .94); Web-Pedagogical-Content Knowledge eight items (α =.95); and Attitudes toward Web-based instruction six items (α = .92).

Technology Integration Scale assesses participants' level of technology integration, dissemination of learning, and perceptions of barriers to integrating technology upon completing the intervention and returning to their home country. This instrument included three subscales, all which were measured on a 1 (do not agree at all) to 5 (definitely agree) Likert scale. The first subscale was Technology Integration, which included eight items. Two questions included short answer responses which were: "Provide a list (if possible) of the types of curriculum goals that technology would most likely be able to achieve:" and "Provide a list (if possible) of the types of curriculum goals that technology *would not* be able to achieve:" An example Likert scale response item was: "Technology can be used to support student group work." The reliability for this subscale was .78. The second subscale was Dissemination of Learning, which included six questions. An example question is, "I will be able to train my colleagues on how to use specific software." Three questions also had follow-up responses, for example: "Please state the types of software you will be able to train your colleagues on:" The reliability for this subscale was .96. The third and final subscale was Barriers to Integrating Technologies. This subscale included nine questions (e.g., "My students do not have sufficient access to technology at their homes".). The reliability for this subscale was .41.

Results

Repeated measures ANOVAs were run to investigate the differences between pre, post, and follow up scores. In terms of the OTSES and TPACK, no significant time differences emerged. In terms of the PTKTT, however, a significant time effect was detected Wilks' Lambda, .018, $F(12,3) = 13.88$, $p = .03$. Univariate statistics revealed that significant differences exist for all of the individual subscales: Technology Knowledge ($p = .03$), Pedagogical Knowledge ($p < .001$), Pedagogical Content Knowledge ($p = .02$), Technological Content Knowledge ($p = .04$), Technological Pedagogical Knowledge ($p < .001$), and Technological and Pedagogical Content Knowledge ($p < .001$). Paired samples t-tests were conducted to investigate the direction of the findings. The results showed that all of the subscales under Teachers Knowledge of Teaching and Technology had changed between pre to post scores and the pre to follow up scores. There were no changes from post to follow up scores, suggesting that teacher efficacy and technology changes from pre to post were maintained at follow up. Specifically, Technology Knowledge ($p = .01$; $p = .005$), Pedagogical Knowledge ($p = .001$; $p < .001$), Pedagogical Content Knowledge ($p = .005$; $p = .05$), Technological Content Knowledge ($p = .02$ $p = .04$), Technological Pedagogical Knowledge ($p < .001$; $p < .001$), and Technological and Pedagogical Content Knowledge ($p < .001$; $p < .001$) all increased from pre to post as well as pre to follow up, respectively. Please see Table 2 for the means and standard deviations of the PTKTT as well as the changes from pre to post and post to follow up.

Table 1: Survey Means and Standard Deviations

	Pre		Post		Follow-Up	
	M	(SD)	M	(SD)	M	(SD)
Online Technologies Self-Efficacy Scale						
Internet Competencies	3.84	(.29)	3.97	(.09)	3.96	(.10)
Synchronous Interaction	3.68	(.76)	3.85	(.31)	3.93	(.20)
Asynchronous Interaction I	3.87	(.27)	3.96	(.08)	3.99	(.04)
Asynchronous Interaction II	3.58	(1.00)	3.77	(.48)	3.84	(.33)
Technological and Pedagogy Content Knowledge						
Web General	4.86	(.32)	4.72	(.97)	4.61	(.82)
Web Communicative	4.35	(1.08)	4.65	(.78)	4.66	(.98)
Web Content Knowledge	4.54	(.67)	4.56	(.99)	4.55	(.99)
Web Pedagogical Content Knowledge	3.71	(1.34)	4.31	(.95)	4.50	(1.03)
Attitude toward web-based instruction	4.82	(.32)	4.86	(.26)	4.73	(.96)

Table 2: Teachers Knowledge of Teaching and Technology

	Pre		Post		Follow Up	
	M	(SD)	M	(SD)	M	(SD)
Technology Knowledge	3.42	(.89)	3.73	(.96)	3.91	(.76)
Pedagogical Knowledge	3.80	(.50)	4.20	(.47)	4.25	(.45)
Pedagogical Content Knowledge	3.80	(.68)	4.35	(.48)	4.27	(.70)
Technological Content Knowledge	3.63	(1.01)	4.20	(.77)	4.22	(.65)
Technological Pedagogical Knowledge	3.41	(.94)	4.26	(.63)	4.41	(.50)
Technology Pedagogy and Content Knowledge	3.50	(.59)	4.25	(.77)	4.27	(.59)

In terms of the technology integration survey responses collected at follow-up, the results showed that participants perceived that technology integration was important in their teaching efforts ($M = 4.76$, $SD = .35$) and reported high levels of information dissemination ($M = 4.49$, $SD = .76$). In contrast, participants generally reported low levels of barrier perceptions ($M = 2.38$, $SD = .45$).

Table 3: Technology Integration

	Follow-up	
	M	(SD)
Technology Integration	4.76	(.35)
Dissemination of Learning	4.49	(.76)
Barriers to Integrating Technology	2.38	(.45)

The Technology Integration Scale included open-ended questions. These were analyzed by looking at frequency of responses in order to determine if there was consistency in the responses.

The first question asked participants to provide a list of the types of curriculum goals that technology would most likely be able to achieve. Seventeen participants responded to this question, the majority with multiple responses. Table 4 provides the frequency of responses.

Table 4: Curriculum Goals Technology Can Help to Achieve

Response	Number of Responses
Critical Thinking/Learning How to Learn	11
Differentiation	8
Collaboration	7
Learner Autonomy	5
Multicultural Understanding	4
Literacy Skills (Reading/Writing/Digital)	4
Active Learning/Engagement	3
Global Access	2

The second open-ended question asked the participants to provide a list of the types of curriculum goals that technology would not be able to achieve. Sixteen teachers responded to this question. However, five of these 16 indicated they felt there were no curriculum goals that technology would not meet. In other words, they felt technology was appropriate for all of their curriculum goals, if integrated appropriately. Table 5 provides the frequency of responses.

Table 5: Curriculum Goals Technology Cannot Help to Achieve

Responses	Number of Responses
None, all goals can be met	5
Social Skills, Face to face interaction	2
Experiential Learning	2
Close Reading, Grammatical Structure	2

Participants were asked to provide a list of the types of ideas they felt they could share with their colleagues. Seventeen participants responded to this question. Although many listed specific technologies (i. e. digital stories, wikis, blogs, video editing), others addressed technology integration and strategies for differentiation. Table 6 provides a frequency of responses to this question.

Table 6: Type of Ideas Able to Share with Colleagues

Responses	Number of Responses
Integration of Technology in the Classroom	9
Differentiation of Instruction	5
WebQuests	5
Digital Stories	4
Blogs	3
Rubrics	2
Video	2

Participants were asked to list barriers that they thought would prevent them from effectively integrating technology in their school or class. Seventeen participants responded to this question. Of these, four indicated they did not have any barriers to integrating technology. Table 7 provides the frequency of responses for this question.

Table 7: Barriers to Technology Integration

Responses	Number of Responses
Lack of Access (computers, Internet, software, technical support)	8
Colleagues' Resistance to Technology	5
No Barriers	4
Lack of Teaching Time/Preparation time	4
Structure of the Educational System (exam focused)	2

Discussion

The results of the study indicate that the PDMIE had a lasting effect on the Greek teachers. These effects went deeper than technology knowledge and self-efficacy. The biggest gains made from pre to post were in the area of pedagogy (see Web Pedagogical Content Knowledge, Pedagogical Knowledge, and Technological Pedagogical Knowledge). The Greek teachers experienced new ways of teaching through their university seminars and through their field experiences in the U.S. classrooms. For some of the teachers, they were exposed to student-centered activities for the first time. Throughout the project, they wrestled with how best to teach their students. Despite their concerns they were willing to try some of the strategies they saw once they returned to Greece. As a result, the gains made in pedagogy were maintained during the follow-up surveys.

Another interesting finding is the four teachers who indicated there were no barriers to integrating technology within their context. These four teachers were technology users prior to participating in this project (this was not the case for all of the teachers). These four were also teaching in more affluent parts of Greece and had access to technology that other teachers did not. Although this explains their level of comfort with technology, it does not address the other barriers identified by their colleagues. A follow-up needs to be done with these four teachers to explore deeper why they do not perceive the structure of the educational system or their colleagues' resistance to technology to be barriers to implementation.

Classified as *Progressive Innovators* (Amanatidis, 2011), these teachers present a positive stance on technology pedagogy, flexibility and collaboration with others. A number of the teachers have continued their collaboration with colleagues from this professional development program by co-authoring papers and presenting their work within Greece. Several of the teachers are also interested in furthering their education and have applied to the PhD. Program at the university where this project took place.

Although we cannot predict the final outcome of PDMIE, the seeds of change have been planted in Greece and the 19 teachers who participated in the project are having a lasting impact on the system. These 19 teachers expressed receptiveness to change their teaching practice and to consider alternative ways to integrate technology. As a result other teachers and K-12 students in Greece are benefiting from their experiences.

Limitations of the Study

This study examines the effectiveness of PDMIE on a sample size of 19 Greek teachers. The results of this study are limited to the contexts and experiences of this sample population. Repeated implementation would indicate whether the results are specific to this cohort or provide greater generalizable knowledge. The data is self-reported by the teacher participants which creates a potential validity threat. In-class teacher observations in their local contexts would provide greater data and a possible hands-on opportunity to address the teachers' concerns about implementing their learned knowledge in their teaching. Finally, a needs analysis may be conducted to directly assess the individual participants' abilities throughout the implementation of the program.

Lessons Learned

Based on the results of this study and our experience, the following lessons are provided for those interested in creating international professional development projects:

- Pre-program orientation, preferably within the home country, should be conducted by the faculty implementing the project. Because we were unable to do the pre-program orientation, the participants received inaccurate information, which led to confusion and concerns. Conducting the pre-program orientation enables participants to understand the goals and various components of the project and the expectations of the faculty and program director. It also enables the faculty to learn more about the participants and to tailor the program to their needs.

- The quality of the school-based field experience coupled with the expertise of the master teachers in the classroom was instrumental in the success of this program. Hosting schools and teachers extended multiple opportunities for learning and participation. This led to the development of joint understanding between themselves and the international group.

- Instructors and participants in this project continued to communicate and share information upon return to the home country. This ongoing support enabled the teachers to implement strategies in their own context and extended their learning.

References

Amanatidis, N. (2011). INSET (in service training) of Greek primary school teachers in the acquisition and promotion of pedagogic practices and competences in the use of ICT (information and communications technology) in-classroom teaching. In T. Bastiaens & M. Ebner (Eds.), *Proceedings of World Conference on Educational Multimedia, Hypermedia and Telecommunications 2011* (pp. 3257-3262). Chesapeake, VA: AACE.

Bandura, A. (1986). *Social foundations of thought and action: A social cognitive theory.* Englewood Cliffs, NJ: Prentice-Hall.

Bandura, A. (1997). *Self-efficacy: The exercise of control.* New York: W. H. Freeman and Company.

Dunn, K. E. and Rakes, G. C. (2010). Learner-centeredness and teacher efficacy: Predicting teachers' consequence concerns regarding the use of technology in the classroom. *Journal of Technology and Teacher Education, 18*(1), 57-83.

Kitsantas, A., Sprague, D., Shaklee, B. (2011). Exploring the impact of a professional development model on teacher efficacy toward technology integration. In Pyrini, N. (Ed.) *Readings in Technology Proceedings of ICICTE 2011.* Rhodes, Greece

Lee, M. H., & Tsai, C. C. (2010). Exploring teachers' perceived self efficacy and technological pedagogical content knowledge with respect to educational use of the World Wide Web. *Instructional Science, 38*, 1-21.

Miltiadou, M., & Yu, C. H. (2000, October). Validation of the online technologies self-efficacy survey (OTSES). Paper presented at the Association for Educational Communications and Technology (AECT) International Convention, Denver CO.

Pearson, D. & Smart, K. (2011). International educators professional development: A one year follow up study. In M. Koehler & P. Mishra (Eds.), *Proceedings of Society for Information Technology & Teacher Education International Conference 2011*, 2897-2901. Chesapeake, VA: AACE.

Schmidt, D. A., Baran, E., Thompson, A. D., Koehler, M. J., Mishra, P., & Shin, T. (2009-10). Technological Pedagogical Content Knowledge (TPACK): The Development and Validation of an Assessment Instrument for Preservice Teachers. *Journal of Research on Technology in Education,* 42(2), 123-149.

Teo, T. (2009). Modeling technology acceptance in education: A study of pre-service teachers. *Computers & Education, 52*(2), 302-312.

Watson, G. (2006). Technology professional development: Long-term effects on teacher self-efficacy. *Journal of Technology and Teacher Education, 14*(1), 151-166.

Acknowledgements

This project is funded by the Bureau of Educational and Cultural Affairs of the United States (U.S.) Department of State, Award #S-ECAAS-08-CA-204 (55). The ideas reflected represent those of the authors and are not endorsed by the U.S. Department of State. The authors would like to recognize the contributions of Drs. Rebecca Fox and Anastasia Samaras and Ms. Jessica Turner for their invaluable support of the Greek Teacher Professional Development program. Our work would not have been possible without their active involvement.

Interactive white boards: Is it worth it? Use in Four Western PA K-12 Schools

Yehuda Peled
Western Galilee and Ohalo Colleges, Israel
ypeled@macam.ac.il

Mandy Medvin
Westminster College, PA, USA
medvinm@westminster.edu

Linda Domanski
Westminster College, PA, USA
domanslp@westminster.edu

Abstract: This research examines teacher attitudes and fears about interactive whiteboard (IWB) use as related to perceived classroom implementation to enhance student engagement and achievement. The research took place in four western PA school districts. Nearly 78 percent of all teachers surveyed reported using the IWB either "Often" or "All the time" and 75 percent of them reported using an IWB for two or more years. These combined data suggest that the districts in this study are investing in IWB technology and the majority of teachers are using IWBs on a regular basis for instruction. Number of years and frequency the IWB technology was used in the classroom was strongly related to levels of training and support the teachers believed they received, teachers' sense of self-efficacy and the perceived value of IWB technology as a useful tool, and teachers' perceptions about the positive effect that integrating IWBs had on student achievement.

Introduction

Over the last five years, school districts across the country have been acquiring and implementing Interactive Whiteboards (IWB) and other technological tools through grants, stimulus funding, state initiatives, and by directly designating district monies for innovative instructional resources. The districts in this sample are thought to be a representative sample of many typical school districts nationwide with respect to location, numbers of teachers, levels of education, and the recent introduction of IWBs for instructional purposes.

Although there is a growing body of research related to the use of IWBs, evidence regarding the effects of IWBs on student achievement is limited. This study will describe teacher attitudes toward the use of IWBs and begin to examine how teachers implement the technology to enhance student engagement and achievement. The survey was administered to K-12 teachers and administrators of four western PA school districts, each in varying phases of IWB implementation; it was used to explore teacher attitudes regarding the use of the IWB as a pedagogical tool and its perceived influence on teaching and learning.

IWBs are large, touch-sensitive boards, which control a computer connected to a digital projector. They were originally developed for office settings (Higgins, Beauchamp & Miller, 2007) and are a relatively new technology to education. Most conclusions from literature reviews reported the following benefits of IWBs: supports ease of integration of ICT in classroom teaching; offers flexibility and saves time because a wide range of web-based resources can be applied; allows reuse of adapted and customized content; makes teaching more stimulating for the teacher partly because of the availability of source materials; facilitates addressing diversity; learners show more task-oriented behavior; contributes to the (eventual) reduction of workload because materials can be easily shared; encourages and assists lesson preparation; allows replay of events and reviews of processes; inspires teachers to change their teaching methods and facilitates the adoption of other ICT applications (Beauchamp & Parkinson, 2005; Koenraad, 2008). In addition, IWB use affords students additional opportunities to participate and cooperate; lessons are viewed as being attractive, clear, efficient and dynamic presentations which in turn promote learner engagement and motivation; enables learners to be more creative when making presentations for fellow students and thus promotes their self-confidence (Beauchamp & Parkinson, 2005; Koenraad, 2008). Disadvantages reported include the cost factor and matters of a more technical nature. The literature review reveals a clear preference for IWB use by both teachers and pupils (Higgins et al., 2007; Smith, Higgins, Wall, & Miller, 2005). Higgins et al. (2007) conclude their review by stating that the use of the IWBs may be the most significant change in the classroom learning environment in the past decade and the relationship between multi-modal pedagogy, multi-modal technologies and gesture as part of our communications armory is an emerging and increasingly investigated area of research into teaching and learning.

Over the last three years, IWBs have been installed in an increasing number of classrooms in western Pennsylvania. Administrators have supported the use of this technology and educators have begun to incorporate this technological tool into daily instruction. Many teachers find IWB-use motivating because it can provide easy access to digital materials to enrich their lessons (Balanskat, Blamier, & Kefala, 2006; Zadelhoff, 2007). Yet teachers may vary in their ease of implementation and comfort level with use. The current study examines teacher attitudes and fears about white board learning and use as related to perceived classroom implementation to enhance student engagement and achievement.

The theoretical frame work for this research is based on two areas of research: (1) The TPACK model which attempts to identify the nature of knowledge required by teachers for technology integration in their teaching, while addressing the complex, multifaceted and situated nature of teacher knowledge (Mishra & Koehler, 2006). It is "a way of thinking" about the knowledge teachers need to understand to integrate technology, pedagogy and content effectively together into their classrooms (Koehler & Mishra, 2008), and (2) the role of schools as environments that encourage the teachers' professional growth (Demertzi, Bagakis & Georgiadou, 2009; Kelceoglu, 2008). The success of innovative approaches to education in general and of utilizing technology in classrooms in particular, is heavily dependent on the school's environment and organization, and on the principal's attitude towards the proposed change (Varma, Husic & Linn, 2008). The principal is increasingly expected to take a lead role in supporting teachers to adopt technology-based innovations that support learning and instruction (Bowyer, Gerard & Marx, 2008) for his or her school.

Principals set up their priorities and preferences within their daily workload based on a personal vision, building needs, or district-wide long term strategic plans and goals (Foster, Loving & Shumate, 2000). There are varying definitions for administrative styles (Hunter-Boykin & Evans, 1995) and for change leading (Foster et al., 2000). The most successful systemic reform efforts succeed where the local organization either invents or assumes ownership of the core ideas in the reform (Honey & McMillan-Culp, 2000). In these reforms, principals often set goals and directions rather than receive them from a higher authority.

A school that has successfully integrated computers and information technology into its learning environment can be characterized by (1) an educational approach that was decided upon by all the teachers (Solomon, 2000; Yuen, Law & Wong, 2003), (2) intense pervasive support for conducting changes from the school's administration, and most importantly, (3) the technology is incorporated into the pedagogical approach rather than the educational framework subverting itself to the technology (Solomon, 2000). When incorporating information technology into the educational framework, the school's characteristics reflect those of its principal (Wiggins, 1970).

Research Questions

(1) What are teachers' perceptions of IWB training and support as related to perceived value of IWB use in the classroom? (2) How do teachers' attitudes influence perception of student achievement through the use of IWB as a teaching tool? (3) Does training and support influence teacher IWB anxiety? (4) What aspects of TPACK influence teacher perceptions of student achievement? (5) How are administrative attitudes reflective of teacher perceptions?

METHODS

Participants

Four local K-12 public schools in western Pennsylvania participated in this study of IWB use. Schools were selected that (a) had an administrator willing to participate and (b) were in varying stages of IWB implementation based on prior interviews with a study co-author who was a technology specialist. Over 400 educators were employed in the districts surveyed and a total of 130 teachers voluntarily responded to the online surveys made available over a two week period in March of 2011. In terms of education level, 46.2% of respondents had a bachelor's degree, 53% had a masters' degree, and .8% had a Ph.D. For grades taught, 43% of respondents taught in grades K-6th, and 57% of respondent worked with students in grades 7th-12th.

Response rates from each school varied, and were as follows: school 1 = 76, school 2 = 27, school 3 = 20, and school 4 = 7. Schools with low response rates indicated that only teachers who were using the technology responded. Teachers from two schools did not provide information on gender; therefore, we did not do any analyses regarding that variable.

Responses were combined to provide an overview of IWB use across schools. Key administrators and technology leaders were subsequently interviewed to obtain information about each district's strategic plans for technology acquisition and integration into their curriculum, and their responses were summarized.

Measures

A search of the literature indicated that few teacher surveys were available to evaluate teacher perceptions of IWB use in the schools for teaching and the impact on student achievement. Therefore, in this study we either modified surveys that focused on computer use or created our own measures based on theoretical or review papers in the literature. Chronbach's alpha was used to calculate reliability, and many of these scales were based on other instruments with already demonstrated validity. All items on the surveys were reviewed by professionals familiar with IWB use in schools, and pilot testing with student teachers was done to ensure that the wording of the surveys was clear.

Five scales were included in the on-line survey: (1) teacher attitudes towards support and training (based on Solomon, 2000, alpha = .76, 9 items, "I feel that the administration is supportive of my work in using the IWB for teaching"), (2) teacher self-efficacy concerning IWB use (based on Gibson & Dembo, 1984; Kellenberger,1996; alpha = .75, 9 items, "I would be able to help a student having difficulty on the IWB"), (3) perceived value to the teacher (based on Kellenberger, 1996; alpha = .88, 13 items, "Time spent preparing lessons for use on the IWB is an efficient use of my time"), and (4) impact on student achievement (based on information from Kennewell, Tanner, Jones & Beauchamp, 2008; Koenraad, 2008; alpha = .86, 10 items, "My students learn better when using the IWB"). These items were answered on a likert scale of 1 to 5 (1 = *strongly disagree*, 5 = *strongly agree*). Several items were reverse scored to prevent automatic responding (e.g., "I do not think that IWBs are a valuable addition to the classroom"). In addition, a fifth scale measuring teacher IWB anxiety was modified from a computer anxiety survey developed by Bradley and Russell (1997). The IWB anxiety measure used a different likert scale (1 = *doesn't concern me at all*, 5 = *extreme concern*) to evaluate statements about things that could go wrong (alpha = .93, 12 items, "Getting stuck and not knowing what to do" and "Breaking the IWB or associated materials"). Demographic questions also addressed teacher gender, grade(s) taught, education, length of time using the IWB (1 = *less than a year*, 6 = *greater than five years*), and frequency of use in the classroom (1 = *never*, 5 = *all the time*).

Findings

Based on a review of current literature, the initial predictions of the study included premises that: (1) teachers who have used the IWB longer and more frequently would report higher levels of training and support; (2) teachers who have used the IWB longer and with a higher frequency would report a greater sense of self-efficacy for using IWB technology, value its use, report higher levels of student achievement, and have lower anxiety about using IWB technology; (3) teachers who report higher levels of training and support would also report higher self-efficacy, perceived value, higher student achievement, and lower levels of anxiety regarding IWB use; (4) teachers who exhibit higher self-efficacy would value IWB use more and have lower levels of anxiety about the technology. We also explored which aspects of training and support influenced IWB anxiety and teacher perceptions of student achievement.

Part I: Characteristics of Sample

The entire sample was examined with respect to length of time and frequency using IWBs and level of teacher education. An investigation of the "length of use" responses indicated that nearly 75 percent of the teachers reported using an IWB for a period of from two to greater than five years. Similarly, even though there were a range of responses for the query "How frequently have you been using and IWB?" responses indicated that nearly 78 percent of the teachers reported using the IWB either "*Often*" or "*All the time*". These combined data suggest that the schools included in this study are investing in IWB technology and that the majority of teachers are using the tool on a regular basis for instruction.

School districts in Western Pennsylvania have been integrating IWB technology into their classrooms over the last five years. Districts have been acquiring this technology through funded grants, stimulus funding, state technology initiatives, and by directly designating district monies for innovative technology resources. In examining the "length of time" measure more closely, responses confirmed that IWBs have been phased into use; the overall length of time the highest percentage of teachers reported using IWBs varied among the four school districts from less than a year to just over 1 year in one district to between 2 and 3 years in two other districts, and between three to five years in another district. On the whole, however, the highest percentage of teachers in most school districts report having used IWBs for two or more years (see Tables 1 and 2 below).

Table 1: Length of time teacher report using the IWB.

N = 130	< 1 year	1 year	2 years	3 years	5 years	< 5 years
Frequency	20	12	26	39	16	17
Percent	15.4	9.2	20.0	30.0	12.3	13.1

Table 2: Frequency of use in the classroom

N = 129	Never	Rarely	Sometimes	Often	All the time
Frequency	6	3	20	42	58
Percent	4.5	2.2	14.9	31.3	43.3

Part II: Effects of Length of Use, Frequency of Use, And Teacher Education on Study Variables

A core focus of this study was to examine school factors that influenced the use of IWBs in the classroom. For length of use, our results found that the longer IWB technology was used in the classroom, the higher the levels of training and support the teachers believed they received, their sense of self-efficacy and the perceived value of IWB technology as a useful tool, and the better the teachers' perceptions about the positive effect that integrating IWB technology had on student achievement (see Tab. 3 below). It was also found that anxiety levels about using IWB technology decreased the longer teachers used IWBs; conversely, teachers who reported being anxious about using the technology used it less often.

Frequency of use was also related to the study variables in a similar pattern. The results showed that teachers who used IWB technology more frequently in their classrooms had higher levels of training and support, teacher self-efficacy, perceived value of IWB technology and beliefs about its positive impact on student achievement. Levels of teacher education were not related to the study variables.

Table 3: Correlations between length and frequency of use in classroom, teacher education, and study variables.

	Training and support	Teacher self-efficacy	Teacher perceived value	IWB anxiety	Student achievement
How long used in classroom	.31*** N = 130	.52*** N = 128	.38*** N = 128	-.38*** N = 128	.37*** N = 127
Frequency of use	.23** N = 129	.59*** N = 127	.43*** N = 127	-.36*** N = 127	.38*** N = 126
Teacher Education	-.09 N = 129	-.15 N = 128	-.05 N = 128	.12 N = 128	-.05 N = 127

*=.05, **=.01, ***=.001

Part III: Analyses of the Relationships Among Study Variables

Intercorrelations among our variables of interest, training and support, teacher self-efficacy and perceived value, student achievement and IWB anxiety revealed that most were statistically significantly related. These findings indicate that each of the variables we have identified clearly have an impact on how IWBs are used in the classroom, in support of the study predictions (see Tab. 4 below). The one exception is the relationship between student perceived achievement and IWB anxiety. At this stage of analysis, this particular finding may indicate that instruction takes place and students "learn" regardless of any anxiety a teacher may have about implementing IWB technology in his or her classroom. It is interesting that IWB anxiety was relatively low in this sample.

Table 4: Means, standard deviations, and intercorrelations among study factors.

	Training & support	Teacher self-efficacy	Teacher perceived value	IWB anxiety	Student achievement	Mean (SD)
Training and support	___	.48*** N = 128	.42*** N = 128	-.18* N = 128	.43*** N = 127	3.80 (.67)
Teacher self-efficacy	___	___	.71*** N = 128	-.42*** N = 128	.66*** N = 127	3.79 (.58)
Teacher perceived value	___	___	___	-.21* N = 128	.75*** N = 127	4.09 (.58)
IWB anxiety	___	___	___	___	-.15 N = 127	1.75 (.71)
Student achievement	___	___	___	___	___	3.69 (.62)

Note: Standard deviations are included in parentheses.
*=.05, **=.01, ***=.001

In order to further understand the role of teacher anxiety related to IWB use, and to understand how districts can reduce teacher anxiety, individual training and support items were examined in relationship to IWB anxiety. The two most important training and support items focused on technological aspects of training "I have not received enough training to use the IWB effectively in the classroom" ($r = -.32$, $p < .001$), and "The IWB is easy to set up and use" ($r = -.21$, $p < .05$). More specifically, teachers who believe their training and support were sufficient had lower levels of IWB anxiety. In turn, training and support was definitely a concern for those teachers who believed they did not have sufficient training and support to implement use of the IWB effectively in their classroom. Likewise, the easier the IWB is to set up and use, the lower the IWB anxiety. Interestingly, responses to open-ended questions included at the end of the survey gave credence to this finding – if a teacher perceived that the IWB was easy to set up and use, he or she had less anxiety about using it, while the converse is likely also true. Therefore, across all school districts, ensuring that there is sufficient mentoring and instruction for IWB use and simplifying the mechanics of using IWBS in the classroom should be part of any long range strategic technology plan.

A final question to be examined from the quantitative data is which aspects of training and support influenced teacher perceptions of improvement in student achievement. In examining items related to the technological aspects of the training and support scale, three were significantly correlated with student achievement, "Other teachers support me in learning the technical aspects of the IWB" ($r = .35$, $p < .001$), "I have access to the IWB in the classroom whenever I need it" ($r = .19$, $p < .05$), and "The IWB is easy to set up and use" ($r = .39$, $p < .001$). For pedagogical aspects, two items show positive correlations with student achievement, "Collaboration with other teachers is more meaningful when using the IWB than for traditional classroom activities" ($r = .24$, $p < .01$), and "Other teachers support me in using the pedagogical aspects of the IWB" ($r = .48$, $p < .001$). In addition, administrative support was also important "I feel that the administration is supportive of my work in using the IWB for teaching" ($r = .24$, $p < .01$). Clearly, teacher perceptions of both pedagogical and technological potentially influence student achievement, but administrative support is also valuable. Therefore, the second part of our study examines teacher-administrative investment via the TPACK model.

Summary of Findings

1. Teachers who perceived higher levels of school training and support had higher perceived IWB value, IWB self-efficacy, and perceptions of student achievement from using the IWB.
2. Higher levels of training and support, particularly the technological aspects, and higher teacher self-efficacy, and perceived value were related to lower levels of IWB anxiety.
3. Both pedagogical and technological aspects of training and support led to higher perceived student achievement.
4. IWB anxiety and perceptions of student achievement were not related.
5. The data collected revealed similar patterns in three of the four school districts. Nearly 78 percent of all teachers surveyed reported using the IWB either "Often" or "All the time" and 75 percent of them reported using an IWB for two or more years. These combined data suggest that the districts in this study are investing in IWB technology and the majority of teachers with access to IWBs on a regular basis for instruction.

Following the quantitative findings, we interviewed the school principals and superintendents of the school districts. The interviews were based on the data accumulated from the questionnaires.

Districts' Findings Related To Leadership and the TPACK Model

1. School #1 has invested heavily in the TPACK Model and designed their implementation program based on this framework over a 5+ year period which results in teachers' understanding of the pedagogical benefits of IWB use in their classrooms. School leadership spoke in one voice and transmitted a clear vision of having a 21st century learning environment accompanied by extensive technical and pedagogical support available for faculty members. As part of their contract, teachers agreed to participate in yearly technological professional development activities such as the *Lunch and Learn* one hour sessions and the two day *Summer Technology Academy* the district hosts every August. Teachers in this district also discussed their habits of regularly mentoring one another and sharing prepared IWB lessons within grade levels.
2. School #2 has bought into the TPACK Model and has been in the implementation phase for 3+ years. There is a clear focus on school's objectives in regard to IWB implementation as part of Technology integration and immersion

in teaching. As with School #1, the administration is aware of the TPACK Model and uses it as a philosophy for approaching technology integration; but it is doubtful that the teachers are aware of or could identify the TPACK Model as the basis for their use of similar best practices with technology.
3. School #3 is just beginning to implement technology integration in the high school, but lags behind in training opportunities, and has a limited number of IWBs in the elementary school. Knowledge of the TPACK Model was neither articulated during the interviews with administration nor by IT personnel.
4. School #4 subscribes to the TPACK philosophy and promotes best practices while actively working to diversify its approach by incorporating multiple technologies in varied ways to enhance instruction.

Discussion and Conclusion

The goal of this study was to examine IWB use across several school districts and identify those factors that enhance or impede classroom practices and student achievement. Our findings support our initial predictions for the most part, and demonstrate that higher levels of training and support for teachers by school districts affects teachers' perceived IWB self-efficacy, perceived value, and anxiety. Training and support, self-efficacy, and perceived value, in turn, lead to higher levels of teacher reported student achievement related to IWB use. Districts that continue to provide training for teachers should find that the educational benefits of IWB use in the classroom continue to increase over time, and that their investment in this technology is valuable. Even though the frequency of use varied from district to district, it was encouraging to discover that the technology is being well-used and the overall frequency of use is reasonably high. It is encouraging, though, that teacher IWB anxiety did not influence the teachers' perceptions of student achievement.

The teachers surveyed repeatedly mentioned that district leadership and support played an important role in making the shift to incorporate IWB technology into their daily instructional repertoires. Teacher attitudes and fears about using technology and its subsequent impact on learning are critical aspects to study in today's performance driven educational milieu.

Although most school administrators acknowledged that their long term technology strategic plan is based on the TPACK model, it seems that neither the *Technological Content Knowledge* (TCK) interaction nor the *Pedagogical Content Knowledge* (TPK) interaction is formally or intentionally addressed as part of the long term school technology integration plan. On the other hand, teachers reported that "Other teachers support me in using the pedagogical aspects of the IWB" which suggests a high level of IWB use for instruction, as the teachers found it necessary to address the TPK interaction of IWB use. In regard to the TCK interaction, there is no clear evidence whether it is given attention at the teachers' level. It is suggested that school administrators continue to encourage and support the practice of this TPACK element by enabling small teams of either discipline related or grade level teachers such as the science, math, and language teachers, to have regular common technology planning time to promote effective mentoring and increased use of IWBs for daily lessons. This practice would allow teachers to have an opportunity to discuss the merits of specific content and practice various ways to use the technology more effectively with like-minded colleagues to address each teacher's unique teaching challenges.

Currently, both in-service and pre-service teachers are being taught to use IWBs and other technology tools for instructional purposes. Since educators have all been wading into the waters of technology recently, it is probable that the findings generated by this study represent situations in other districts where teachers are just beginning their technological journeys or are well on their way and looking for new ideas to integrate IWBs into daily use. In light of these findings we intend to continue monitoring the above schools in order to see the impact over time on the immersion of IWBs in these schools.

References

Balanskat, A., Blamier, R., & Kefala, S. (2006). *The ICT impact report: A review of studies of ICT impact on schools in Europe*. (European Communities, European Schoolnet, Belgium). Retrieved Nov. 16, 2010 from http://insight.eun.org/shared/data/pdf/impact_study.pdf.:

Beauchamp, G., & Parkinson, J. (2005) Beyond the 'wow' factor: Developing interactivity with the interactive whiteboard. *School Science Review*, *86*(316), 97-103.

Bowyer, J., Gerard, L., & Marx, R. (2008). Building leadership for scaling science curriculum reform. In Y. Kali, M. C. Linn and J. E. Roseman (Eds.), *Designing coherent science education: Implications for curriculum, instruction, and policy* (pp. 123-152). New York: Teachers College Press).

Bradley, G., & Russell, G. (1997). Computer experience, school support and computer anxieties. *Educational Psychology*, *17*(3), 267-285.

Demertzi, V., Bagakis, G., & Georgiadou, S. (2009) School voices in leadership for learning within the Greek context, *International Journal of Leadership in Education*, *12*(3), 297-309.

Foster, E.S., Loving, C. C., & Shumate, A. (2000). Effective principals, effective professional development schools. *Teaching and Change*, *8*(1), 76-97.

Gibson, S., & Dembo, M. H. (1984). Teacher efficacy: A construct validation. *Journal of Educational Psychology*, *76*, 569-582.

Higgins, S., Beauchamp, G., & Miller, D. (2007). Reviewing the literature on interactive whiteboards. *Learning, Media and Technology*, *32*(3), 213–225.

Honey, M., & McMillan-Culp, K. (2000). Scale and localization: The challenge of implementing what works. In Honey M. and Shookhoff C. (Eds.), *The wingspread conference on technology's role in urban school reform: Achieving equity and quality* (pp. 41–46). Racine, WI: The Joyce Foundation, The Johnson Foundation, and the EDC Center for Children and Technology.

Hunter-Boykin, H. S., & Evans, V. (1995). The relationship between high school principals' leadership and teachers' morale. *Journal of Instructional Psychology*, *22*(2), 152-167.

Kelceoglu, I. (2008). Personal and institutional factors affecting first year elementary teachers use of technology. In K. McFerrin et al. (Eds.), *Proceedings of Society for Information Technology & Teacher Education International Conference 2008* (pp. 2064-2067). Chesapeake, VA: AACE. Retrieved Nov. 18, 2011 from http://www.editlib.org/p/27506.

Kellenberger, D. W. (1996). Preservice teachers' perceived computer self-efficacy based on achievement and value beliefs within a motivational framework. *Journal of Research on Computing in Education*, *29*(2), 124-140.

Kennewell, S., Tanner, H., Jones, S., & Beauchamp, G. (2008). Analyzing the use of interactive technology to implement interactive teaching. *Journal of Computer Assisted Learning*, *24*, 61-73.

Koehler, M. J., & Mishra, P. (2008). Introducing TPCK. AACTE Committee on Innovation and Technology (Ed.), *The handbook of technological pedagogical content knowledge (TPCK) for educators* (pp. 3-29). New York: Routledge.

Koenraad, A. L. M. (2008). *Interactive Whiteboards in educational practice: the research literature reviewed*. Retrieved November 12, 2010 from http://www.callinpractice.net/IWB/Research/overview-of-research-literature/at_download/file.

Mishra, P., & Koehler, M. J. (2006). Technological pedagogical content knowledge: A framework for integrating technology in teacher knowledge. *Teachers College Record*, *108*(6), 1017-1054.

Smith, H. J., Higgins, S., Wall, K., & Miller, J. (2005). Interactive whiteboards: boon or bandwagon? A critical review of the literature. *Journal of Computer Assisted Learning*, *21*, 91–101.

Solomon, G. (2000). *Technology and education in the age of information*. Haifa: Zemora-Bitan.

Varma, K., Husic, F., & Linn, M. C. (2008). Targeted support for using technology-enhanced science inquiry modules. *Journal of Science Education and Technology*, *17*(4), 341-356.

Wiggins, T. W. (1970, March). *Conceptualizing principal behavior in the school climate: A systems analysis*. Paper presented at the American Educational Research Association Annual Meeting, Minneapolis, MN. (ERIC Document Reproduction Service No. ED041387)

Yuen A. H. K., Law N., & Wong K. C. (2003). ICT implementation and school leadership: Case studies of ICT integration in teaching and learning. *Journal of Educational Administration*, *41*(2), 158-170.

Zadelhoff, T., van (2007). *InformatiewijzerDigitaleSchoolborden. Kennisnet / ICT op School*. Retrieved November 16, 2010 from http://www.kennisnet.nl/cpb/po/praktijkinbeeld/bestanden/infowijzer-digitale-schoolborden.pdf (In Dutch).

Issues in the Transformation of Teaching with Technology

Shelley Goldman
sgoldman@stanford.edu

Robert Lucas
Stanford University
United States
robert.lucas@gmail.com

Abstract: The study gave voice to teachers' thoughts about teaching and learning in the 21st century. Teachers were interviewed about how they used classroom technologies, the demands and pressures they faced, and how they addressed calls for 21st century skills. A semi-structured protocol was used to interview 25 teachers from 11 states and four international sites. Using open coding and a constant comparative method, the teachers' most significant issues, accomplishments, and thoughts were identified. Almost every teacher felt pressured to cover standards and prepare students for tests, and they saw those demands as a higher priority than engaging in 21st century teaching and learning. They used a variety of technologies but generally had not transformed their teaching with them. The TTT teachers expressed a hope for teacher education and professional development that would point them to the future with technology and new kinds of learning.

Introduction

Today's students will be called to participate in a society where problems are increasingly complex and technological change becomes ever more rapid. Leaders in business, science, and technology—even the U.S. President—argue that such a world demands enhanced skills of innovation, communication, and collaboration. Our education system must focus on developing these capacities, and technology represents not only an important tool for doing so but an integral aspect of how these skills will be practiced in the 21st century.

While many are addressing these new goals, one organization, the Partnership for 21st Century Skills (P21), has developed a particularly influential educational agenda. P21 contends that the central economic competitiveness issue is to create an aligned, 21st century public education system that prepares students, workers and citizens for the future. The organization defines a set of interconnected skills that must be integrated into K-12 education for it to address these imperatives. They include: creativity and innovation; communication and collaboration; critical thinking; digital citizenship; and information, media and technology skills (2008).

The overall goal of the *Teaching for Tomorrow Today* study (TTT) was to give voice to teachers about how they define, think about, and work to bring 21st century learning to their students. We interviewed the teachers about the demands they face on a daily basis and about how those demands interact with notions such as 21st century skills and classroom technology use.[1]

The TTT study reveals that teachers have heard and understood these imperatives. However, when they must decide between teaching 21st century skills and responding to the standards-and-accountability systems so pervasive in schools, accountability takes precedence. Almost every teacher we interviewed felt pressure to cover standards and "prepare students for tests." Even so, they found the 21st century skills arguments compelling. Many, especially those in public schools, attend to these new learning goals while meeting current demands even when test-based accountability is high and resources are low. Overall, the teachers reported handling existing demands, pressures, and traditions for teaching and learning in their schools while also trying to open up new opportunities for students. The TTT teachers expressed a hope for teacher education opportunities that would point them to the future with technology and new kinds of teaching and learning.

The Study

The interview study utilized a semi-structured interview protocol. All of the teachers answered the same questions and were prompted to elaborate on their responses. Most of the interviews lasted between 60 and 80 minutes, giving teachers time to explain their thoughts and give plenty of examples. The interviews were conducted using Skype and audio recording, making possible a geographically diverse sample. Several teachers added thoughts by email following their interviews. 25 teachers from 11 states in the US and four international sites participated. They ranged from first-year teachers to one who was in his 42nd and final year of teaching. On average, the teachers had 14 years of classroom experience. Six teachers were in preschools and elementary schools, 11 taught in the middle grades, seven were high school teachers, and one taught both middle and high school. All subjects were represented, including English and language arts, science, math, history and economics, art, choir, English language development, special education, and technology.

Data Analyses

Analyses of the interviews proceeded through several phases. After transcription, two coding processes helped to begin theory building. The first was an open coding process for each interview where the research team identified topics, ideas, opinions, and teachers' stories. This process generated 400 topic codes. Then co-occurrence of codes for each teacher and across all teachers was tracked. Those re-occurring and co-occurring codes generated categories and aided in the search for patterns, structures, and defining ideas. One section of the interview consisted of 20 statements about technology and education, which interviewees evaluated and then commented on. Coding of their responses resulted in running analysis metrics across the 25 teachers. Teachers' elaborations on these questions were also open coded. In the second analysis, the teachers' most significant issues, themes, and accomplishments were identified in each of the codes and categories. Significant themes were those that seemed common among the teachers, that were "outliers" or novel, or that emerged from an absence of expected responses. The research team asked, "What could these responses mean?" Once all of the explanatory possibilities were checked, a category or instance might have been designated as a theme—an interpretation based on comparing data. These analyses made it possible to characterize the most significant messages from teachers in terms of commonness or amplitude. Quotations and implications from the teachers' accumulated knowledge and practice are included to capture their wisdom of practice.

Findings

The findings are presented in three sections. In Part I, the results are organized by questions asked about technology beliefs. There is also discussion of the technologies the teachers currently use in their classrooms. In Part II, a sample of questions is provided and highlights about technology use are reviewed. In Part III, questions and findings relating to teachers experiences with and views of 21st century learning are reviewed.

Part I. Teachers on Technology

The researchers read 20 statements about technology, asking teachers for one of the following responses: "agree," "disagree," "some combination—both disagree and agree," or "no opinion." The belief statements were drawn from those used by Forsell in a survey of teachers (2011). Study teachers responded and then were asked to elaborate on their responses. Examples of the statements included: *Technology increases productivity*; *Working with technology makes people feel isolated from each other*; *All students should have an opportunity to learn to use technology at school*; and, *Students use technology in order to avoid doing more important schoolwork*. Since teachers answered the statements within a Likert-scale framework, the statements that received strong agreement or disagreement are presented quantitatively and qualitatively.

Where Teachers Agreed

The teachers were in widespread agreement with eight of the 20 statements. More than 75% agreed with the following assertions (listed from greatest agreement to least agreement):

Technologies provide different ways of accomplishing a given task. - 100% agreed

All students should have an opportunity to learn to use technology at school. – 96% agreed

> I agree 175 percent, and I think that given the state of the 21st century and the rapid development of technology, that it is a major...issue of equality that all students from all different demographics have access to technology so that they will be prepared for the jobs and skills of the 21st century.

> I especially agree on that because of the school I teach at, which is a rural school, and there are a lot of students there that don't have access to technology at home, and school's the only place where they learn to use computers and...do stuff online.

Technology helps students acquire new knowledge effectively – 96% agreed

> It's just amazing...how much information you could be exposed to in a day. With that comes a really big responsibility to be channeling what you're learning towards things that are valid.

Technology increases productivity – 91% agreed

Students should learn to use technology outside of school. – 86% agreed

> I agree with that when circumstances permit. I have worked with families who don't have technology in the home and who have gone the extra mile to go to the library to expose their children to types of technology. Also students are having a lot of informal interactions with technology at home with iPod Touches and cell phones and things like that. I think it puts the onus too much on the families in situations where that's not possible. Although it is something that we see even in low-income demographics, that they are having that type of experience.

Today's students learn better with technology. – 84% agreed

The use of technology increases student motivation for class – 80% agreed

> My middle school students were always so much more excited about an assignment if they were going to get to use the computer to either type it, or research it, or find pictures to illustrate it.... Putting a computer in their hands made it more exciting, period.

The use of technology makes a lesson more interesting – 76% agreed

> You can present stuff in ways that appeal to [students]. You can present stuff visually...It allows you more choices with how you present things...I can just do so many things really quickly that help the kids...get it more in a language that they understand.

Where Teachers Disagreed

A few other statements were roundly rejected—especially propositions about the negative effects of technology. More than three quarters of our interviewees disagreed with all of these statements:

Technology hinders creativity in students – 83% disagreed

> I think it probably heightens creativity. I think it makes it easier for kids to be creative…I don't think it hurts kids' creativity at all.

Technologies encourage students to be lazy. –76% disagreed

Several interviewees noted that while students may use technology while being lazy, technology is not the cause:

> It completely depends on the way the student uses it…If a kid was say more keen on playing videogames or watching TV rather than doing his other homework, which maybe wouldn't involve technology, I wouldn't say that technology is responsible. I would say it's probably the parents that let him sit on the computer and let him watch the TV instead of doing the homework.

Teachers saw school as a place where all children should learn with technology. A pattern of responses showed teachers' particular sensitivities towards issues of access and equity. They believe that technology learning in out-of-school settings is also important but recognize that there are great disparities in access. They see school as a necessary equalizer.

Teachers worried about when and how much to use technology. They also wanted to better understand how to harness it to help in their specific teaching contexts. They grappled with getting access to technology at schools. Many still share computers and equipment or must sign up in advance to take their students to a technology lab.

Teachers downplayed their technology fluency, and there was huge variation in how they portrayed their own use of technology. Even teachers who reported that they were not "big" technology users still used classroom technologies, especially with project work. Presentation software, Internet, and video are staples; Interactive White Boards (IWBs) are proliferating. Most teachers have computers, smart phones and other devices at home. Many are social networkers, and almost all engage the Web in support of their work.

Overall, the teachers grappled with finding the proper niches for technology in their classrooms. They enjoyed seeing technology motivate students to do important or deep work, but they also worried about the ways in which technologies can distract students and pull them away from the central ideas being taught.

Part II. Technology Use

After the belief statements, the interviews moved to a semi-structured format. Example technology questions included: *What technologies do you use regularly both at home and at school? What access to technology do you have in school? Can you give an example of some activity you have done with technology? What access do you think your students have at home?*

The most common response, by 18 interviewees, concerned use of a personal computer. This was noteworthy because prior research suggests that teachers who have personal computers are more likely to meaningfully integrate technology into their classroom practice (Forsell 2011, Wozney et al. 2006). In this sample, the most widely used technologies reflected notions of teaching as information delivery. Ten teachers mentioned their Interactive White Boards (IWBs), and an 11th was awaiting delivery. Six teachers used document cameras, and one technology coach hoped to purchase them school-wide. In use, these devices were depicted as the evolution of the overhead projector, minus the plastic transparencies. One teacher complained that half of the teachers at his school used IWBs "superficially," for tasks such as displaying school announcements. Another said that without proper training, IWBs became "glorified projectors." In addition to those teachers using IWBs and document cameras, five teachers told us that they have LCD projectors that display their computer screens.

Generally, the technologies represented traditional pedagogical models, with teachers delivering information to their students. Multimedia aids may enhance or supplement classroom lessons and lectures, but they generally have not transformed teaching and learning. Eight interviewees mentioned using PowerPoint or similar presentation software. Eight also talked about showing videos, often from YouTube. Several teachers mentioned that their IWBs go unused or are put to very traditional purposes.

Technologies may influence teacher practice, but they do not wholly determine it. Only a few teachers were taking on new uses that transformed their teaching. In one project, students created PowerPoint-style presentations and shared them in class. Another teacher described a student presentation with embedded YouTube videos. On the one hand, this work simply extended the didactic model, with students lecturing. On the other hand, it engaged the student more actively as producers of the learning content. One teacher described her school's experience with IWBs:

> When the school was set up, it was like this ultramodern green building, and we all have Smart Boards in our room, but, they had some 1950s person set up the rooms, so, all the desks were individual desks, and they were all in rows, and the teacher's desk was in the front of the room and then there was a stationary computer on that desk that was hooked into the outlets in the floor. So that's the only place you can use the computer from to project; so old fashioned. And so, many of us moved our desk away from the front of the room and use our chairs in all different kinds of configurations.

Although IWB technologies are designed to increase interactivity and to facilitate creative and collaborative approaches to learning, their use mostly reflected more traditional, teacher-led models of pedagogy. The counterexample of IWB use was in evidence as well. One teacher became dedicated to exploring IWB interactivity. She downloaded the IWB software onto student laptops, engaged students in designing their own "flipcharts," and then combined them into large, media- and content-rich presentations, teaching tools, activities and archives. She also regularly used the "voting" capabilities of IWBs to increase participation in problem solving and discourse during lessons.

Some technologies, such as media production tools, allow students to take a more active role in their own learning. These tools were mentioned infrequently. Four teachers mentioned blogs, which were generally used for communication within the class. One teacher used a blog for posting assignments and announcements, and three permitted students to post. Four mentioned video production, but in only one case did students edit. Four mentioned Skype, but always in reference to personal use.

Cell phones were mentioned frequently, by 14 different interviewees, but not generally in the context of student learning. Two reported using their phones to stay in touch with students and parents. Two iPhone users talked about using apps in class, such as "games . . . to reinforce a skill" or "a goal-setting app, for students where, if they meet a certain goal for a day, they can uncover a puzzle piece." One teacher told us, "The cell phone thing has been a battle. We initially had this policy [of] . . . 'We see your phone out; it'll be taken from you.'" But at his school, as phones become more versatile, attitudes have begun to change:

> If they're doing a science project … they can take photos with their own cell phone, even upload them to Flickr or to the class Website or the blog. But we're making slow progress getting teachers out of the mindset that this is gonna be a bad thing that the kids can have.

A half-decade after the excitement around MIT's One Laptop Per Child project, and nearly a decade after Maine's much-praised 1:1 laptop program, the vision is far from reality in this sample. Only two interviewees had anything approaching a 1:1 ratio. One of these had a classroom set of computers, and another's school bought laptops for students who could not afford them. The dominant configuration was far more traditional. Nine had one or a few computers in the classroom, 12 had to sign up for occasional computer lab use, and 11 had IWBs. iPads were a frequent topic of discussion, mentioned by five, although only two of those actually had them for classroom use. One teacher, whose school had an iPad set, gave a mixed report on their value.

When asked to imagine ideal scenarios, teachers saw technologies as consistent with project-based learning and 21st century skills. As a practical reality, however, the dominant mode of technology use is better depicted as an enhancement of teacher-led instruction. Some of the teachers made innovative, cooperative uses of limited tools, while most appropriated technologies in traditional ways. In Part III, the teachers' desires to provide more student-centered opportunities are considered. The results revealed a gap between how teachers would like to be teaching and the ways they actually teach with and without technology. Technology was a bit player for most in practice, yet it played a major supporting role in their visions of what teaching could be. Teachers imagined working with technologies to give students the power to actively produce and construct knowledge.

Part III. 21st Century Skills

There are increasing calls for 21st century learning in schools, and educators are attempting to translate these messages about educating for the future into real school change (Chen 2010, Trilling & Fadel 2009). In its mission statement, the Partnership for 21st Century Skills describes itself as an organization that prepares students for "a global economy that demands innovation" (2008). P21 stresses the continued importance of the traditional *Three Rs* (reading, writing and arithmetic), but adds to them a set of "learning and innovation skills" called the *Four Cs* (critical thinking and problem solving, communication, collaboration, and creativity and innovation). Using these P21 skill sets, we sought to determine whether and how the ideas of 21st century teaching and learning had penetrated the awareness of our interviewees. Examples of questions included: *Have you heard of 21st century skills? What do you think they are? Let's take the 4Cs one at a time. Are you working on any of these 4 Cs in your teaching? Can you describe how?*

The teachers were broadly familiar with the idea of 21st century skills. Only three said they had never heard the phrase. Of the rest, a handful (four to six) were aware of the idea but requested a definition (in which case, we read one from P21). The others were more confident in their understanding of 21st century skills. Said a teacher from an urban California school:

> Yes, I have heard of them, and I can explain to you what my perspective is. When I think of 21st century skills, I think of ways that we can prepare students to be ready for problems . . . we haven't experienced, and to solve these problems, to also work in fields and do jobs that don't exist. So I think of 21st century skills in two major domains, and I would think of those first as skills related to technology, things that my students will know more than I know now. . .

Teachers were asked to comment on the traditional *Three Rs* and to relate them to the *Four Cs* promoted by the P21 project. In general, teachers accepted the importance of the *Three Rs* but found them incomplete.

Not all teachers were addressing 21st century skills. One teacher reported being hard-pressed to raise standardized test scores that she teaches mostly basic skills:

> In our district, reading skills, writing skills, math skills are so low that in order to have them pass something, you directly teach to the tests. And I'm not saying it's the right way to go, but that's the only success that we've seen – kind of inundating with just the way the test is formatted and giving them feedback back and forth on the actual tests is where we've seen the most success – not that we've had great success. I'll be perfectly honest. I don't do an awful lot of critical thinking lessons, probably because I have such a difference in students in a given class.

Other teachers find certain 21st century skills less applicable to their grade levels or subject areas. For the most part, the *Four Cs* encompassed many of these teachers' broader concerns and gave them license to go beyond basics. There was near unanimity about the *Four C's* importance. Two teachers mentioned the importance of speaking in addition to writing. Teachers expressed frustration with their attempts to teach 21st century skills and occasionally spoke up for educational goals that were not included, but they never directly challenged the value of the *Four Cs* as educational goals.

As mentioned above, several teachers were concerned with helping students develop communication skills that go beyond formal writing. For some, that meant formal speaking skills—participating in seminar discussions or giving presentations to groups. Three spoke of navigating new media and communication platforms like Facebook, email, and texting. As an English teacher in Peru noted, "Kids—their world has a lot more images, and that's also a type of language". Teachers said it was important that students learn to consider the audience, platform, purpose, and levels of formality in both spoken and written work. The teachers repeatedly spoke about new technologies as providing opportunities to give and receive feedback, especially on publicly posted work. A high school English teacher described such a project:

> Rather than the traditional role of the student writing something and giving that to me, where I'm the only person that sees it, and I'm the only person giving them feedback—we post our writing to a network where it's viewable by everybody. And I've noticed that they put more effort into things that they write because they know people are reading it. And a lot of times, they'll kind of ratchet it up, make it more exciting than it would have been otherwise because they're careful with their titles, what they're gonna call something because they wanna grab people's attention and have people reading their work.

On a recent poster project, he allowed students to leave feedback for each other and concluded, "They were very respectful in the comments they left and brutally honest, way more honest than I could have been as a teacher." A middle school math teacher and technology specialist assigned students to create audio podcasts and post them so others could "sit and listen to them, and then provide feedback." The students then asked other teachers to do this kind of project. A high school English teacher spoke admiringly of a colleague's project in which students created a museum about Renaissance artists and musicians and then critiqued each other's work. These discussions about production and feedback with new technologies represented one of the more promising, concrete strategies to emerge in discussions about the *Four Cs*.

Obstacles to Implementation

Teachers generally supported the *Four Cs* as goals, but they identified a number of obstacles to implementation. Five identified conflicts between 21st century skills learning and mandates to address the standards and standardized tests, especially because of the focus on learning facts stressed by some of the tests.

Three interviewees identified teachers as part of the issue. One commented that teachers are accustomed to being in control of the classroom. Another stressed the lack of opportunities to collaborate, and at least a few mentioned a lack of technology skills. One teacher mentioned the idea that teachers think they must "know" what they teach and that educating towards the *Four Cs* brought uncertainty: "There's kind of a culture of fear. Teachers can be afraid of doing the wrong thing and looking stupid in front of their kids."

The teachers were grappling with the dilemmas of accountability—both to tests and to their students. Their philosophical stances and visions encompassed the idea of 21st century learning, but their efforts were limited by the demands placed on them by everyday school realities. There was still a great distance to be traveled for 21st century ideas to become a reality.

Summary and Discussion

How did the teachers think about educating students for the future? In what ways did their current practices align with their visions of what is needed? Many assumptions about education for the future go hand in hand with arguments for 21st century skills, project learning, and learning with—and transformed by—technology. Together, these represent a complex array of moving parts for schools to navigate. The group of teachers we interviewed led us to believe that technology may be one of the key levers. From their points of view, technologies are present and expected, and there is strong belief that schools need to play a major role in getting students access to learning with technology. Each of the teachers had their "go to" technologies, and projects especially enabled some highly interactive, student engaged, constructivist content and technology use. Still, most of the teachers were not using technology to transform their teaching or their students' learning. Gaps between technology beliefs and classroom practices had been identified previously (Judson 2006), and we see this as a continuing theme.

In *Rethinking Education in the Age of Technology*, Collins and Halverson observe that although the technological revolution has taken over the workplace and our lives at home, it has not yet transformed school learning (Collins & Halverson 2009). They offer suggestions for rethinking education in an age of radical change, suggesting technologies can help make these shifts. The New Media Consortium (2011) also predicts how technologies—such as social networking, games, mobile devices, Open Educational Resources, electronic texts and augmented reality—will drive learning into the future with demands for any-time, any-place, customized learning outside of the school and across the lifespan.

We learned that the 21st century arguments and the role of technology were not lost on the teachers, who found them extremely compelling and felt that schools were in need of change. Many were trying to organize 21st century learning experiences for their students while still meeting current commitments and demands. This was especially true for teachers working in public schools, where accountability demands are high and resources are in short supply. Teachers were attempting to open up student-centered learning opportunities by using projects, social networking tools and other technology, group work, and student production activities. The teachers had in mind learning experiences that stressed communication, creativity, problem solving and a bit of innovation. They were well aware that the future was bearing down on their students, yet their first priorities were to respond to immediate pressures to meet established standards.

Teachers seemed deeply rooted in the present, both in their minds and, more importantly, in their teaching practices. They were trying to do the best they could, given the constraints and demands of their situations. Furthermore, they were not asked, able, or equipped to think about what the needs of their students would be ten or twenty years from now. It was not in their purview to predict and teach to an uncertain future.

The teachers expressed the need for leadership and guidance in creating new visions, teaching practices, and learning spaces. They were aware of the distance they would need to travel. They wanted clear directives to be established with corresponding accountability demands and roadmaps to change. The gaps between technology access and use, changes in teaching and learning, and 21st century visions need to be closed. Teacher education is needed to support these new teaching and learning practices.

References

Chen, M. (2010). *Education nation: Six leading edges of innovation in our schools*. San Francisco, CA: Jossey-Bass.

Collins, A. & Halverson, R. (2009). *Rethinking education in the age of technology: The digital revolution and schooling in America*. New York: Teachers College Press.

Forsell, K.S. (2011). *Technological pedagogical content knowledge: Relationships to learning ecologies and social learning networks*. Stanford University. Unpublished Doctoral Dissertation.

Judson, E. (2006). How teachers integrate technology and their beliefs about learning: Is there a connection? *Journal of Technology and Teacher Education, 14*(3), 581-597. Retrieved from http://www.editlib.org/p/6046.

New Media Consortium. (2011). *2011 horizon report*. New Media Consortium.

Partnership for 21st Century Skills. (2008). 21st century skills, education & competitiveness: A resource and policy guide. Tucson, AZ: Partnership for 21st Century Skills. Retrieved from www.p21.org.

Trilling, B. & Fadel, C. (2009). *21st century skills: Learning for life in our times*. San Francisco, CA: Jossey-Bass.

Wozney, L., Venkatesh, V. & Abrami, P. (2006). Implementing computer technologies: Teachers' perceptions and practices. *Journal of Technology and Teacher Education, 14*(1), 173-207. Retrieved from http://www.editlib.org/p/5437.

Notes

1 The project was made possible by a grant from the Oracle Education Foundation.

A Study of the Effectiveness of Technology Integration Training on Student Achievement

Scott Elliot
selliot@segmeasurement.com

Cathy Mikulas
SEG Measurement
United States
cmikulas@segmeasurement.com

Abstract: The purpose of this study was to investigate the impact of online technology integration training for teachers on student achievement. We investigated the following question: Do students in classes whose teachers use online technology integration training achieve greater increases in Reading and Mathematics skills than a comparable group of students in classes whose teachers do not use online technology integration training? Additionally, the study explored the results by gender and ethnicity. Using a quasi-experimental, pre-post design, this study compared growth in Reading and Mathematics skills. The findings indicate that students in classes whose teachers used technology integration training show greater learning gains than students in classes whose teachers did not use the online technology integration training.

Background and Purpose

Improving students' academic skills remains a core goal of the schools. While debates rage regarding what constitutes appropriate school outcomes, growth in academic skills, particularly in the core content areas, remains a critical part of the educational mission. At the same time, the tools available to achieve this goal are changing—most notably, technology.

The students we see in the classroom today are "digital natives." They have grown up with technology around them rather than being forced to learn the technology later in life (Prensky, 2010). Technology is not just important to these students; it is an integral part of their lives. But, despite the ubiquity of technology in society as a whole and in students' daily lives, technology often remains at the periphery of the school. One often cited reason of this, is that teachers often lack the knowledge and skills to use technology effectively. Teachers not only need to understand how to use technology in their teaching, they need to understand how to help students use technology to help guide their own learning, both within and outside the classroom (Collins and Halverson, 2009).

Schools need the right tools for professional development to improve teachers' technology skills, teachers' ability to develop those skills in students, and teachers' integration of technology with students to facilitate learning. The single greatest impact on improved student achievement is increased teacher education (Borthwick and Pierson, 2008). The research is clear: students achieve more when taught by teachers who receive technology training. In a 1999 study reported by Schacter, students with teachers receiving any technology training during the past five years academically outperformed their peers whose teachers had not had any technology training during that period. Owen, Farsali, Knezak, and Christensen (2005) conducted a large-scale study of technology and student learning in Irving Texas. The conclusion? Students learn more, and report being more engaged, in schools that are actively engaged in professional development for teachers focused on technology use and the application of technology to new ways of teaching and learning.

Still, most of the 8 million U.S. teachers do not have the skills necessary to teach today's tech savvy students. One study suggests that fewer than 7% of schools have teachers who are technologically literate enough to effectively integrate technology into their lessons (Sparks, 2006). This 2006 study by Sparks also found that 36% of the schools provide no professional development for technology and another 29% provide only 1-14 hours a year.

The 2011 Horizon Report on the outlook for education technology confirms this picture. Digital literacy among teachers is identified as the number one challenge faced by education. "The challenge is due to the fact that despite the widespread agreement on its importance, training in digital literacy skills and techniques is rare in teacher education and school district professional development programs." "As teachers begin to realize that they are limiting their students by not helping them to develop and use digital media literacy skills across the curriculum, the lack of formal training is being offset through professional development or informal learning, but we are far from seeing digital media literacy as a norm."

Fortunately, professional development offers a solution to this lack of technology knowledge and mixed attitudes toward technology, regardless of the cause. Professional Development provides the basis for increasing teacher knowledge of technology, and expanding their repertoire of instructional practices (Killion and NSDC, 2002). There is an emerging consensus on what makes for successful professional development. For example, Harris' (2007) review of successful professional development programs suggests that professional development is most successful when it:
- is conducted in school settings,
- is linked to school-wide change efforts,
- is teacher planned and teacher assisted,
- provides differentiated learning opportunities for participants,
- is focused on teacher-chosen goals and activities,
- exhibits a pattern of demonstration/trial/feedback,
- is concrete,
- is ongoing over time, and
- provides for ongoing assistance and support.

The growing role of technology in education on the one hand, and the lack of teacher training in this important area on the other, is what gave rise to this research. This research study sought to investigate the impact of technology integration training for teachers on student academic growth. This study compares the academic achievement of students in classes whose teachers were provided with technology integration training to students in classes where teachers were not provided with this training.

Study Overview

During the 2010-2011 school year we evaluated the impact of teacher technology training on student achievement. Specifically, we compared the growth in academic skills of students in grades 6, 7 and 8 in classes whose teachers participated in online technology integration training (Treatment Group) to those in classes whose teachers did not participate in this training (Control Group). The study compared student academic growth in the Treatment and Control Groups between the beginning and end of the 2010-2011 school year.

We investigated the following two questions: 1). Do students in classes whose teachers participated in technology integration training show larger gains in Reading and Mathematics skills than a comparable group of students whose teachers did not participate in the training? 2). Do students of different gender and ethnic backgrounds differ in their Reading and Mathematics gains when their teachers participate in technology integration training?

Study Sample

Approximately 1,000 students in 42 classrooms in Minnesota, Missouri, and Texas participated in the study. Students enrolled in classes whose teachers participated in online technology integration training constituted the Treatment Group. Students enrolled in classes whose teachers did not participate in the training constituted the Control Group. There were approximately 629 students in the Treatment Group and approximately 240 students in the Control Group. The table (Tab. 1) shows the number of students in each gender, ethnic, and grade category. (The total number of students listed for each background variable may be different since some schools were unable to provide complete background information.

Variable	Number (N) of Students	Percentage of Students
GENDER		
Male	435	52%
Female	401	48%
Total (All Gender)	836	
ETHNICITY		
Caucasian	680	83%
African American	25	3%
Hispanic	59	7%
Asian/Pacific Islander	15	2%
Mixed Race and Other	45	6%
Total (All Ethnicity)	824	
GRADE		
Grade 6	166	19%
Grade 7	312	36%
Grade 8	390	45%
Total (All Grades)	868	

Table 1: Demographic Profile of Student Participants

Comparability of Study Groups. Student pretest scores were used to compare the initial Reading Comprehension and Mathematics levels for students in both the Treatment and Control Groups. The Treatment and Control Groups were comparable in ability. There were no statistically significant differences in the Means between the Treatment and Control groups for Reading Comprehension (T=-.55, df=1/855, p<.58) or Mathematics (T=-.10, df=1/837, p<.92). There were no statistically significant differences in the Standard Deviations (Variances) of the Treatment and Control Groups for Reading Comprehension (F=1.90, df=1/855, p<.17) or Mathematics (F=.14, df=1/837, p<.71).

Gender and Ethnicity. The number of female and male students in both the Treatment and Control were computed and compared. A statistical comparison of the two study groups shows that the Treatment Group and Control Group were comparable with respect to gender. There were no statistical differences in the expected and observed frequencies for gender (chi square =3.59 df=1, p<.06). The number of Caucasian and Non-Caucasian students in both the Treatment and Control were computed and compared. A statistical comparison of the two study groups shows that there was a statistically significant difference in the ethnic composition of the Treatment Group and Control Group (chi square =.13.14, df=1, p<.01). While there were statistical differences, there was still significant representation of both Caucasian and Non-Caucasian students in both the Treatment and Control Group.

Description of the Pretest and Posttest

The academic growth of students was operationalized as the gains in Reading Comprehension and Mathematics ability between pre and posttest. The students participating in the study were measured using the Reading Comprehension and Mathematics Stanford Achievement Test™, Tenth Edition (SAT 10), Abbreviated Battery, Form A, 2002. The SAT 10 was used as both the pretest and posttest measure; students took the SAT 10 in September or October 2010 at the beginning of the school year and then again at the end of May or in June 2011 at the end of the school year.

The reliability of the SAT 10 ranges from .89 to .97 (KR-20 reliability coefficient; Harcourt, 2002). Several validity studies conducted for the SAT 10 have found strong evidence for the validity of SAT 10 scores (SAT 10 Technical Manual, Harcourt, 2002).

Description of the Treatment

The Treatment in this study was teacher's use of technology integration training. Technology integration training is professional development services designed to assist teachers in integrating technology into their curriculum and instruction. Technology integration training includes learning the basics of using the technology and using the technology to support instruction. Moreover, technology integration training seeks to support teachers in integrating technology into classroom practice. The implementation of technology integration training for this study relied on the Atomic Learning Platform.

The Atomic Learning solution is an online tool providing a library of thousands of short, online video tutorials and curriculum examples showing successful integration of technology. Atomic Learning's 21st Century Skills Collection includes professional development resources and curriculum materials to empower educators to infuse 21st century skills into the classroom. The collection includes access to 21st Century Skills online training and resources, assessments with prescriptive training paths, classroom technology integration projects, technology workshops, and progress reports. The Technology Skills Collection consists of thousands of tutorials on more than two hundred software applications for both Macintosh and Windows platforms. The Atomic Learning platform is available through an annual subscription with unlimited use.

The teachers in this study were given access to the Atomic Learning platform and were encouraged to use the online training and materials for their instruction throughout the year. The teachers were not required to use the platform for a particular amount of time each week or to use specific materials. Instead, the teachers were able to use the platform as they determined would be most effective for their instruction. Teachers could select the workshops, tutorials, lesson plans, or projects for their use in their classroom instruction. This unconstrained use of the tool allowed for an authentic use of the platform as intended by its developers. Teachers could plan their own use and implementation of the information and materials available in the system throughout the school year, could seek help and support through the system, and could work at their own pace. Those teachers who confirmed use of the platform throughout the school year were included in the study.

Study Design

The goal of this study was to compare the growth in Reading and Mathematics skills between students whose teachers received online technology integration training and those students whose teachers did not participate in this training. Students' growth in Reading and Mathematics skills was measured by comparing their scores on the Stanford 10 pretest at the beginning of the study to their scores on the Stanford 10 posttest administered at the end of the study. The results were compared statistically using Analysis of Covariance (ANCOVA). The study employed a pre-post, Treatment-Control Group design. Since the students were not randomly assigned to the groups, this is considered a quasi-experimental design.

Data Collection

Teachers participating in the study were provided with the Stanford 10 pretest booklets and administration manuals in September 2010, and administered the pretests according to the administration instructions provided. In May, 2011, at the end of the school year, teachers administered the Stanford 10 posttest. The Stanford 10 pretest and posttest results were compared as a basis for evaluating the growth reported in this study.

Teachers also self-reported regarding their use of the platform throughout the school year. Those teachers who used the platform were included in the study. Sixty percent of the teachers used the platform for more than 10 distinct training sessions, workshops, or tutorials.

Findings

The overall growth in Reading Comprehension and Mathematics skills as measured by the Reading Comprehension and Mathematics subtests of the SAT 10 for those students in the Treatment Group was compared to the Reading Comprehension and Mathematics subtests of those students in the Control Group. Multivariate Analysis of Covariance (MANCOVA) was used to evaluate the difference in a composite Reading Comprehension and Mathematics skill score (dependent variable) between the Treatment and Control Groups (independent variable) controlling for the initial Reading and Mathematics levels of the students (covariate). The SAT 10 pretest scores were used as the covariate to place students in the Treatment Group and Control Group on the same baseline. The comparisons were based on 527 Treatment Group students and 208 Control Group students for whom both pretest measures and both posttest measures were available.

The results show a significant difference in a composite of the SAT 10 Reading Comprehension and Mathematics subtest posttest scores between the Treatment Group and the Control Group (df=2/730; F=12.01; p<.01) when initial Reading and Mathematics skills are controlled. The results, using Pillai's Trace, are summarized in the table (Tab. 2) below.

Effect		Value	F	Hypothesis df	Error df	Significance	Partial Eta Squared
Intercept	Pillai's Trace	.074	28.961	2	730	.01	.07
Reading Pretest	Pillai's Trace	.386	229.793	2	730	.01	.39
Mathematics Pretest	Pillai's Trace	.535	420.082	2	730	.01	.54
Study Group	Pillai's Trace	.032	12.011	2	730	.01	.03

Table 2: Multivariate Analysis of Covariance Comparison of Treatment and Control Group Reading Comprehension and Math Posttest Scores

To provide a more complete understanding of these results for the separate Reading and Mathematics skill areas, the individual effects were examined separately using ANCOVA (Tab. 3).

Source	Dependent Variable	Type III Sum of Squares	df	Mean Square	F	Significance	Eta Squared
Corrected Model	Reading Posttest	952659.870[a]	3	317553.290	366.27	.01	.60
	Mathematics Posttest	1.383E6	3	460961.420	491.14	.01	.67
Intercept	Reading Posttest	45983.559	1	45983.559	53.04	.01	.07
	Mathematics Posttest	16181.086	1	16181.086	17.24	.01	.02
Reading Pretest	Reading Posttest	390209.889	1	390209.889	450.07	.01	.38
	Mathematics Posttest	7340.052	1	7340.052	7.82	.01	.01
Mathematics Pretest	Reading Posttest	50252.555	1	50252.555	57.96	.01	.07
	Mathematics Posttest	789462.570	1	789462.570	841.15	.01	.54
Study Group	Reading Posttest	17794.234	1	17794.234	20.52	.01	.03
	Mathematics Posttest	8770.932	1	8770.932	9.35	.01	.01
Error	Reading Posttest	633777.129	731	867.000			
	Mathematics Posttest	686083.850	731	938.555			
Total	Reading Posttest	3.455E8	735				
	Mathematics Posttest	3.493E8	735				
Corrected Total	Reading Posttest	1586436.999	734				
	Mathematics Posttest	2068968.109	734				

Table 3: Analysis of Covariance Comparison of the Treatment Group and Control Group Reading Comprehension and Mathematics Posttest Scores

Reading Comprehension Growth. The SAT 10 Reading Comprehension subtest scores, for those students in classes with teachers participating in technology integration training (Treatment Group) were compared to the SAT 10 Reading Comprehension subtest scores of those students in classes whose teachers did not participate in the training (Control Group). ANCOVA was used to evaluate the difference in Reading subtest scores between the Treatment and Control Groups controlling for the initial reading proficiency levels of the students. The SAT 10 pretest scores were used as the covariate to place students in both groups on the same baseline.

The results show a significant difference in Reading Comprehension between the Treatment Group and the Control Group (df=1/734; F=20.52; p<.01) when initial Reading proficiency is controlled. The average Reading Comprehension subtest score for students in the Treatment Group (Mean= 687.10) was significantly greater than the average Reading Comprehension subtest score achieved by students in the Control Group (Mean= 676.16). This represents an effect size of +.24 (Cohen's d).

Mathematics Growth. The SAT 10 Mathematics subtest scores, for those students in classes with teachers participating in technology integration training (Treatment Group) were compared to the SAT 10 Mathematics subtest scores of those students in classes whose teachers did not participate in training (Control Group). ANCOVA was used to evaluate the difference in Mathematics subtest scores between the Treatment and Control Groups controlling for the initial mathematics proficiency levels of the students. The SAT 10 pretest scores were used as the covariate to place students in the Treatment Group and the Control Group on the same baseline.

The results show a significant difference in Mathematics between the Treatment Group and the Control Group (df=1/734; F=9.35; p<.01) when initial Mathematics proficiency is controlled. The average Mathematics subtest score for students in the Treatment Group (Mean= 689.46) was significantly greater than the average Mathematics subtest score achieved by students in the Control Group (Mean= 681.79). This represents an effect size of +.14 (Cohen's d).

We examined whether there were any differences in growth between male and female students between the Treatment and Control Groups (main and interaction effects). To this end, the overall growth in Reading and Mathematics skills for the Treatment Group was compared to the overall growth in Reading and Mathematics skills within the Control Group as measured by the SAT 10. MANCOVA was used to evaluate the difference in a composite reading and mathematics score between the Treatment and Control Groups of different genders controlling for the initial skill levels of the students. The SAT 10 pretest scores were used as the covariate to place students in the Treatment Group and the Control Group on the same baseline. The gender comparisons were based on 362 male students and 344 female students.

The main effect for study group memberships (Treatment and Control Group) was confirmed; there was a significant difference in a composite of the SAT 10 Reading Comprehension and Mathematics posttest scores between students in the Treatment and the Control Group when initial Reading and Mathematics proficiency levels are controlled ($F=12.39$; $df=2/699$; $p<.01$). There were no significant main effects for gender ($F=1.25$; $df=2/699$; $p<.29$) or the interaction between gender and study group membership ($F=.17$; $df=2/699$; $p<.84$).

Effect	Value	F	Hypothesis df	Error df	Significance	Partial Eta Squared
Intercept	.077	29.26	2	699	.01	.08
Reading Pretest	.365	200.61	2	699	.01	.37
Mathematics Pretest	.524	385.03	2	699	.01	.52
Study Group	.034	12.39	2	699	.01	.03
Gender	.004	1.25	2	699	.29	.01
Study Group by Gender	.000	.17	2	699	.84	.00

Table 4: Multivariate Analysis of Covariance Comparison of Treatment and Control Group by Gender and Reading and Mathematics Posttest Scores

We examined whether there were any differences in growth between students in different ethnic groups between the Treatment and Control Groups (main and interaction effects). To this end, the overall growth in Reading and Mathematics skills for the Treatment Group was compared to the overall growth in Reading and Mathematics skills within the Control Group as measured by the SAT 10. MANCOVA was used to evaluate the difference in a composite reading and mathematics score between the Treatment and Control Groups of different ethnicities controlling for the initial skill levels of the students. The SAT 10 pretest scores were used as the covariate to place students in both groups on the same baseline. The ethnic comparisons were based on 583 Caucasian students and 111 Non-Caucasian students.

The main effect for study group memberships (Treatment and Control Group) was again confirmed; there was a significant difference in a composite of the SAT 10 Reading Comprehension and Mathematics posttest scores between students in the Treatment and the Control Group when initial Reading and Mathematics proficiency levels are controlled ($F=8.63$; $df=2/691$ $p<.01$). There were no significant main effects for ethnicity ($F=2.25$; $df=2/691$; $p<.11$) or the interaction between ethnicity and study group membership ($F=.64$; $df=2/691$; $p<.53$). This indicates that teachers' participation in technology integration training was equally effective for students of different ethnic groups.

Effect		Value	F	Hypothesis df	Error df	Significance	Partial Eta Squared
Intercept	Pillai's Trace	.078	29.13	2.000	691	.01	.078
Reading Pretest	Pillai's Trace	.367	199.89	2.000	691	.01	.367
Mathematics Pretest	Pillai's Trace	.526	383.85	2.000	691	.01	.526
Study Group	Pillai's Trace	.024	8.63	2.000	691	.01	.02
Ethnicity	Pillai's Trace	.006	2.25	2.000	691	.11	.006
Study Group by Gender	Pillai's Trace	.002	.634	2.000	691	.53	.002

Table 5: Multivariate Analysis of Covariance Comparison of Treatment and Control Group by Ethnicity and Reading and Mathematics Posttest Scores

Summary/Conclusion

During the 2010-2011 school year, we conducted a year-long, multi-site study with approximately 1,000 6th, 7th, and 8th grade teachers and students, in 42 classrooms in Minnesota, Missouri and Texas, to evaluate the impact of teacher technology integration training on student achievement. The implementation included a portfolio of online tools to assist teachers in providing technology integrated instruction to foster student achievement and college and career readiness. The results show that students in classes whose teachers participate in technology integration training learn significantly more than students in classes whose teachers do not participate in this training.

Students in classes with teachers who participated in the training showed about a year more of growth in Reading and in Mathematics, than students in classes with teachers that did not participate in the training. These estimates are based on the average gains seen by students at the 50th percentile at grades 6, 7 and 8 provided by Harcourt (2002). The Treatment Group students showed statistically greater gains in Reading Comprehension (11 scale score points; Effect Size= .24) and Mathematics (7 scale score points; Effect Size=.14) than the Control Group classes. While these effect sizes are modest, they are meaningful given the representation of three states and considering the indirect nature of the treatment on student learning.

These effects suggest that providing teachers with online technology integration training that can be used independently has an impact on student Reading Comprehension and Mathematics skills growth. The solution was found to be equally effective for boys and girls and for students of different ethnicities.

In addition, teachers using the Atomic Learning platform reported an increase in technology use and increased technology integration in the classroom. Several teachers reported an increased willingness to use technology in the classroom and several teachers integrated mobile devices such as iPads and iPods.

Supplementary studies would provide further clarification on the effectiveness of the Atomic Learning platform and whether various implementation models used by teachers affects student achievement. One factor that could be modified would be to have multiple treatment groups, each varying on the particular prescription of use of the platform including amount of use and specific materials to use. Students in all grade levels could be included in the studies. Teacher level gains in technology skills could be evaluated using pre and post measures. Student level gains in technology as well as gains in the respective subject areas could be evaluated. These additional studies would help gather information with regards to how changes in the amount or nature of use of the online technology integration training impacts teacher and student performance.

References

Borthwick, A. and Pierson, M. (2008). Transforming Classroom practice: Professional Development Strategies in Educational Technology. Washington, D.C: ISTE.

Collins, A and Halverson, R. (2009). Rethinking education in the age of technology. New York: Teachers College Press.

Harcourt Assessment (2002). Stanford Achievement Test Series™, Tenth Edition, Technical manual: San Antonio, Texas: Harcourt Assessment.

Harris, J. (2007). Educational technology professional development models: A taxonomy of combinable choices. Paper presented at the National Educational Computing Conference, Atlanta, GA.

Johnson, L., Adams, S., and Haywood, K., (2011). The NMC Horizon Report: 2011 K-12 Edition. Austin, Texas: The New Media Consortium.

Killion, J. and National Staff Development Council (2002). Assessing impact: Evaluating staff development. Oxford, OH: National Staff Development Council.

Owen, A., Farsali, S., Knezak, G. and Christensen, R. (2005). Teaching in the One-to-One Classroom: It's not about laptops, it's about empowerment. Learning and Leading with Technology, 33, 12-16.

Prensky, M. (2010). Teaching Digital Natives. Partnering for real learning. Thousand Oaks, CA: Corwin Publishers.

Schacter, J. (1999). The impact of educational technology on student achievement: What the most current research has to say. www.mff.org/pubs/ME161.pdf

Schrum, L. (2010). Considerations of technology and teachers. The best of JRTE. Washington, D.C.: International Society of Technology in Education.

Sparks, D. (2006). Plugging educators into technology. www.nsdc.org/library/publications/results/res2-99tech.cfm.

Yoon, K. S., Duncan, T., Lee, S. W.-Y., Scarloss, B., & Shapley, K. (2007). Reviewing the evidence on how teacher professional development affects student achievement (Issues & Answers Report, REL 2007–No. 033). Washington, DC: U.S. Department of Education, Institute of Education Sciences, National Center for Education Evaluation and Regional Assistance, Regional Educational Laboratory Southwest. Retrieved from http://ies.ed.gov/ncee/edlabs.

Cognitive Presence Characteristics of Online and Face-to-face Discussions in a Blended Course

Petrea Redmond
University of Southern Queensland
Australia
redmond@usq.edu.au

Abstract: This paper will describe the cognitive presence pre-service teachers demonstrate during online and face-to-face discussions. Through a case study approach it will explore student cognitive presence in one Early Childhood Leadership course taught in a blended mode. Pre-service teachers' contributions in online and face-to-face discussions were analyzed using Garrison, Anderson and Archer's (2000) cognitive presence indicators from the Community of Inquiry Framework. This study found that pre-service teachers' cognitive presence was more frequent at the exploration level in both face-to-face discussions and online posts. The study also found that having a third party analyze the online and face-to-face elements of the course and report the results back to the instructor provided a powerful tool for instructor reflection and catalyst for change in pedagogical practice.

Introduction

Irrespective of the mode of delivery, a goal of teaching and learning in higher education is to maintain a high level of both cognitive engagement and intellectual rigor. Blended and online courses have new dynamics that both instructors and students alike need to become familiar with in order to exploit the benefits that the technology affords. The online component of a blended course provides a number of advantages including flexibility, convenience of participation, and a more permanent record of the discussion, unlike face-to-face discussion which is fleeting.

Tiene (2000) and Wang and Woo (2007) have used anecdotal evidence or survey instruments to investigate the reactions or perceptions of students in face-to-face discussion and made comparison to online discussions . These studies explored elements such as access, support, timing, mode of expression, visual cues, and overall student satisfaction. The goal of this study was to explore the difference between pre-service teachers' level of cognitive presence in face-to-face and online discussion within a blended course. The levels of cognitive presence are related to the depth of critical thinking at each level. This study will focus on the quality of discourse in relation to critical thinking.

Blended Learning

Blended learning has been described in the literature and enacted in practice in a range of ways. It was explained broadly by Mantyla (2001) as "taking two or more presentation and distribution methods and combining them to enhance the learning content and experience for the learner" (p. 3). Whereas, Graham (2005) stated that "[b]lended learning systems combine face-to-face instruction with computer-mediated instruction" (p. 5) . Allan and Seaman (2010) quantified blended learning as having 30 – 79% of the content online. They went on to comment that it is a course "that blends on-line and face-to-face delivery. [A] substantial proportion of the content is delivered online, typically uses online discussions, and typically has a reduced number of face-to-face meetings" (p. 8).

In the blended learning environment, discussions occur in both face-to-face and online modes. Face-to-face discussion has the flexibility and capacity to provide immediate feedback, both verbally and non-verbally. The interpretation of non-verbal communication mediates ongoing participation, particularly when the audience is unclear. There is also a perception of efficiency in face-to-face discussion. Face-to-face discussion provides prompt response to questions whereas online discussions require a longer time frame. This, however, enables time for reflective responses (Garrison & Kanuka, 2004; Meyer, 2003; Vaughan & Garrison, 2005).

Discussion in the online space enables observation of text online. The persistent nature of online discussion (Ng & Cheung, 2007), in that it remains or is accessible after the discussion, enables participants to return to the discussion to review it and in fact restart the discussion. Online discussion enables a participant to gain ongoing feedback from peers and instructors in a way that is not possible in face-to-face classes where students may feel inhibited to participate and/ or are restricted by time. Furthermore, students are also able to start new discussions online without the knowledge or approval of the instructor. This can lead to discussion that is very student-directed rather than instructor-led (Henri, 1992; Stacey & Gerbic, 2007). Is there or should there be a difference in the expectation of cognitive presence students exhibit face-to-face and online?

Cognitive presence

Garrison, Anderson and Archer's (2000) Community of Inquiry Framework is a contemporary tool for researching and conceptualizing online and blended learning. A Community of Inquiry provides "an environment that is supportive intellectually and socially, and with the guidance of a knowledgeable instructor, students will engage in meaningful discourse and develop personal and lasting understandings of course topics" (Rourke & Kanuka, 2009, p. 21). Figure 1 presents the Community of Inquiry Framework elements and indicates the interrelationship among them.

Figure 1: Community of Inquiry (Garrison & Anderson, 2003, p. 28)

The Community of Inquiry Framework consists of "three critical elements in the experience of conducting higher education using online communications media – Social Presence, Cognitive Presence, and Teaching Presence" (Garrison, Anderson, & Archer, 2010, p. 5). Social Presence is "the ability of participants in a community of inquiry to project themselves socially and emotionally as 'real' people" (Garrison et al., 2000, p. 94). Teaching presence is "the design, facilitation, and direction of cognitive and social processes for the realization of personally meaningful and educationally worthwhile learning outcomes" (Anderson, Rourke, Garrison, & Archer, 2001, p. 5). The final element of the framework is cognitive presence described as "the intellectual environment that supports sustained critical discourse and higher order knowledge acquisition and application" (Garrison & Anderson, 2003, p. 55)Cognitive presence reflects the intellectual climate and critical thinking within the learning. It is concerned with the "discourse in the initiation, construction and confirmation of meaningful learning outcomes" (Garrison, 2003, p. 50). Cognitive presence provides a framework to assess the quality of the inquiry, the levels of critical thinking and discourse, and can be mapped to four different phases as shown in Table 1 below. Each phase has a number of indicators that exemplify the types of contributions participants make to the discussion.

Cognitive Presence Phases	Indicators
Triggering Event	Recognise problem
	Sense of puzzlement
Exploration	Divergence – within the online community
	Divergence – within a single message
	Information exchange
	Suggestions for consideration
	Brainstorming
	Leaps to conclusions
Integration	Convergence – among group members
	Convergence – within a single message
	Connecting ideas, synthesis
	Creating solutions
Resolution/Application	Vicarious or real world application of solutions/ideas
	Defending solutions

Table 1: Cognitive Presence indicators (Garrison & Anderson, 2003)

The role of the instructor is to design and "build the discussion from problem recognition through to exploration, integration and resolution" (Garrison & Anderson, 2003, p. 62). High levels of cognitive presence require learners to have active and scholarly engagement with the course content, their peers, and the instructor in a way that promotes critical thinking and enables deep learning.

Critical thinking

Critical thinking has been described by Lipman (2003) as *"thinking that strives to be impartial, accurate, careful, clear, truthful, abstract, coherent,* and *practical.* Critical thinking is practical in the sense that it is *applied"* (p. 58). He goes on to suggest that it includes "reasoning and argumentation, with deduction and induction, with form, structure and composition" (Lipman, 2003, p. 261).

Critical thinking is a key outcome of higher education, it "is not just limited to the one-off assessment of a statement for its correctness, but a dynamic activity, in which critical perspectives on a problem develop through both individual analysis and social interaction" (Newman, Webb, & Cochrane, 1995, p. 61). This social interaction comes in the form of discussion which can occur face-to-face or online, and in blended courses would occur in both environments. Online discussion can promote critical thinking, clarify information, justify and link ideas (Marra, Moore, & Klimczak, 2004; Newman et al., 1995).

There have been a number of studies (Marra et al., 2004; Newman et al., 1995) that have identified that online discussion can promote critical thinking, clarify information, justify and link ideas. Meyer's (2003) early study, which explored graduate students' face-to-face and online discussions, suggested that students display more critical thinking in online discussions. Newman, Webb and Cochrane (1995) found "more new ideas emerged in face-to-face seminars, and more ideas in the computer conferences were important, justified or linked together" (p. 57). However, there is a shortage of literature that has analyzed and compared the quality of face-to-face and online discussion, in terms of the levels of critical thinking, in blended undergraduate courses.

Research Context

This study investigated the discussion contributions of final year pre-service teachers studying in an Early Childhood Leadership course at a regional Australian University. Students were enrolled in a blended course where face-to-face discussion was extended online to expand the time for discussion and deepen students' knowledge. The instructor was a novice educator in the online and blended environments. The online space was largely a repository of information and made space for unstructured online discussions. The researcher was not the instructor of the course. This study investigated the variation in the pre-service teachers' contributions in online and face-to-face discussion.

Of the 20 people in the tutorial group within this case study all students consented to be videoed in their face-to-face classes but only thirteen students consented to an analysis of their online discussions for the purpose of this research. The contributions of any student who did not provide consent were removed from the data. All participants were female, including the instructor.

There was no summative assessment of the pre-service teachers' online contributions, although the instructor did indicate an expectation that they would post in the online discussions as part of their weekly engagement with the course. There was also no mandate for students to attend face-to-face classes.

Method

Both face-to-face and online discussion contributions by the pre-service teachers were explored though content analysis. Pre-service teachers' utterances, both online and face-to-face, were analyzed using the cognitive presence phases shown above in Table 1. The indicators served as examples of the type of content within utterances at each phase as well as the complexity of the critical thinking they were demonstrating. The instructor was not the researcher. The items were coded by the researcher and then several months later recoded by the researcher to determine the reliability of the coding. The same coder was used for the coding of the online and face-to-face discussions. The coder had previously used the coding framework in her PhD research (unpublished) with an Intra-rater reliability (or agreement level) of 92% using Holsti's (1969) coefficient reliability.

The face-to-face classes were videoed and then analyzed using the software Studiocode. The archived online discussions were also analyzed using the cognitive presence phases. Both online and face-to-face sessions selected for analysis occurred in the middle of the semester, after students and the instructor had established social presence and prior to the major assessment item being due. In the face-to-face classes only the first hour was coded. The second half of the face-to-face time involved guest speakers. This time was largely taken over by the speaker presenting with only a few student questions at the end.

The unit of analysis for the online discussions was deemed to be each post, where the author decides on the length and content of the utterance. Weltzer-Ward (2011) claimed that using a post as a unit of analysis provided "reliable and valid analysis" (p. 18). It was much more difficult to identify a unit of analysis in face-to-face discussions. However, it was decided that each speaker's utterances would become one unit of analysis irrespective of the length of that utterance. That is, each time a participant spoke it was deemed a unit of analysis irrespective of content or length of contribution to the discussion. This seemed to align with the selection for the unit of analysis for online posts in that each contribution was different in length but the content and length was chosen by the pre-service teacher rather than the instructor or the researcher.

To build an understanding of the cognitive presence made visible by pre-service teachers in discussions, the following question guided the study: What is the difference in the quality of the contributions between online and face-to-face discussions?

After the initial data collection and analysis a semi-structured interview was held with the instructor as part of the member checking process. "Member checking is a particularly powerful technique for determining the trustworthiness of interpretations that involves asking informants ... to check on the accuracy of the themes, interpretations, and conclusions" (Bergman, 2008, p. 109). The aim of the interview was to confirm the reliability of the researcher's understanding of the data and also to gain the instructor's perspective on the results.

Results and Discussion

The pre-service teachers availed themselves of the learning opportunities at a time and place that suited them. It was observed that most students attended face-to-face classes and read online posts, however only half of the students actually contributed actively in discussion in either mode. Chen and Looi (2007) also found that few students shared their ideas in face-to-face classes even when invited to do so by the instructor. They commented that "[d]uring the 3-hour session, normally less than 10 learners expressed their ideas to their peers" (p. 316).

The instructor was a novice in the online and blended modes of instruction. The role of the online space for this blended course was to provide a repository for course documents and space for online discussions. The instructor had minimal design experience of how best to utilize the online space to enhance face-to-face activities. While the coded sessions were identified by the instructor as a tutorial they were highly lecture-orientated, meaning they were instructor-led with less student talk than might be expected. Although the instructor articulated that she aspired to a constructivist approach, being new in the blended environment, she may well have reverted her teaching to a more instructivist mode. This aligns with the research of Weaver, Green, Rahman and Epp (2009) who found that in their exploration of face-to-face and online communication in chemistry classes that "[t]he instructor directed the discourse in both environments" (p. 15) and that the "discourse was similar in structure to traditional classroom lectures. The instructor acted as a lecturer and explained a topic to the students" (p. 10).

In both face-to-face and online environments the discussion was usually one-to-one rather than one-to-many. This may have been an outcome of the teaching presence displayed by the instructor as a beginner instructor in the blended mode. Teaching presence was also coded however it is not the focus of this chapter. The instructor and students provided limited visual cues online e.g. emoticons. It was apparent that in face-to-face discussions non-verbal feedback was much more overt.

Table 2 below provides an analysis of the pre-service teachers' contributions to discussions, both face-to-face and online. It indicates the percentage of discussion contributions at each phase of cognitive presence.

Phase of cognitive presence	Face-to-face	Online
Trigger	13%	6%
Exploration	83%	76%
Integration	4%	18%
Resolution	0%	0%

Table 2: Percentage of utterances at each phase of cognitive presence

The pre-service teachers were more likely to participate at the exploration phase of cognitive presence in both the face-to-face and online environments. Many of their comments related to the information exchange indicator where participants shared personal narratives, literature or resources, and asked questions of clarification. One pre-service teacher posted, "*I have had a look on the internet for strategic plans with a search mainly focusing on child care centers. I have not read in detail all these examples but I wanted to share them. [URLs provided].*" The following quote is another example of a pre-service teacher's response coded at the exploration phase, "*Thank you for clarifying that – one trend that did come up was ... It's a bit bewildering to me that ... My experience has been that ... Has anyone else had similar experiences?*"

Previous studies have also found that the exploration phase of cognitive presence has the highest proportion of online postings (Garrison, Anderson, & Archer, 2001; Gorsky, Caspi, Antonovsky, Blau, & Mansur, 2010; Kanuka & Anderson, 1998; Luebeck & Bice, 2005; Redmond & Mander, 2006; Vaughan & Garrison, 2005). The high frequency of exploration posts could be due to the fact that participants do not have to demonstrate high levels of critical thinking at this stage and these types of posts are 'easier' than those at the next phases. Possibly some students felt comfortable sharing their experiences and perspectives on topics without validating their remarks.

The face-to-face discussion resulted in higher levels of triggering (13%) and exploration (83%) responses when compared to online. However, online discussion proved to stimulate more integration contributions (18%) than face-to-face (4%). Sadly, within this cohort no contributions were observed at the final phase of cognitive presence - that of resolution. In both modes of discussion students were more likely to contribute at a surface or low level of critical thinking.

The higher proportion of triggering contributions in face-to-face discussions could be because face-to-face discussions are more suited to collecting ideas. The instructor may well have designed the face-to-face environment to achieve this focus. It is possible that participants used the face-to-face arena to unpack the problem and then little further discussion around the triggering phase was required online.

In their investigation of undergraduate online and face-to-face discussions Ellis, Goodyear, Prosser and O'Hara (2006) found that in both online and face-to-face discussions students were more likely to post at a surface level rather than a deep level. The online discussions, however, were more likely to have a higher percentage of contributions at a deeper level.

The second most common contributions in online discussions were those coded as integration phase where participants blended information from multiple sources and connected different experiences and ideas. Lesley stated:
> *I agree with you that E.C. professionals have a great responsibility to educate our students. Leadership versus Management is a crucial part in being able to deliver children's ... After reading ch 1, Demystifying leadership by John Zenger it is apparent also that a leader is instrumental in ... I have worked in schools where ... The school I work in now has a principal who is a leader in many ways.*

The higher contributions of integration online could be due to the fact that online discussion provides participants with the time to reflect on the contributions of others and the course content, and connect the ideas they have collated. In the face-to-face classes students can only bring forward those facts, experiences etc that they can recall off the top of their head, as the instructor provided very little time for students to form a response to questions. Also, students did not access their notes, text or other sources of information when responding to the face-to-face questions, unlike their responses within the online environment where students did take the time to source additional information and resources prior to responding. The online responses demonstrated more of an informed voice than the face-to-face responses.

Abrams's (2005) study investigating critical thinking in graduate courses found that there was a difference in the face-to-face and online contributions of the students. Their face-to-face contributions were "based only on their own experiences and personal beliefs rather than on pertinent literature on content or research design" (¶ 46); however in online contributions the "students provide[d] their peers with detailed, critical feedback, suggestions for improvement and information from other resources" (¶ 48).

Overall this study has found that the types of student contributions to discussions differed in nature when comparing face-to-face and online discussions, which aligns with the research of Weaver et al., (2009). Another finding of this study is that it is more likely to find higher levels of critical thinking online rather than in face-to-face discussion, supporting the research of Newman et al. (1995). Within online discussions the participants were more likely to: demonstrate the ability to identify important statements; bring in outside knowledge and experience; link ideas; and justify their comments. This is most likely because the online environment provides the participants with more time and ease of access, to search for more information, literature, resources, or examples, and to link to previous and new ideas resulting in a more informed and higher cognitive level of contribution.

A secondary outcome of this study was in relation to the instructor's pedagogical practice after viewing the data analysis. At the semi-structured interview the instructor was shown the breakdown of the data and was surprised at the number of low level responses in both the online and face-to-face modes.

In the online forums it was noted that the instructor responded immediately (when possible) to the student posts. That had the effect of shutting down conversation and the online discussions were simply one-to-one discussions held publically. After viewing the data the instructor made some immediate changes to her pedagogical practice. There was a paradigm shift in how she communicated with students online (and also in the way she designed the next course offering). The instructor waited for students to respond to each other before stepping in and encouraged students back into the conversation in her posts. The following is an example of the instructor's post after viewing the student data:

> "I want you to dig deeper ... you have made some interesting observations about the end result of great leadership but what is happening within the organisation to get it to this stage? What practices are occurring? What method is the leader using?"

It appears that the opportunity to see an analysis of her teaching, completed by a third party, was the catalyst for the instructor to question and reflect on her online practice resulting in immediate and longer term transformation of practice. The opportunity for the instructor to discuss with the researcher how their philosophy and practice had been constructed, deconstructed and reconstructed resulted in significant and purposeful adjustments by the instructor, this was an unexpected yet favorable outcome of this study.

Conclusion

There are a number of limitations regarding this study. First, one needs to be cautious about making generalisations. Although similar findings have resulted in research from online courses at the graduate level, these findings are specific to the context of this course, with this instructor and this particular cohort of students. As the instructor gains more experience and skills in teaching in both blended and online modes, the results may well be different. Second, the number of participants was very small. Third, it is difficult to determine what one face-to-face session might be equivalent to in terms of online discussion. To avoid this problem in this study, percentages were used rather than raw numbers of contributions at each phase. For the purposes of this chapter, the design of the discussions, both online and face-to-face, were not investigated. Exploration of the design of the discussion might have revealed a possible cause/effect relationship between instructor and student posts.

Irrespective of the mode of discussion the pre-service teachers participated at a low or surface level. The exploration phase of cognitive presence, being the second of four phases, was the dominant type of contribution made by the students. The online discussion resulted in higher levels of integration posts where the students synthesized and connected ideas from multiple sources. Further exploration of the teaching presence would be required to explore how discussions can be moved to higher levels of cognitive presence.

Although there is a desire for students to contribute at higher levels of critical thinking, it is normally not evidenced until the end of the course within assessment responses. Instructors need to be more active and have a range of pedagogical strategies in the design and facilitation stages so as to promote higher levels of critical thinking in both online and face-to-face discussions.

References

Abrams, Z. (2005). Asynchronous CMC, collaboration and the development of critical thinking in a graduate seminar in applied linguistics. *Canadian Journal of Learning and Technology, 31*(2), 23-47.

Allen, I. E., & Seaman, J. (2010). *Learning on Demand: Online Education in the United States, 2009*. Needham, MA: Sloan Consortium.

Anderson, T., Rourke, L., Garrison, D. R., & Archer, W. (2001). Assessing teacher presence in a computer conferencing context. *Journal of Asynchronous Learning Networks, 5*(2), 1-17.

Bergman, M. (2008). Introduction: Whither Mixed Methods? In M. Bergman (Ed.), *Advances in Mixed Methods Research* (pp. 1-7). Thousand Oaks, CA: SAGE.

Chen, W., & Looi, C. (2007). Incorporating online discussion in face to face classroom learning: A new blended learning approach. *Australasian Journal of Educational Technology, 23*(3), 307-326.

Ellis, R., Goodyear, P., Prosser, M., & O'Hara, A. (2006). How and what university students learn through online and face-to-face discussion: conceptions, intentions and approaches. *Journal of Computer Assisted Learning, 22,* 244-256.

Garrison, D. R. (2003). Cognitive presence for effective asynchronous online learning: The role of reflective inquiry, self-direction and metacognition. In J. Bourne & J. C. Moore (Eds.), *Elements of Quality Online Education: Practice and Direction* (Vol. 4, pp. 47–58). Needham, MA: The Sloan Consortium.

Garrison, D. R., & Anderson, T. (2003). *E-learning in the 21st century: a framework for research and practice*. New York: Routledge Falmer.

Garrison, D. R., Anderson, T., & Archer, W. (2000). Critical inquiry in a text-based environment: computer conferencing in higher education. *Internet and Higher Education, 2*(2-3), 87-105.

Garrison, D. R., Anderson, T., & Archer, W. (2001). Critical thinking, cognitive presence, and computer conferencing in distance education. *American Journal of Distance Education, 15*(1), 7-23.

Garrison, D. R., Anderson, T., & Archer, W. (2010). The first decade of the community of inquiry framework: A retrospective. *The Internet and Higher Education, 13*(1-2), 5-9.

Garrison, D. R., & Kanuka, H. (2004). Blended learning: Uncovering its transformative potential in higher education. *The Internet and Higher Education, 7*(2), 95-105.

Gorsky, P., Caspi, A., Antonovsky, A., Blau, I., & Mansur, A. (2010). The Relationship between Academic Discipline and Dialogic Behavior in Open University Course Forums *International Review of Research in Open and Distance Learning 11*(2), 49-72.

Graham, C. R. (2005). Blended learning systems: Definition, current trends, and future directions. In C. J. Bonk & C. Graham (Eds.), *The handbook of blended learning: Global perspectives, local designs* (pp. 3-21). San Francisco, CA: Pfeiffer.

Henri, F. (1992). Computer conferencing and content analysis. In A. R. Kaye (Ed.), *Collaborative Learning Through Computer Conferencing: The Najaden Papers* (pp. 117-136). Berlin: SpringerVerlag.

Holsti, O. (1969). *Content analysis for the social sciences and humanities*. Reading, MA: Addison-Wesley.

Kanuka, H., & Anderson, T. (1998). Social interchange, discord and knowledge construction. *Journal of Distance Education, 13*(1), 57-74.

Lipman, M. (2003). *Thinking in education* (2nd ed.). Cambridge: Cambridge University Press.

Luebeck, J. L., & Bice, L. R. (2005). Online Discussion as a Mechanism of Conceptual Change among Mathematics and Science Teachers. *Journal of Distance Education, 20*(2), 21-39.

Mantyla, K. (2001). *Blending E-learning: the power is in the mix*. Alexandria, VA: American Society for Training & Development.

Marra, R. M., Moore, J. L., & Klimczak, A. K. (2004). Content analysis of online discussion forums: a comparative analysis of protocols. *Educational Technology Research and Development, 52*(2), 23-40.

Meyer, K. A. (2003). Face-to-face versus threaded discussions: The role of time and higher-order thinking. *Journal of Asynchronous Learning Networks, 7*(3), 55-65.

Newman, D. R., Webb, B., & Cochrane, C. (1995). A content analysis method to measure critical thinking in face-to-face and computer supported group learning. *Interpersonal Computing and Technology, 3*(2), 56-77.

Ng, C., & Cheung, W. S. (2007). Comparing face to face, tutor led discussion and online discussion in the classroom. *Australasian Journal of Educational Technology, 23*(4), 455-469.

Redmond, P., & Mander, A. (2006). *Online mentoring of pre-service teachers: exploring cognitive presence*. Paper presented at the Society for Information Technology & Teacher Education 17th International Conference Annual, Orlando, Florida.

Rourke, L., & Kanuka, H. (2009). Learning in Communities of Inquiry: A Review of the Literature. *Journal of Distance Education, 23*(1), 30.

Stacey, E., & Gerbic, P. (2007). Teaching for blended learning—Research perspectives from on-campus and distance students. *Education and Information Technologies, 12*(3), 165 -174.

Tiene, D. (2000). Online discussions: A survey of advantages and disadvantages compared to face-to-face discussions. *Journal of Educational Multimedia and Hypermedia, 9*(4), 69-382.

Vaughan, N. D., & Garrison, D. R. (2005). Creating cognitive presence in a blended faculty development community. *The Internet and higher education, 8*(1), 1-12.

Wang, Q., & Woo, H. (2007). Comparing asynchronous online discussions and face-to-face discussions in a classroom setting. *British Journal of Educational Technology, 38*(2), 272-286.

Weaver, G., Green, K., Rahman, A., & Epp, E. (2009). An Investigation of Online and Face-to-Face Communication in General Chemistry. *International Journal for the Scholarship of Teaching and Learning, 3*(1), 1-22.

Weltzer-Ward, M. L. M. (2011). Content analysis coding schemes for online asynchronous discussion. *Campus-Wide Information Systems, 28*(1), 56-74.

Generalized Checklist Significance in Improving Timeliness in Asynchronous Distance Education

Terence Cavanaugh
Educational Leadership, School Counseling, & Sport Management
University of North Florida
United States
t.cavanaugh@unf.edu

Marcia Lamkin
Educational Leadership, School Counseling, & Sport Management
University of North Florida,
United States
m.lamkin@unf.edu

Haihong Hu
Leadership Studies
University of Central Arkansas
United States
HHu@uca.edu

Abstract: In response to novice online learners in distance learning courses submitting work late and missing elements of various assignments, research on using generalized checklists as a strategy or tool to assist students in doing their work and submitting that work on time was undertaken. This generalized assessments checklist for distance learning students taking an asynchronous course was designed using the READ-DO checklist design standards and distributed to by email on a weekly basis. The checklist was found to be statistically significant as a strategy in improving submission times for asynchronous distance learning students.

Introduction

Asynchronous, Internet-based, distance learning (DL) courses have become common in the delivery of postsecondary education. During the 2007–2008 school year, 20% of undergraduates and 22% of graduate students took DL courses in the U.S. (USDOE-NCES 2011), numbers that have consistently grown in the recent past. These web-based learning environments require more learner self-control and proactive learning to construct knowledge and acquire skills, and that self-regulation can be a critical element for student's success (Schunk & Zimmerman 1998), and so it is important that they develop or instructors provide instructional self-monitoring tools to better support students in the distance learning environment. The use of checklists can be an effective self-regulation or monitoring strategy for improving student assignment completion and on time submission in the asynchronous project-based distance learning classes. In a recent project it was found that a generalized assignment checklist, designed according FAA and CAAA checklist design guidelines, and sent to students on a weekly basis had a significant impact of improving the students' submission time.

In this project, instructors participating in a number of asynchronous distance learning courses in a graduate educational leadership program that had noticed a trend among many students of failing to submit all of the associated course assignments by the listed deadlines. While many students had submitted all of their work on time, often others were components of their weekly assignments, such completing the week's major project, but failing to participate in the online discussion for that week. Interviews with the students revealed that they thought that they had completed all the assigned elements for a given session, but that they must have forgotten or overlooked elements of the session's assignments. Additionally it was found that a good portion of the students did not have much experience with distance learning. Since effective online practices for project-based learning for online classes like these at this university require a variety of project experiences (NACOL 2007; Sloan-C n.d.), the loss of any assigned element damages the continuity of the students' learning and possible success. Therefore, a search for a strategy to assist the students in their online classes was undertaken.

Checklists & Design

While there are numerous reasons that students may select online courses, such as increased convenience or access, many novice distance learners may lack the necessary experiences or appropriate strategies to be successful in such an environment. In this project, the students in the participating classes were all working full time, so it was already understood that they were constantly busy and that there could be any number of issues affecting their cognitive load. The checklist strategy being implemented in the classes was based on the work of Atul Gawande's (2009) success in surgical reform, where it was also found that before using checklists, steps were often forgotten in implementation during surgery, which was considered to be similar to the situation that was occurring with the distance learning students - forgotten or missed elements. Education research has found that lack of management skills, mismatch between learners' interest and course structure, can cause students to be unsuccessful in distance learning programs (Chyung 2001; Kember et al. 1991). A search for distance learning assignment checklists was done, and many different kinds of checklists were found, but they did not appear to address the overall issue, instead most were specific assignment focused or were not assignment related, i.e. course or student preparation for distance learning. To help overcome the self-management gap, a generalized checklist for distance learning students in an online asynchronous course was developed to be a strategy or job-aid to assist the student and remind them of the different assignment components of an online course and make these explicit to the student. The checklist developed for the online learners was to be a resource to support the learner's educational needs beyond the provision of content, instead to assist as a self-monitoring tool or strategy for the students. The checklist was to help the individual student identify gaps in their own attention or comprehension concerning online course elements, then assists them in overcoming those gaps in their online classes.

The design of any checklist is dependent on the intended checklist purpose and associated problem. The generalized checklist for the online class was created following the specification elements of the Federal Aviation Authorities (FAA) and the Civil Aviation Authority (CAA) guidelines for checklist design including structural layout and readability, (FAA 1995; FAA 2007; CAA 2000; CAA 2006). The final design of the checklist was to make it quick to use, not be too long, or difficult to read, but it still would need to represent all the required elements for students to be successful in assignment completion. Aviation and medical checklists are usually either DO-CONFIRM or READ-DO checklists (Gawande 2009; FAA 1995). As the checklist being developed was for students to work with on their own, a READ-DO format was used, along with the associated instructions for using the checklist. The checklist developed was also of the "normal" checklist classification (FAA 1995), with a listing of action items to be performed, but not necessarily representing sequential or procedural steps, and was to act as a self-monitoring reminder for the various elements that students would be working on during the session.

The included elements of the generalized checklist for distance learning students were based on the instructors' own experiences and on analysis of various online course assignment structures. This checklist provides the students a guide or job aid in procedural performance of the common elements and activities that take place in the online learning environment. Based on the reviewed literature and reports from aviation (Degani & Wiener 1990; Degani & Wiener 1993), the generalized checklist of assignments for distance learning students was to assist the students by providing them with a framework tool to: serve as a strategy to prevent errors; be a memory aid to enhance task performance; standardize the tasks; and serve as a quality control tool. The checklist assists the student in recognizing the multiple areas of work that occur in asynchronous classes – long and short term projects, discussions or other interactive elements, and readings, and with such a tool increase the timeliness of submissions.

Methodology & Results

To investigate the effectiveness of the generalized checklist, the instructors participating in this study used a split half design, randomly assigning DL students into the two groups: the experimental group of students received a generalized checklist of five items on a weekly basis, while the student control group did not. The checklist was emailed weekly from course professors to members of the experimental group approximately four days before the listed assignment deadlines. The control group also received a reminder note concerning session assignment being due, but lacking the checklist. The email sent to the experimental group contained the checklist within the email message, with an attachment that contained a printable version of the checklist. The students were encouraged to print out the attachment, to create a more concrete representation of what they were to do. They were also encouraged to interact with the checklist – to add extra details, to mark the times elements were competed, and to write any other notes or thoughts that they had. Here is a sample email sent to the experimental group:

> *Here is a checklist for this week to help you get organized with this session's work and get it in on Monday. Print out the attached checklist and keep it around. Don't just read though the list, instead, interact with it. Try going through the assignments folder and writing in the activities into the ACTION STEPS section for yourself to better track your own assignments. When you have completed a section, check it off to help you keep track of your work in the online class. You can add more sections to be done if you need to. Review your assignments in Blackboard or from the syllabus to find more detail on your required work.*
>
> *1) Read this week's reading materials*
> *2) Review this week's online content materials*
> *3) Participate in this week's collaborative elements (the discussion/blogs/wikis/etc.)*
> *4) Complete this week's assignments to turn in*
> *5) Review progress on your long term projects.*

In order to assess the effect of the checklist on the timeliness of student submissions during the study, instructors tracked the submission times of each student's assigned work and compared those to the assigned submission times for all assignments for the four courses, with an experimental student population (n) of 56 students over the course of an entire semester. To simplify the data collection, basic date comparisons were used, so all submission values were by day counts, days before the deadline being positive, and days after being negative values. Before analyzing the data, outliers of submissions that were more than one week on either side of the assigned due date were removed, as it was supposed that the checklist in a given week could have no impact on those submission times.

The use of the generalized checklist in this study was found to significantly influence assignment submission timeliness. An initial descriptive analysis of results to examine students' submission patterns that might have been influenced by the checklist noted a mean ($\bar{x}$) that was almost twice as large for the experimental compared to the control (see Table 1).

Experimental		Control	
Mean	1.593521127	Mean	0.743209302
Standard Error	0.371623347	Standard Error	0.357687187
Median	1	Median	1
Mode	0	Mode	1
Standard Deviation	5.423664195	Standard Deviation	5.244723688
Sample Variance	29.4161333	Sample Variance	27.50712657
Kurtosis	12.19216484	Kurtosis	6.110010658
Skewness	-2.476335856	Skewness	-1.674543784
Range	44	Range	41
Minimum	-34	Minimum	-29
Maximum	10	Maximum	12
Sum	339.42	Sum	159.79
Count	213	Count	215

Table 1: Descriptive statistics from one of the instructor's courses

t-Test: Independent sample Assuming unequal variances		
	Experimental	Control
Mean	1.683294798	1.088799
Variance	13.61654679	15.51507
Observations	346	358
Hypothesized Mean Difference	0	
df	701	
t Statistic	2.067360311	
p (T<=t) one-tail	0.019533338	
t Critical one-tail	1.647030228	
p (T<=t) two-tail	0.039066677	
t Critical two-tail	1.96335382	

Table 2: Results from t-Test analysis of all courses

An independent samples t-test of the data was conducted to evaluate the hypothesis that students who received checklists submitted assignments in a more timely fashion than students in the control group. This t-test analysis assumed unequal variances between the student average submission scores for the two groups (see Table 2). The results across all courses and instructors showed a statistically significant difference according to t-test analysis with a p value equal to 0.039. The results of the t-test for this study indicated a statistically significant difference in the timely submission of assignments in these online courses, based on the distribution of the generalized checklist to the students between experimental and control groups. Analysis of the students' means and standard deviations for the two independent samples found an effect size (Cohen's d) of 0.159 during the semester of treatment.

Significance & Impact

Students who received checklists were found to be timelier in submitting their work than those who did not receive a checklist. This effect was noted even when both control and experimental groups received reminder notes concerning work completion. The checklist appears to assist the student as a monitoring and completion tool. Glouberman and Zimmerman (2002) provided distinctions among different kinds of problems: simple, complicated, and complex. While simple problems are identified as having a few basic steps; complicated problems have reductive characteristics and can be broken down into a series of simple problems; and complex problems have emergent characteristics that may change with each situation. For an asynchronous project based designed course, a single assignment, such as a discussion posting, could be considered a simple problem, but often during each session of an online course students have numerous elements and projects that they are working on: read from a text, review online course materials, participate in discussions, write reviews, complete simulations, analyze data, and possibly more, some of which may be short term, while others are long term projects. In such an online learning environment, each session can become a complicated problem for the student, a larger problem that can be reduced to smaller problems. The generalized checklist that was developed appeared to successfully serve as a structural tool to break down the larger "problem" into manageable tasks. While the success of checklists as a self-monitoring tool is limited by the willingness of the student in using it, the costs in time and effort by the instructor to provide the checklist to the students are small. Limitations of this study include the relatively small sample size, sampling adequacy and local application, as the 56 participants were from a single college, and only a few were located outside the immediate region; this may limit generalizability of the findings to other locations, colleges, and programs. A study involving multiple programs in multiple locations over time might provide more generalizable information; nonetheless, these results provide support for using a distributed generalized checklist to students to improve timeliness submission of their work and perhaps keep them more on task in their learning. For online courses and programs to be successful, instructors need to go beyond just the content, and provide students the experiences and tools to allow them to become successful.

One interesting aspect of the project that occurred during the next semester was actually in a different course, which had members from the previous experimental group. Within the first few weeks, the instructors of the other course were receiving questions from students asking why they had not yet received their checklists. When informed that they now had learned the use of the checklist as a strategy for self-monitoring that they could use on their own, they indicated that they would rather still receive the general statement and checklist on the regular basis through their email. One of the instructors who teaches a distance learning course early in the program sequence now incorporates the use of the generalized checklist for all of his students. To save time and to make sure that the checklist is sent each week to all students, and based on the fact that every checklist is the same, that instructor uses an email scheduling tool, setting it up so that the weekly checklist emails are be automatically sent to the students.

Conclusion

Using structured generalized checklist in online instruction appears to be an effective resource, providing students with an easy to use self-monitoring tool, one that standardizes performance and actions in the online learning environment. Since there is a zero materials cost to implement the checklist resource, and with applications such as email scheduling, it is even possible to set up a whole course's checklist emails for a semester in just a few minutes; the checklist can be an effective, efficient, and cost effective tool in assisting students to complete the various aspects of an online class, and improve their submission times. The printed checklist provides a concrete resource to novice online student awareness of the expected elements instead of relying on memory alone, helping them in completing the various elements found in an online class, and when presented to the students was associated with a significant improvement in submission time. We encourage distance learning instructors who have students that are novices to the DL environment or are having self-monitoring issues to consider integrating the generalized checklist that was used in this project or some adaptation.

References

CAA (Civil Aviation Authority). (2000) Guidance on the design, presentation, and use of electronic checklists. CAP 708. Safety Regulation Group. Retrieved September 22, 2011 from http://www.caa.co.uk/docs/33/CAP708.PDF

CAA (Civil Aviation Authority). (2006) Guidance on the design presentation and use of emergency and abnormal checklists. CAP 676. Safety Regulation Group. Retrieved September 22, 2011 from http://www.caa.co.uk/docs/33/CAP676.PDF

Chyung, S. Y. (2001). Systematic and systemic approaches to reducing attrition rates in online higher education. *The American Journal of Distance Education, 15*(3), 36-49.

Degani, A. and Wiener, E. L. (1990) Human factors of flight deck checklists: the normal checklist. NASA Contractor Report 177549. Retrieved September 30, 2010 from http://ntrs.nasa.gov/archive/nasa/casi.ntrs.nasa.gov/19910017830_1991017830.pdf

Degani, A. and Wiener, E. L. (1993) Cockpit checklists: concepts, design, and use. *Human Factors* 35(2): 28–43. Retrieved September 30, 2010 from http://ti.arc.nasa.gov/m/profile/adegani/Cockpit%20Checklists.pdf

FAA (Federal Aviation Administration). (1995). *Human performance considerations in the use and design of aircraft checklists.* Office of Safety Services, Safety Analysis Division. Retrieved September 20, 2011 from http://www.faa.gov/about/office_org/headquarters_offices/avs/offices/afs/afs200/branches/afs210/training_aids/media/checklist.doc

FAA (Federal Aviation Administration). (2007). Order 8900.1 CHG 0 Vol. 3, Ch. 32, Sect. 12. Aircraft checklists for 14 CFR parts 121/135. Retrieved September 20, 2011 from http://fsims.faa.gov/PICResults.aspx?mode=EBookContents

Gawande, A. (2009). *The checklist manifesto: How to get things right.* New York: Metropolitan Books.

Glouberman, S. & Zimmerman, B. (2002). Complicated and complex systems: What would successful reform of Medicare look like? Retrieved September 28, 2011 from http://investisseurautonome.info/PDF-Downloads/COMMENT-INVESTIR-RENDEMENT-INDEX/doc.1590-%20Zimmerman%20Glouberman%202002%20Health_Care_Commission_DP8.pdf

Kember, D., Murphy, D., Siaw, I., & Yuen, K. S. (1991). Towards a causal model of student progress in distance education: Research in Hong Kong. *The American Journal of Distance Education, 5*(2), 3-15.

NACOL (North American Council for Online Learning). (2007). *National Standards for Quality Online Teaching.* Retrieved July 15, 2011, from http://www.inacol.org/resources/nationalstandards/NACOL%20Standards%20Quality%20Online%20Teaching.pdf

Schunk, D. H., & Zimmerman, B. J. (1998). Conclusions and future directions for academic interventions. In D. H. Schunk & B. J. Zimmerman (Eds.), *Self-Regulated learning: From teaching to self-reflective practice.* New York, NY: The Guilford Press.

Sloan-C. (n.d.). Quality framework narrative, the 5 pillars. Retrieved July 15, 2011 from http://sloanconsortium.org/Quality_Framework_Narrative_5_pillars

USDOE-NCES (U.S. Department of Education, National Center for Education Statistics). (2011). The condition of education (COE). Retrieved July 15, 2011 from http://nces.ed.gov/programs/coe/index.asp

Learning Motivation and Student Academic Dishonesty – A Comparison Between Face-To-Face And Online Courses

Yehuda Peled
Department of Education, Western Galilee College
Department of Science and Environmental Studies, Ohalo College
Israel
ypeled@macam.ac.il

Casimir Barczyk
Purdue Calumet
USA
barczyk@calumet.purdue.edu

Yovav Eshet
yovave@wgalil.ac.il

Keren Grinautski
School of Management, Haifa University
Methodology studies, Western Galilee College
Israel
Kereng@wgalil.ac.il

Abstract: This study explores student academic dishonesty in the context of traditional and distance-learning courses in higher education. Data from 1,376 Students enrolled in colleges or universities in the U.S. and Israel were surveyed to assess their motivational orientation and their willingness to commit various acts of academic misconduct. Findings indicate that students' propensity to engage in academic dishonesty is explained by an extrinsic motivational orientation, participation in face-to-face type courses, and their age. Students were inclined to commit acts of dishonesty if they were (1) extrinsically, rather than intrinsically motivated to learn; (2) engaged in traditional face-to-face, rather than online courses; and (3) younger in age, rather than older. In addition, students in face-to-face courses had a statistically significantly higher propensity to engage in academic dishonesty than their counterparts in distance learning courses – a finding similar in both the U.S. and Israel. Implications for further research are discussed.

Introduction

Academic dishonesty continues to be a pervasive problem on college campuses, with the majority of students having engaged in it at some point during their collegiate career (Stuber-McEwen, Wiseley & Hoggatt, 2009). With the rapid growth of distance learning involving the Internet, there is a greater opportunity for individuals to engage in plagiarism, particularly where there is little or no personal contact between students and faculty (Robinson-Zañartu et al., 2005; Walker, 2010). Kelley and Bonner (2005) suggested that students who feel close to their professors tend to be more honest. However, the ability for faculty to develop a strong rapport with students becomes more difficult in the onlinxe learning environment. Students who feel "distant" from others are more likely to engage in deceptive behaviors, such as cheating (Burgoon, Stoner, Bonito & Dunbar, 2003; George & Carlson, 1999; Rowe, 2004). Online courses, as contrasted with traditional classroom courses, may serve to exacerbate these feelings of separation and thus, may contribute to the incidence of academic dishonesty (Heberling, 2002; Kennedy, Nowak, Raghuraman, Thomas & Davis, 2000; Stuber-McEwen et al., 2005). In contrast, there are some reports suggesting there is less academic dishonesty in nontraditional (i.e., online) learning as compared to traditional learning settings. The reason for this latter finding is that academic dishonesty may be associated with the extrinsic motivation that drives students in traditional classroom courses (Greenberger, Lessard, Chen & Farruggia, 2008). Online students may be more intrinsically motivated or able to learn independent of traditional classroom settings, which could substantially reduce their desire to cheat (Stuber-McEwen et al., 2009).

Motivation and E-learning

"To be motivated means to be moved to do something" (Ryan & Dec, 2000, p. 54). People vary in their motivational level and orientation, i.e., people have different amounts and different kinds of motivation (Deci & Ryan, 1998, 1999; Deci et al., 1991). Human motivation can be placed along a continuum of self-determination, from which one can distinguish whether its origins are internal or external to the subject (Moreno, González-Cutre & Chillón, 2009). According to Deci and Ryan's (1985) Self-Determination Theory (SDT), there are two types of motivation: intrinsic and extrinsic, which are based on the different reasons or goals underlying an action. Intrinsic motivation refers to doing something because it is inherently interesting or enjoyable, while extrinsic motivation refers to doing something because it leads to an enjoyable but external and separable outcome (Ryan & Deci, 2000). In other words, an intrinsically motivated person is moved to act because of the fun or challenge it entails, while an extrinsically motivated person is moved to act because of external prods, pressures, or rewards. Differences in the quality of learning and creativity can be traced to motivational orientation. Self-determined motivation was found to be related to more interest, effort, positive emotions, satisfaction, and commitment by students (Ryan & Deci, 2000).

The Organismic Integration Theory (OIT) (Deci & Ryan, 1985) suggests that intrinsic and extrinsic motivations can be viewed as extremes on a continuum. Between these polar extremes are additional types of motivation that vary according to level of self-determination, i.e., the more one internalizes the reasons for an action and assimilates them to the self, the more one's extrinsically motivated actions become self-determined and more internalized (Ryan & Connell, 1989; Ryan & Deci, 2000). Motivation type that follows internal motivation is regulation through identification. This is the most autonomous or self-determined form of extrinsic motivation. Here, a person considers his activity as important and beneficial and he carries it out, although he does not enjoy it. In the next type of internal regulation on the motivation scale, which is still quite controlling - introjected regulation - individuals begin to internalize the reasons for their actions, but they do things in order to avoid feelings of guilt or anxiety or to attain ego-enhancements or pride (Moreno et al., 2009). Moving further away from internal motivation, external regulation behaviors are performed to satisfy an external demand or to obtain an externally imposed reward contingency. Externally regulated behavior is usually experienced as controlled or alienated, and the actions have an external perceived locus of causality (deCharms, 1968). Finally, amotivation refers to a state where intention to act appears to be absent. Individuals might feel amotivation when they do not value an activity (Ryan, 1995), do not feel that they are competent to perform a certain chore or act (Deci, 1975), or do not believe it will yield a desired outcome (Seligman, 1975; Rovai, Ponton, Wighting & Baker, 2007).

Motivation plays an important role when one chooses to participate in an online course (Moore & Kearsley, 2005; Rovai et al., 2007) as intrinsic motivation is considered to be a significant predictor of persistence and achievement in distance education (Coussement, 1995; Fjortoft, 1996). In contrast, Grolnick and Ryan (1987) found that controlling environments reduce a student's sense of autonomy, decrease intrinsic motivation, and result in poorer attitudes and performance in the classroom. A meta-analysis by Deci, Koestner, and Ryan (1999) confirms that virtually every type of expected tangible reward made contingent on task performance undermines intrinsic motivation. George and Carlson (1999) contend that as the distance between a student and a physical classroom setting increases, so does the frequency of online cheating. Their assumption, coupled with the belief that academic misconduct is more pervasive in the virtual classroom (Stuber-McEwen et al., 2005) led us to question whether there is (1) a higher incidence of cheating in online courses as compared to traditional on-campus face-to-face courses; and (2) a relation between the student's motivation, type of course, and attitude towards academic misconduct. Thus, the purpose of this research is to explore the connection between self-reported frequency of academic dishonesty in the virtual classroom and students' learning motivation. Another purpose is to examine, for the first time, the issue of academic dishonesty from a cross-cultural perspective, i.e., by comparing online and face-to-face students in U.S. and Israeli institutions of higher learning.

Examining the issue of students' motivation both in online and face-to-face courses is important because of the implications for instructors in teacher education and other fields. It is widely recognized that teaching online is a different experience than teaching face-to-face and requires new skills and techniques. The online learning environment is qualitatively different than the traditional face-to-face classroom environment. Many authors argue that the online environment promotes more learner-centered instruction, requiring instructors to share control of the learning process with students (e.g., Jolliffe, Ritter, & Stevens, 2001; Palloff & Pratt, 1999; Shearer, 2003), which is essential when presenting material to intrinsically motivated learners. University level teachers clearly need education in learning how to play a more facilitative role, which can be a significant departure from their normal teaching style and require a shift in thinking related to control of the learning process. Teaching in the online environment "challenges previous practice with regard to assessment, group interaction and student/teacher dialogue" (Ellis & Phelps, 2000, p. 2) and "necessitates a new model of instructor (Cohen, 2001, p. 31) required for successful interaction with internally-motivated students.

This presents a pedagogical imperative for teacher education aimed at the ranks of instructors through full professors. With better training and development, faculty members can use the technology of online education to reach their students, and in so doing, reduce the incidence of academic dishonesty.

Based on the foregoing, we hypothesize that there will be differences in level of motivation between students that learn in traditional settings and those that are e-learners in motivation and propensity toward academic dishonesty. Specifically, e-learners will show higher levels of intrinsic motivation and less propensity toward academic dishonesty than learners in traditional face-to-face settings.

Method

Participants: The sample consists of 1,574 participants with 803 from two American academic institutions and 771 from four Israeli academic institutes. About two thirds (65%) of the participants were women and about a third (35%) were men. The age ranged from 17 to 59 (X = 26.4 years). Approximately a quarter of the participants (26%) were freshmen, a third (32%) sophomores, a fifth (20%) juniors, a fifth (19%) seniors, and 3% were graduate students. Approximately, half of the participants (46%) were Christians, 38% were Jews, and 16% were Muslims. 13% of the participants were excluded from the analysis because their survey instruments were incomplete or carelessly completed. The final data set consisted of 1,376 participants.

Survey Instrument: The first part of the survey instrument contained 16 items that were compiled from the Academic Self-Regulation Questionnaire (SRQ-A) (Ryan & Connell, 1989). The questionnaire examines four types of motivation: external regulation, introjected regulation, identified regulation, and intrinsic motivation. The participants responded to these questions using a five-point Likert scale where 1 corresponded to "Not at all true" and 5 corresponded to "Very true." The reliability of this questionnaire, measured by Cronbach's alpha, was 0.79. The second part of the survey instrument contained questions that examined academic integrity using the Academic Integrity Inventory (Kisamore, Stone & Jawahar, 2007). These questions inquired about students' likelihood to engage in various forms of academic misconduct, such as inappropriate collaboration on assignments or copying from others on a test. The participants responded to these questions using a five-point Likert scale where 1 corresponded to "Very unlikely" and 5 corresponded to "Very likely." The reliability of this questionnaire, measured by Cronbach's alpha, was 0.75. The survey instrument also contained a series of demographic questions that related to the participants' age, gender, and type of course enrollment (elective versus required and online versus face-to-face).

Procedure: In order to encourage the participants to think in the frame of a specific type of course, we administered a printed version of the survey instrument in the traditional face-to-face courses and an online version of the survey instrument in the e-learning courses. The survey instruments were coded and grouped according to the location of the participants' college or university (USA or Israel).

Results

Table 1 summarizes the results of independent sample t-test analyses, which indicate that there were significant differences in the level of motivation between students taking face-to-face courses and those taking e-learning courses.

These differences were found for three of the four motivational orientations (introjected, identified, and intrinsic) in the U.S. and all four orientations (extrinsic, introjected, identified, and intrinsic) in Israel.

Country	Motivation type	Course type	N	Mean	S.D.	T-Test
USA	Extrinsic	E-learning	287	2.61	0.65	0.023
		Face-to-Face	476	2.61	0.62	
	Introjected	E-learning	287	3.23	0.60	**2.727****
		Face-to-Face	477	3.11	0.56	
	Identified	E-learning	287	3.77	0.42	**4.827****
		Face-to-Face	477	3.61	0.51	
	Intrinsic	E-learning	287	2.82	0.62	**9.039****
		Face-to-Face	475	2.37	0.74	
Israel	Extrinsic	E-learning	293	2.37	0.61	**2.138***
		Face-to-Face	316	2.48	0.65	
	Introjected	E-learning	293	2.88	0.61	**15.503****
		Face-to-Face	316	2.13	0.57	
	Identified	E-learning	293	3.61	0.54	**44.606****
		Face-to-Face	318	1.53	0.61	
	Intrinsic	E-learning	293	2.85	0.66	**9.784****
		Face-to-Face	316	2.31	0.70	
Overall Sample	Extrinsic	E-learning	580	2.49	0.64	**1.956***
		Face-to-Face	792	2.56	0.64	
	Introjected	E-learning	580	3.05	0.63	**8.855****
		Face-to-Face	793	2.72	0.74	
	Identified	E-learning	580	3.69	0.49	**19.925****
		Face-to-Face	795	2.78	1.16	
	Intrinsic	E-learning	580	2.84	0.64	**13.241****
		Face-to-Face	791	2.35	0.73	

***$P<0.001$, **$P<0.01$, *$P<0.05$

Table 1: Differences in motivational level by course type, motivational orientation, and country

The data in Table 1 indicate that, in general, students in e-learning courses had statistically significantly higher levels of intrinsic motivation than those in face-to-face courses. In the overall sample, there was a statistically significant difference in level of extrinsic motivation with students in e-learning courses having lower levels as compared to students in face-to-face courses. This difference in level of extrinsic motivation was not found for students in the U.S.

Table 2 summarizes the results of independent sample t-test analyses, which indicate that there were statistically significant differences in students' likelihood to engage in academic dishonesty based on the type of course in which they were enrolled. Specifically, it was found that students in face-to-face courses were more likely to engage in acts of academic dishonesty than their counterparts in e-learning courses.

Country	Course type	N	Mean	S.D.	T-Test
USA	E-learning	287	2.03	0.83	**10.334*****
	Face-to-Face	468	2.73	0.99	
Israel	E-learning	291	2.33	0.95	**2.601***
	Face-to-Face	311	2.52	0.86	

***P<0.001, **P<0.01, *P<0.05

Table 3 summarizes the results of a Stepwise Regression analysis used to explain the effect of motivational orientation on academic dishonesty. Likelihood to engage in acts of academic dishonesty served as the dependent variable and motivational orientation along with socio-demographic factors served as the independent variables. The hypothesis that students' propensity to commit dishonest acts would be related to type of course (face-to-face versus online) and motivational orientation was supported.

	Predictors	β	t	F	R^2	$R^2\Delta$
Step I	Country (0=USA, 1=Israel)	-0.089	**2.460***	18.719***	0.115	==
	Teaching Method (0=E-learning, 1=Face-to-face)	0.355	**7.194*****			
	Gender (0=Female, 1=Male)	0.018	0.537			
	Age	-0.106	**3.203****			
	Course type (0=Optional, 1=Required)	0.030	0.822			
	Average Grade	-0.085	1.950			
Step II	Country (0=USA, 1=Israel)	-0.105	1.439	12.498***	0.127	0.012
	Teaching Method (0=E-learning, 1=Face-to-face)	0.351	**7.009*****			
	Gender (0=Female, 1=Male)	0.012	0.367			
	Age	-0.098	**2.914****			
	Course type (0=Optional, 1=Required)	0.028	0.786			
	Average Grade	-0.077	1.745			
	Extrinsic Motivation	0.124	**3.377****			
	Introjected Regulation	-0.081	1.592			
	Identified Regulation	0.032	0.404			
	Intrinsic Motivation	0.007	0.182			

***P<0.001, **P<0.01, *P<0.05, N=867

Table 3: Stepwise Regression analysis – Motivational orientation, type of course, and socio-demographic variables as predictors of academic dishonesty

The results of the regression analysis indicate that approximately 13% of the variance in students' propensity to engage in academic dishonesty is explained by motivational orientation, type of course, and age. Specifically, students' likelihood to engage in dishonest acts was found to vary directly with level of extrinsic motivation and participation in face-to-face type courses (as opposed to e-learning type courses) and inversely with age. Simply put, the regression results show that the only motivational orientation found to explain students' likelihood to engage in academic dishonesty was the extrinsic category. The more students are extrinsically motivated, the more likely they are to engage in academic dishonesty. Course type was also found to explain academic dishonesty. According to the results, students in face-to-face course were more prone to engage in academic dishonesty than students in e-learning courses. Finally, age of students was found to explain academic dishonesty, with younger students inclined to cheat more than older students.

Discussion and conclusion

The results of this study confirms that although there is a greater opportunity for individuals to engage in plagiarism, particularly where there is little or no personal contact between students and faculty which stems from the rapid growth of distance learning (Robinson-Zañartu et al., 2005; Walker, 2010) and in spite of Kelley and Bonner's (2005) suggestions that students who feel close to their professors tend to be more honest and Greenberger et al. (2008) findings that there is lower tendency to be involved in deviance activity in online courses. The results are also in accordance with the findings of Greenberger et al. (2008), who suggested that academic dishonesty can be explained by extrinsic motivation. Our findings indicate that of the four types of motivational orientations, extrinsic motivation is the only type that explains academic dishonesty in sample populations of American and Israeli students. Furthermore, Stuber-McEwen et al. (2009) found that there is less overall cheating in the virtual classroom than in traditional classroom settings. They explained that students may have a higher motivation to learn or able to learn independent of the structure typical in traditional classroom settings, which could substantially reduce their desire to cheat. Our study found that e-learning students manifest significantly higher levels of intrinsic motivation than traditional classroom students – a result noted in both the U.S. and Israel student groups. Consistent with Stuber-McEwen et al. (2009), we also found that e-learners were less likely to engage in acts of academic dishonesty as compared to face-to-face learners – a finding most likely related to their being intrinsically motivated in their course work. One possible explanation for these results is that more intrinsically motivated students self-select online as opposed to traditional classroom courses. Since less than 6% of higher education students are enrolled in online courses, they most likely are innovators and early adopters who, according to Rogers' (2003) diffusion of innovations theory, may be more internally motivated by factors such as intellectual curiosity. Another possible explanation for the higher levels of intrinsic motivation observed in e-learning students as compared to students in face-to-face courses is that online instruction facilitates increasing levels of intrinsic motivation. Zhang's (1998) research suggests that the e-learning medium provides a learning environment that "emphasizes intrinsic motivation, self-sponsored curiosity and creative situated learning" (p. 4). This rationale is consistent with the Cognitive Evaluation Theory (Deci & Ryan, 1985), which posits that intrinsic motivation is maximized when individuals feel competent and self-determining in dealing with their environment. Ryan and Deci (2000) pointed out that "interpersonal events and structures (e.g., rewards, communications, feedback) that conduce toward feelings of competence during action can enhance intrinsic motivation for that action because they allow satisfaction of the basic psychological need for competence" (p. 58). It is important to note that this research study examined academic dishonesty in e-learning and face-to-face settings in two culturally different countries – the USA and Israel. The findings were consistent across student groups in both countries. As such, these findings should be interpreted as having greater generalizability and not limited by cultural specificity.

The findings of this study have implications for university-level teacher education. Because online learners are more intrinsically motivated, faculty need to be educated in principles of instructional design to cater to this group of students. They need to understand how learning at a distance differs from face-to-face instruction and design their courses in ways to capture their students' desire to learn. Among other things, this will foster a climate of respect for honesty in the classroom. Similarly, faculty teaching face-to-face need to better understand their students and attempt to design their courses so that they can become intrinsically motivating. Consistent with the meta-analysis by Deci, Koestner, and Ryan (1999), faculty can be developed through mentoring and learning on how to make course material and activities more interesting. This would reduce the expected tangible rewards associated with task performance -- a connection that undermines intrinsic motivation and fosters academic dishonesty.

Limitations and implications for further research

This study has two potential limitations. The first relates to the methodology which involved the use of self-report measures. While the student-participants completed their survey instruments anonymously, self-report has the potential of introducing a social-desirability bias. Survey respondents may want to answer questions in ways that make them appear as good as possible. They may respond to questions in a socially desirable way and perhaps over-report behaviors considered appropriate by researchers and under-report inappropriate behaviors. The nature of the survey and the method of its administration most likely prevented participants in this study from knowing the research questions or desired responses. While the possibility for this bias exists, the probability that it had a significant effect on the study's findings is very low.

The second limitation of this study relates to the inclusion of students from only two countries. While the results with respect to self-reported propensity to engage in academic dishonesty and motivational orientation were robust and similar in both the U.S. and Israel, the results could have had greater external generalizability if students in online and face-to-face courses from more countries were included in the research design.

There is an opportunity to further this line of research on academic dishonesty and distance education by including students from more countries having different cultural orientations. Additional research should examine whether other factors might explain the difference between online and face-to-face learners in their propensity to engage in academic dishonesty.

References

Adcock, L., & Bolick, C. (2011). Web 2.0 tools and the evolving pedagogy of teacher education. *Contemporary Issues in Technology and Teacher Education*, 11(2), 223-236.

Burgoon, J., Stoner, M., Bonita, J., & Dunbar, N. (2003). *Trust and Deception in Mediated Communication.* 36th Hawaii International Conference on Systems Sciences, 44a.

Cohen, D. E. (2001). The role of individual differences in the successful transition to online teaching. *Journal of Instruction Delivery Systems*, 15(3), 30-34

Coussement, S. (1995). Educational telecommunication: Does it work? An attitude study. (ERIC Document Reproduction Service No. ED391465)

deCharms, R. (1968). *Personal Causation.* New York: Academic Press.

Deci, E.L. (1975). *Intrinsic Motivation.* New York: Plenum.

Deci, E.L., & Ryan, R.M. (1985). *Intrinsic Motivation and Self-Determination in Human Behavior.* New York: Plenum.

Deci, E.L., & Ryan, R.M. (1991). A motivational approach to self: Integration in personality. In Dienstbier, R. (Ed.), *Nebraska Symposium of Motivation,* 38 (pp. 237-288) Lincoln, NE: University of Nebraska Press.

Deci, E.L., Koestner, R., & Ryan, R.M. (1999). A meta-analytic review of experiments examining the effects of extrinsic rewards on intrinsic motivation. *Psychological Bulletin,* 125, 627-668.

Deci, E.L., Vallerand, R.J., Pelletier, L.G., & Ryan, R.M. (1991). Motivation in education: The self-determination perspective. *The Educational Psychologist*, 26, 325-346.

Ellis, A. & Phelps, R. (2000). Staff development for online delivery: A collaborative, team based action learning model. *Australian Journal of Educational Technology*, 16(1), 26-44; p. 26.

Fjortoft, N.F. (1996). Persistence in a distance learning program: A case in pharmaceutical education. *American Journal of Distance Education*, 10(3), 49-59.

George, J., & Carlson, J. (1999, January). *Group Support Systems and Deceptive Communication.* Speech presented at 32nd International Conference on Systems Sciences, Hawaii.

Greenberger, E., Lessard, J., Chen, C., & Farruggia, S. (2008). Self-entitled college students: Contributions of personality, parenting, and motivational factors. *Journal of Youth and Adolescence*, 37(10), 1193-1204.

Grolnick, W.S., & Ryan, R.M. (1987). Autonomy in children's learning: An experimental and individual difference investigation. *Journal of Personality and Social Psychology,* 52(5), 890-898.

Heberling, M. (2002). Maintaining academic integrity in on-line education. *Online Journal of Distance Learning Administration*, 5(2). Retrieved October 1, 2004 from: http://www.westga.edu/~distance/ojdla/spring51/heberling51.html.

Jolliffe, A., Ritter, J., & Stevens, D. (2001). *The online learning handbook: Developing and using web-based learning*, Sterling, VA: Kogan Page.

Kelley, K., & Bonner, K. (2005). Distance education and academic dishonesty: Faculty and administrator perception and responses. *Journal of Asynchronous Learning Network*, 9, 43-52.

Kennedy, K., Nowak, S., Raghuraman, R., Thomas, J., & Davis, S.F. (2000). Academic dishonesty and distance learning: Student and faculty views. *College Student Journal*, 34, 309-314.

Kisamore, J.L., Stone, T.H., & Jawahar, I.M. (2007). Academic integrity: Therelationship between individual and situational factors on misconduct contemplations. *Journal of Business Ethics,* 75, 381–394.

Moore, M.G. & Kearsley, G. (2005). *Distance education. A systems view*. Belmont, CA: Wadsworth

Moreno, M.J.A., González-Cutre C.D., & Chillón G.M. (2009). Preliminary validation in Spanish of a scale designed to measure motivation in physical education classes: The perceived locus of causality (PLOC) scale. *The Spanish Journal of Psychology,* 12(1), 327-337.

Palloff, R., and Pratt, K. (2001). *Lessons from the cyberspace classroom: The realities of online teaching*. San Francisco: Jossey-Bass.

Robinson-Zañartu, C., Peña, E.D., Cook-Morales, V., Peña, A.M., Afshani, R. & Nguyen, L. (2005). Academic crime and punishment: Faculty members' perceptions of and responses to plagiarism. *School Psychology Quarterly*, 20(3), 318–337.

Rogers, E.M. (2003). *Diffusion of innovations* (5th ed.). New York: Free Press

Rovai, A.P., Ponton, M.K., Wighting, M.J., & Baker, J.D. (2007). A comparative analysis of student motivation in traditional classroom and E-Learning courses. *International Journal on ELearning,* 6(3), 413-432.

Rowe, N. (2004). Cheating in online student assessment: Beyond plagiarism. *Online Journal of Distance Learning*. Retrieved October 5, 2004 from: http://www.westga.edu/~distance/ojdla/summer72/rowe72.html.

Ryan, R.M. (1995). Psychological needs and the facilitation of integrative processes. Journal of Personality, 63, 397-427.

Ryan, R.M., & Connell, J.P. (1989). Perceived locus of causality and internalization: Examining reasons for acting in two domains. *Journal of Personality and Social Psychology,* 57, 749-761.

Ryan, R.M., & Deci, E.L. (2000). Intrinsic and extrinsic motivations: Classic definitions and new directions. *Contemporary Educational Psychology,* 25, 54-67.

Seligman, M. (1975). *Helplessness: On Depression, Development, and Death*. San Francisco: W. H. Freeman.

Shearer, R. (2003). Instructional design in distance education: An overview. In M. G. Moore & W. G. Anderson (Eds.), *Handbook of Distance Education*. Mahwah, NJ: Lawrence Erlbaum Associates.

Stuber-McEwen, D., Wiseley, P., & Hoggatt, S. (2009). *Point, Click, and Cheat: Frequency and Type of Academic Dishonesty in the Virtual Classroom*. Retrieved September 26, 2011from: http://www.westga.edu/~distance/ojdla/fall123/stuber123.html.

Stuber-McEwen, D., Wiseley, P., Masters, C., Smith, A., & Mecum, M. (2005). *Faculty Perceptions versus Students' Self-Reported Frequency of Academic Dishonesty*. Paper presented at the 25th Annual Meeting of the Association for Psychological & Educational Research in Kansas, Emporia, KS.

Walker, J. (2010). Measuring plagiarism: Researching what students do, not what they say they do. *Studies in Higher Education,* 35(1), 41–59

Zhang, P. (1998). A case study on technology use in distance learning. *Journal of Research on Computing in Education,* 30(4), 398-420.

Teacher Credibility: How Presentation Modalities Affect Teacher Education Students' Perceived Credibility of Information

Jenna L. Sexton, Ph.D.
University of Nevada, Reno
Reno, Nevada, USA
jsexton@medicine.nevada.edu

Cleborne D. Maddux, Ph.D.
University of Nevada, Reno
Reno, Nevada, USA
maddux@unr.edu

Abstract: The following research examined whether or not, all else being equal, the modality of information delivery has an impact on its perceived credibility among teacher education students of two age groups: (>25 and <25). A piece of fabricated information was formatted, with the exact same content and from the same source, into three modalities; (a) face-to-face lecture (b) print via paper, and (c) print via World Wide Web. The formatted information was delivered separately to three randomly assigned groups of undergraduate and graduate teacher education students. After the information was delivered the students completed a self-report survey instrument that recorded their perceptions of the credibility of the formatted information. No significance was found between the mean differences in the credibility scores of participants in the two age groups. However, significant main effects for modality were found. The credibility scores were significantly higher for the print via paper modality than both the face-to-face lecture and the print via World Wide Web modalities.

Introduction

The average American consumes 34 gigabytes of digital information outside of work or school every day. This is approximately a 350 percent increase from thirty years ago (Bohn & Short, 2009). During the past few decades the use of digital media for communication and information access has increased significantly and changed many aspects of human interaction in the industrialized world (Biagi, 2004; Schiller, 2007). Vast amounts of information from multitudes of sources can be digitally accessed virtually instantly in organized, portable, and interactive delivery formats (Bohn & Short, 2009; Hamilton & Tee, 2010).

The methods and modalities used by teachers to interact with their students have also changed dramatically over the past few decades (Beauchamp & Kennewell, 2010). Many of today's college courses include Internet assignments, digital media presentations, online research, chat rooms, email, PowerPoint slides, social networking and/or other forms of digital interaction. Although there is still a strong element of the traditional face-to-face lecture format in contemporary college teaching and learning, there are very few courses nationwide that do not use some form of technology as a tool in the process of educating (Bonk, 2010).

With the many benefits that technology has provided educators, there also exists an unprecedented burden due to the fact that, in contrast with traditional media and methods of information exchange, the Internet has no systematic and trusted regulatory entities vetting its content. Therefore, the credibility of sources of information can be difficult to determine. Therefore, today's educators need to assist their students in learning how to locate and determine which information is appropriate and useful and which is not. This requires assuring that students develop skills to ascertain the credibility, relevancy, and accuracy of accessed information (Karmarkar & Tormala, 2010). Standards for determining the credibility of digital information include consideration of its origin, alteration, authorship, etc. (Karmarkar & Tormala,

2010).

An educator's credibility with his or her students is of the utmost importance, and students' perceptions of teachers' credibility are influenced, directly or indirectly, through digital communication and interaction (Myers, 2004; Myers & Bryant, 2004). Research has shown that credible sources have the potential to greatly influence opinions and change attitudes and behaviors. In contrast, sources with low credibility have little influence, regardless of the accuracy of the message (Fogg, 2003; Hovland & Weiss, 1951).

Today's traditional-age college students were born in the 1980's and 1990's and belong to the Millennial Generation, also sometimes referred to as Generation Y, or the Net Generation (Howe & Strauss, 2000; Schiller, 2007). Many of these traditional-age students have a unique relationship with information resources and some have been immersed in digital technologies since birth. This experience has influenced their expectations regarding the ways in which they access, work with, and share information (Prensky, 2001). They are much more likely to use digital media than previous generations when researching a question for either personal or educational purposes. The primary source of their information is often digitally accessed and this may influence the ways in which they approach both learning and communication (Howe & Strauss, 2000).

Many of the Millennial generation of college students grew up with technology and are very adept using it in their interpersonal interactions. In fact it is often their primary and preferred mode of communication with their peers (Howe & Strauss, 2000; Reith, 2005; Schiller, 2007). Many are quick to share information and collaborate with others in ways that bypass traditional "top-down" processing. This may have had a significant impact on their ability to assess credibility because they are the first generation that has had significantly more access to information sources than their parents.

The interactivity inherent in digital communication has resulted in the ability of students to simultaneously take on roles of both information source and receiver, since the medium allows them to casually alter, critique, reconstruct, and share information. This is something that previous generations did not contend with, so no precedent has been set regarding navigating and assessing the digital information realm.

Many Millennials are skilled with digital tools and Internet navigation. Their proficiency with technology may position them to navigate complex digital information successfully (Reith, 2005; Schiller, 2007). However, young people can also be limited in terms of their cognitive and emotional development and may lack the life experience necessary to comprehend the complexities of information credibility. This is a significant factor for educators to consider as they plan their curricula. In previous generations, teachers and others in authority have led the way in assuring young people are equipped with the awareness needed to make sound assessments regarding the information they consume (Howe & Strauss, 2000).

The present study examined whether perceived credibility of information among younger and older teacher education students varies as the modality of information delivery changes. This was accomplished by formatting a piece of fabricated information that was difficult but no impossible to believe into three modalities; (a) face-to-face lecture (b) print via paper, and (c) print via World Wide Web. The formatted information was delivered to three randomly assigned groups of teacher education students who were told the study was designed to assess their comprehension of the material. Each group of randomly assigned students received the information in a different modality on the same evening. After the information was delivered the students were asked to complete an instrument that included some basic demographic information (age and gender) and recorded their perceptions of the credibility of the formatted information.

The Study

More than 120 undergraduate and graduate teacher education students enrolled in educational psychology and human development courses at a large, Land Grant institution in the western U.S. were asked to volunteer to participate in this research project. They were offered extra credit for their participation in the research experiment, but they were not paid. Additionally, in order to ensure the students did not experience coercion, they were offered an alternative, non-research method of earning the same number of extra credit points. The study was approved by the official Institutional Review

Board of the institution. Initially, the students were divided into the two age groups. One third of each age group was then randomly assigned to each of the three modality groups.

A piece of fictitious information that was difficult but not impossible to believe was composed. The information detailed a supposed new initiative involving the implantation of Radio Frequency Identification (RFID) chips into infants. The fictitious information was formatted in three different ways: (a) face-to-face lecture (b) print via paper, and (c) print via World Wide Web. Each format consisted of exactly the same information, and was said to come from the same fictitious source: an entity called the International Scientific Initiatives Group (ISIDG). Each of the three groups of students received the information in a different delivery modality, and the fictitious source was clearly identified with each modality. The print via paper and the print via World Wide Web modalities contained a clear photograph of the lecturer who presented the material to the face-to-face lecture group.

Each of the three groups of students were told they would be participating in a study that was intended to examine comprehension of material across age groups. Each group was given the fictitious RFID implant initiative information in one of the three formats on the same evening but in different rooms. Group 1 received the information in a face-to-face lecture format delivered in a regular classroom by an experienced lecturer. Group 2 received the information in print format as a group in another regular classroom. Group 3 reported to a computer lab where they were given a URL to access the information via the World Wide Web. The information in each format took approximately 10 minutes to deliver. After each of the three groups had been presented with the information they were asked to complete a self-report instrument. Subsequent to each group receiving the information and completing the survey, all participants were debriefed, both verbally and in writing, regarding the minor deception employed and the true intent of the study: to assess the credibility of information across three modalities.

The instrument consisted of demographic information such as age and gender as well as prior knowledge of RFID technology. There were three questions pertaining to the participants' comprehension of the material. In addition, there were five Likert-style survey items pertaining to the participants' perceived credibility of the information. The five credibility items were developed by Philip Meyer in 1988. Meyer developed the five item, 7-point credibility scale through statistical analyses of relevant previous research on the qualities of credibility including the semantic differential scales developed by McCroskey in 1966 (Hovland & Weiss, 1951; McCroskey, 1966; Poindexter & McCombs, 2000) . Variations of the McCroskey scales, such as the Meyer's scale, have been used in academic and media research for over forty years and have become a standard credibility measure. The survey items were structured in a 7-point semantic differential format with the favorable response at the left side. The participants were asked to rank their opinions of bipolar opposite adjectives regarding the credibility of the information they received.

A 2 x 3 factorial ANOVA was used to analyze the collected data. This research design was composed of two Independent Variables (IVs), age: (a) 25 years and under and (b) over 25 years of age, and modality of information delivery (a) face-to-face lecture (b) print via paper, and (c) print via World Wide Web). The dependent variable (DV) was the total credibility scores obtained from the items explained above for each of the three delivery modalities. In addition, this study examined whether reported time spent on the Internet is related to the perceived credibility of information received from the Internet, since that was one of the findings of previous research on other kinds of media delivery of information. All students in the World Wide Web modality group were identified and Pearson's r was calculated to determine the magnitude and direction of the relationship between reported time spent on the Internet (another item on the instrument) and perceived credibility of information received from the Internet.

RQ1: Are there significant mean differences in the credibility scores between participants who are (a) 25 years of age and under, and (b) over the age of 25?
RQ2: Are there significant mean differences in the credibility scores among participants receiving the information across the three delivery modalities?
RQ3: Is there a significant interaction of credibility scores between participant age and delivery modality?
RQ4: Is there a significant relationship between reported time spent on the Internet and perceived credibility of information received via the Internet?

Findings

Seventy-six undergraduate and graduate teacher education students participated in this study. Of the 76 participants, 61% ($n = 46$) were 25 years of age or younger, and 39% ($n = 29$) were over 25 years of age. Thirty-seven percent ($n = 28$) were male, and 62% ($n = 47$) were female.

The original data contained three outliers and violated the assumption of homogeneity of variance. After removal of the three outliers, all of the data assumptions for a parametric analysis (independent observations, homogeneity of variances, and normal distributions of the dependent variable for each group) were met. To investigate whether modality of information delivery had an impact on perceived credibility across the age groups, a 2 X 3 factorial ANOVA was conducted. The means and standard deviations for the total credibility scores as a function of the two factors, modality and age group, are presented in Table 1. No significance was found between the mean differences in the credibility scores of participants under the age of 25 and over the age of 25. Additionally, the ANOVA indicated no significant interaction between credibility scores and age. This means that the relationship of credibility to modality does not change according to age group.

	25 years and younger			Over 25 years of age			Total	
Modality	n	M	SD	n	M	SD	M	SD
Face-to-face	14	19.29	6.082	10	16.90	5.724	18.29	5.931
Print via Paper	17	21.29	4.120	7	25.14	6.594	22.42	5.132
Print via World Wide Web	15	19.33	5.512	9	16.89	6.333	18.42	5.823
Total	46	20.04	5.207	26	19.12	6.999	19.71	5.885

Table 1: Means, Standard Deviations, and n for Total Credibility Score as a Function of Age and Modality

The only significant F was the one for the main effect of modality ($F(2,66) = 5.82$, $p = .005$, $n_p^2 = .150$.) The null hypothesis was rejected only for this research question. Table 2 shows the source table for the factorial ANOVA. Post hoc Tukey's HSD tests showed the print via paper group had significantly higher credibility scores than both the face-to-face lecture group and the print via World Wide Web group at the $p < .05$ level of significance. No significance was found between face-to-face lecture group and the print via Internet group. The relationship between reported time spent on the Internet and perceived credibility of information received via the Internet was not significant ($r = -.097$). The null hypothesis was not rejected for this research question.

Variable and source	SS	df	MS	F	p	n_p^2
Total credibility score						
Modality	362.42	2	181.21	5.83	.01	.15
Age	1.75	1	1.75	.06	.81	.00
Modality * Age	135.77	2	67.89	2.18	.12	.06
Error	2054.37	66	31.13			
Corrected Total	2458.88	71				

Table 2: Source Table for the Two-Way Analysis of Variance for Total Credibility Scores as a Function of Modality of Information Delivery and Age

Conclusions

This research suggests that students perceive differences in identical information received across different modalities. The data show a significant main effect for modality. The print via paper mode of information delivery yielded a significantly higher overall credibility rating than either the face-to-face lecture format, or the print via World Wide Web format.

There was a large modality effect size of $n_p^2 = .150$. The information was uniform across modalities and the presenters followed a very similar script in their delivery. The face-to-face lecture group and the print via World Wide Web group had virtually identical credibility score means across both age groups (25 years and younger and over 25 years of age; see Figure 2 for graphs of means from all three modality groups).

The data show that the students in both age groups found the information to be more credible when delivered to them in a printed paper format than when delivered in a lecture or a World Wide Web format. The credibility scores for the students who were over 25 years of age had a dramatic difference in mean scores across modalities: face-to-face lecture = 16.90, print via paper = 25.14, print via World Wide Web = 16.89 (see Table 2). This group had nearly a 9 point difference in their collective perception of the credibility of the information across modalities. Although the main effect for age was not significant, this trend may indicate the need for further research. Figure 2 presents a line graph of mean scores which suggests that an interaction might be found with larger samples.

The fictitious RFID information was entirely accurate in technical details, although the proposed initiative to implant babies with the chips was not. The credibility score grand mean ($M = 19.71$) of the fictitious RFID initiative information was just under the completely neutral point ($M = 20$). This indicates that the information chosen for this experiment was not entirely implausible, yet not readily acceptable either, and as such served the purpose of the experiment quite well.

There was one qualitative question on the self-report survey which asked whether the participants had any comments regarding the RFID implantation information that was presented; Eighty-five percent of the participants wrote out a comment. The vast majority of the comments voiced opinions against the concept of implanting human beings with RFID chips, most often citing violation of rights and privacy as the reasons.

This research provides evidence that students perceive information to be more credible when it is delivered to them in a print via paper format than when it is delivered in face-to-face lecture or print via World Wide Web formats. The reasons for this surprising finding are unclear. It is possible that there is a tactile component to the perception of information that is delivered in a paper format. Holding a tangible item may enhance perceptions of credibility. Information that is presented in a print via paper format may be associated with information that has been vetted in some way. Newspapers, books, and magazines all have content that is read, checked and approved by several people or groups before it is deemed ready for publication and public consumption. It is possible that students associate printed information with increased credibility due to how printed information has traditionally been produced.

Another possibility may be that a paper delivery is non-interactive and is thus a "take it or leave it" medium. Both face-to-face and World Wide Web formats are inherently interactive. Receivers of information in these formats are accustomed to be able to ask questions and obtain more information with which to form their opinions regarding what is and is not credible. With a paper delivery format, there is no such interaction. It is possible that the absence of further information recourse may impact perceptions of information received.

Further research would be needed to determine why a piece of information might be deemed more credible when it is delivered in a print via paper format rather than face-to-face or over the World Wide Web.

Regardless of the reasons why there might be a difference in perceived credibility across delivery modalities, this research has implications in the field of information technology in teacher education, and especially in the realm of distance and online education. It may benefit educators to consider not only the content of the information they exchange and deliver with their students, but the modality of the information delivery as well. When students enroll in online and distance education courses, they receive the bulk of their curricula via electronic modes of communication. If the results of this study are replicated by others, it may be of benefit for educators to consider incorporating some form of paper exchange or correspondence with their students in addition to their planned curriculum.

Additional research in the area of credibility perception across delivery modalities might be beneficial for the field of information technology in education. Technology is a mainstay in the education system, and in society as a whole, and more understanding of the impact it may have on students' perceptions could provide educators with valuable information to consider in their decisions regarding how and when they use varying forms of technology in their teaching and in their interactions with their students.

This experiment examined the perception of credibility across information delivery modalities. However, there may be other aspects of information perception that are affected by modality. Examining other aspects of information perception across modalities, such as whether or not one modality is more enjoyable, or more interest-holding than others, could provide more insight into the roles that modes of information delivery and interaction have in education and in learning.

Additionally, it may be interesting to examine whether educational level or socioeconomic status has an impact on the perception of credibility across modalities. This research did not find a correlation between time spent on the Internet and perceived credibly of information received from the Internet. However, such a relationship may exist and an experiment conducted with a larger number of subjects could yield a significant result and might answer more questions.

Implications for Teacher Education

This research provides evidence that the modality of information delivery does have an impact on its perceived credibility among students. Print via paper appears to be a more credible medium, particularly with students who are over 25 years of age. This raises questions regarding whether other aspects of information perception may be affected by mode of delivery, and whether it may be a phenomenon that will disappear in time as paper-based information sources become less common. Whether or not these questions are answered, the findings of this experiment may assist future educators in selecting the methods with which they choose to convey information to their students.

While more research is needed, pre-service and in-service teachers should be made aware that the choice of media used to impart information to their students may have an effect on the degree to which their students trust and/or believe that information. When considering the content of their curricula and the delivery modalities available to them, future educators may be able to use the information from this study to become more attentive of the impact that delivery modality may have on their students, and accordingly they may select appropriate modalities for the varying types of information they intend to convey keeping in mind that just because a particular technology may be available does not necessarily mean that its use is appropriate. Knowing that information delivery modality has an effect on students' perceptions of information credibility may be a valuable asset to teacher education students as they progress in their educational programs and become professionals in the field.

References

Biagi, S. (2004). *Media/Impact: An introduction to mass medai*. Belmont, CA: Wadsworth Publishing.
Bohn, R. E., & Short, J. E. (2009). How much information? 2009 Report on American consumers *Global Information Industry Center*: University of California, San Diego.
Bonk, C. J. (2010). For openers how technology is changing school. *Educational Leadership, 67*(7), 60-65.
Fogg, B. J. (2003). *Persuasive technology: Using computers to change what we think and do*. San Francisco, CA: Morgan Kaufmann Publishers.
Hovland, C., & Weiss, W. (1951). The influence of source credibility on communication effectiveness. *The Public Opinion Quarterly, 15*(4), 635-650.

Howe, N., & Strauss, W. (2000). *Millennials rising : the next great generation.* New York: Vintage Books.

Johnson, T. J., & Kaye, B. K. (2002). Webbelievablity: A path model examining how convenience and reliance predict online credibility. *Journalism & Mass Communication Quarterly, 79*(3), 619-642.

McCroskey, J. C. (1966). Scales for the measurement of ethos. *Speech Monograph, 33,* 65-72.

Myers, S. A. (2004). The relationship between perceived instructor credibility and college student in-class and out-of-class communication. *Communication Reports, 17*(2), 129-137.

Myers, S. A., & Bryant, L. E. (2004). College students' perceptions of how instructors convey credibility. *Qualitative Research Reports in Communication, 5,* 22-27.

Poindexter, P., & McCombs, M. (2000). *Research in mass communication: A practical guide.* Boston, MA: Bedford/St. Martin's.

Prensky, M. (2001). Digital natives, digital immigrants: Do they really think differently? *On The Horizon, 9*(6), 1-6. doi: 10.1108/10748120110424816

Reith, J. (2005). Understanding and appreciating the communication styles of the millennial generation. In G. Walzand & Y. Richard (Eds.), *VISTAS; Compelling perspectives on counseling 2005* (pp. 321-324). Portland, OR: Book News.

Schiller, G. (2007). Americans more wired: Survey. *News & Markets.* Retrieved from Reuters website: http://www.reuters.com/article/idUSN2844258220071228

**Journal Articles
Conference Papers
Special Topic Books
Conference Invited Speaker Talks
Videos
Conference Presentation Slides**

EdITLib is your source for 15+ years (with your subscription) of peer-reviewed, published articles (20,000+) and papers on the latest research, developments, and applications related to all aspects of Educational Technology and E-Learning.

Ten (10) Academic Journals including:

- *Journal of Educational Multimedia and Hypermedia*
- *International Journal on E-Learning*
  (Corporate, Government, Healthcare, & Higher Education)
- *Journal of Computers in Mathematics and Science Teaching*
- *Journal of Interactive Learning Research*
- *Journal of Technology and Teacher Education*
- *AACE Journal*
  (electronic)
- *Contemporary Issues in Technology & Teacher Education*
  (electronic)

Four (4) Conferences including:

- **ED-MEDIA** – World Conference on Educational Multimedia, Hypermedia & Telecommunications
- **E-Learn** – World Conference on E-Learning in Corporate, Healthcare, Government, and Higher Education
- **SITE** – Society for Information Technology and Teacher Education International Conference

Adding soon!
- **Global Learn Asia Pacific** – Global Conference on Learning and Technology
- **Global TIME** – Global Conference on Technology, Innovation, Media & Education

Individual subscriptions $19/month

Does Your Library Subscribe?

Free access to abstracts so you can try the Digital Library at no cost!
- Conduct research • Keep current on the latest research and publications in your field
- Access and fully search publications • Create and store personal collections of articles by topic
- Receive table of contents alerts prior to journal publication
- Share article abstracts and search results with colleagues via email and include your comments
- Export citations to BibTex, EndNote, and RefWorks

www.EdITLib.org

Association for the Advancement of Computing in Education

Email: info@aace.org • Phone: 757-366-5606 • Fax: 703-997-8760

www.ingramcontent.com/pod-product-compliance
Lightning Source LLC
Chambersburg PA
CBHW081129170426
43197CB00017B/2806